First World War
and Army of Occupation
War Diary
France, Belgium and Germany

57 DIVISION
Divisional Troops
505 Field Company Royal Engineers
13 February 1917 - 10 June 1919

WO95/2973/2

The Naval & Military Press Ltd
www.nmarchive.com
Published in association with The National Archives

Published by

The Naval & Military Press Ltd

Unit 10 Ridgewood Industrial Park,

Uckfield, East Sussex,

TN22 5QE England

Tel: +44 (0) 1825 749494

www.naval-military-press.com

www.nmarchive.com

This diary has been reprinted in facsimile from the original. Any imperfections are inevitably reproduced and the quality may fall short of modern type and cartographic standards.

© Crown Copyright
Images reproduced by permission of The National Archives, London, England, 2015.

Contents

Document type	Place/Title	Date From	Date To
Heading	WO95/2973/2 505 Field Company Royal Engineers		
Heading	57th Division 505th Field Coy R.E. Feb 1917-Jun 1919		
Heading	War Diary Of The 505th (Wessex) Field Co Re From Feby 13th 1917 To 28 Feby 1917 Volume I		
War Diary	Havre	13/02/1917	14/02/1917
War Diary	Enroute	15/02/1917	15/02/1917
War Diary	Bailleul	16/02/1917	16/02/1917
War Diary	Vieux Berquin	17/02/1917	23/02/1917
War Diary	Aouvean Monde	25/02/1917	25/02/1917
War Diary	Grispot	26/02/1917	28/02/1917
Heading	War Diary Of 505th (Wessex) Fld Co RE From March 1st To 31st 1917 Volume II		
War Diary	In The Field Billet H 18c 3.6. The Corp Area I31c 77 To I20d4-3 Sheet 36	01/03/1917	01/03/1917
War Diary	In The Field	01/03/1917	31/03/1917
Heading	War Diary of 505th (Wessex) Field Co RE From April 1st to April 30th 1917 Volume 3		
War Diary	In The Field Advamer Billets H6d8.8 Rear Farme For transport H 3d 2.3 Sheet 36 N.W. France	01/04/1917	02/04/1917
War Diary	In The Field	03/04/1917	12/04/1917
War Diary	In The Field H6d8.8 Sheet 36 NW. France	13/04/1917	15/04/1917
War Diary	In The Field	16/04/1917	30/04/1917
Heading	War Diary of the 505th (Wessex) Field Coy RE. From May 1st To 31st 1917 Volume 4		
War Diary	In The Field Billet H6d8.8. Sheet 36	01/05/1917	03/05/1917
War Diary	In The Field	04/05/1917	20/05/1917
War Diary	H6d 8.8 Sheet 36	21/05/1917	26/05/1917
War Diary	In The Field Hbd8.8 Sheet 36	27/05/1917	28/05/1917
War Diary	In The Field	29/05/1917	31/05/1917
Miscellaneous	505th (Wessex) Field Co. R.E. Appendix A	31/05/1917	31/05/1917
Miscellaneous	172nd Infantry Brigade. Appendix B	31/05/1917	31/05/1917
Heading	War Diary of the 505th (Wessex) Field Company RE June 1st to June 30th 1917 Volume 5		
War Diary	In The Field H6d88 Sheet 36 France	01/06/1917	05/06/1917
War Diary	In The Field	06/06/1917	07/06/1917
War Diary	In The Field H6d 8.8 Sheet 36	07/06/1917	25/06/1917
War Diary	In The Field	25/06/1917	30/06/1917
Miscellaneous	Special Operation Orders Issued By Major J.E. Tindall. M.C. Commanding 505th (Wessex) Field Co. R.E.		
Miscellaneous	After Order No. 1	11/06/1917	11/06/1917
Miscellaneous	O.C. Battalion.	07/06/1917	07/06/1917
Miscellaneous	Infantry Advance Dumps		
Miscellaneous	Infantry Advance Dumps.		
Miscellaneous	Brigade Reserve Dump.		
Miscellaneous	R.E. Reserve Dumps.		
Map	Sheet 10000 Map Square I		
Map	Scale 1/10000		
Miscellaneous	App B	10/06/1917	10/06/1917
Miscellaneous	505th (Wessex) Field Co. R.E. Appendix C		

Heading	War Diary of the 505th (Wessex) Field Co RE From 1st to 31st July 1917 Volume 6		
War Diary	H6d8.8 Sheet 36 France	01/07/1917	03/07/1917
War Diary	H5a3.6	04/07/1917	19/07/1917
War Diary	In The Field	20/07/1917	31/07/1917
Map			
Miscellaneous	505th (Wessex) Field Co. R.E.		
Heading	War Diary of the 505th (Wessex) Field Coy. R.E. From August 1st To 31st 1917 Volume Seven		
War Diary	H5a3.6	01/08/1917	11/08/1917
War Diary	In The Field H5a3.6	12/08/1917	27/08/1917
War Diary	In The Field	28/08/1917	31/08/1917
Miscellaneous	505th Wessex Field Co R.E.		
Miscellaneous	Fox Trot	29/07/1917	29/07/1917
Miscellaneous	172nd Brigade. 57th Division. XI Corps August 4th 1917		
Heading	War Diary of the 505th (Wessex) Field Co R.E. From September 1st To 30th 1917 Volume Eight		
War Diary	H5a3.6 Sheet 36 France	01/09/1917	14/09/1917
War Diary	A5a3.6 Sheet 36	15/09/1917	20/09/1917
War Diary	Laires	21/09/1917	30/09/1917
Miscellaneous	Strength of Company on 1st September 1917.	30/09/1917	30/09/1917
Heading	War Diary of the 505th (Wessex) Field Coy From October 1st to 31st 1917 volume nine		
War Diary	Laires Sheet 5A Hazebrook 6d1.5	01/10/1917	03/10/1917
War Diary	Matringhem	04/10/1917	04/10/1917
War Diary	Matringhem 6B 92.58 Sheet 5a Hazebrook	05/10/1917	23/10/1917
War Diary	Belgium Sheet 28 NW E24 B.95.80	24/10/1917	31/10/1917
Miscellaneous	Strength Company on 1st October 1917	31/10/1917	31/10/1917
Miscellaneous	Report of Work done for 24 hours ending 6.0 am 1/11/17	01/11/1917	01/11/1917
Heading	War Diary of the 505th (Wessex) Field Co RE From November 1st To 30th 1917 Volume Ten		
War Diary	Belgium 28 NW B24 B95.80	01/11/1917	06/11/1917
War Diary	Sheet 28 NW C13a4.4	07/11/1917	13/11/1917
War Diary	Sheet 28 NW Belgium C13a4.4	14/11/1917	18/11/1917
War Diary	28 NW C13a4.4	19/11/1917	30/11/1917
Miscellaneous	Strength of boy on 1/11/17 8 offs. 207 O.R.		
Miscellaneous	Honours And Awards		
Miscellaneous	D.R.O. 1712 17/11/17		
Miscellaneous	Honours and Awards		
Heading	War Diary of the 505th (Wessex) Fld Co RE December 1st to 31st 1917 Volume Eleven		
War Diary	28 N.W. C13a4.4	01/12/1917	10/12/1917
War Diary	Sheet 27 F.14c8.6	11/12/1917	15/12/1917
War Diary	Sheet 28 NW B11a3.4	16/12/1917	23/12/1917
War Diary	Boesinghe B11a34 Sheet 28 NW	24/12/1917	31/12/1917
Miscellaneous	Strength on 1/12/17 Offs. 7, O.R. 204	31/12/1917	31/12/1917
War Diary	Boesinghe Hampton Camp K214-75	01/01/1918	02/01/1918
War Diary	Laclytte J354.59	03/01/1918	03/01/1918
War Diary	Hrmentteres B30d05.65 Sheet 36	04/01/1918	06/01/1918
War Diary	Pont Nieppe B23b4.1	07/01/1918	17/01/1918
War Diary	Pont Nieppe	17/01/1918	21/01/1918
War Diary	Pont Nieppe B23 B4.1 Sheet 36	22/01/1918	31/01/1918
Miscellaneous	23rd. Inf. Bde. No. C. 914 Apx 1	29/12/1917	29/12/1917
Operation(al) Order(s)	57th Division. C.R.E's. Operation Order No. 14 Apx 2	29/12/1917	29/12/1917

Category	Description	Start	End
Miscellaneous	Distribution		
Miscellaneous	March Table Issued With C.R.E's Operation Order No. 14		
Operation(al) Order(s)	57th Division. C.R.E's. Operation Order No. 15. Apx 3	30/12/1917	30/12/1917
Miscellaneous	Distribution		
Miscellaneous	March Table Issued With C.R.E's. Operation Order No. 15		
Miscellaneous	War Diary Jan 1918 Strength On Jan 1st 1918 Offs. O.R. 208 Apx 4	31/01/1918	31/01/1918
Heading	War Diary Of The 505th (Wessex) Field Co RE From February 1st to 28th 1918 volume thirteen		
War Diary	Pont de Nieppe B23 B.4.1 Sheet 36	01/02/1918	28/02/1918
Miscellaneous	Strength On 1st Feb 1918 Offrs 7 O.R. 202		
Heading	War Diary Of The 505th (Wessex) Field Coy. R.E. From March 1st To 31st 1918 Volume Fourteen		
War Diary	La Hayes Farm Wear Armentleres B28 B65.05 Sheet 36	01/03/1918	05/03/1918
War Diary	B28b65.05 Sheet 36	06/03/1918	19/03/1918
War Diary	H13b.36	20/03/1918	25/03/1918
War Diary	Forr Rompec H13b36	25/03/1918	29/03/1918
War Diary	H13b3.6	29/03/1918	31/03/1918
Miscellaneous	Strength on March 1st 1918 offrs of OR 203	31/03/1918	31/03/1918
Operation(al) Order(s)	57th Division. C.R.E's. Operation Order No. 18 Apx 1	18/03/1918	18/03/1918
Operation(al) Order(s)	57th Division. C.R.E's. Operation Order No. 19 Apx 2	31/03/1918	31/03/1918
Operation(al) Order(s)	March Table To Accompany C.R.E's. Operation Order No. 19		
Heading	57th Divisional Engineers 505th (Wessex) Field Company R.E. April 1918		
Heading	War Diary Of The 505th (Wessex) Field Co R.E. From April 1st To April 30th 1918 Volume Fifteen		
War Diary	Neuf Berquin 5I36.89	01/04/1918	01/04/1918
War Diary	Steenbecque 4F 83.11	02/04/1918	03/04/1918
War Diary	Oppx 3E 80.05 Sus-st Leger 4F 25-85	04/04/1918	08/04/1918
War Diary	Famechon 5F 52.76 Of Sheet 11 Lens C20cI-1 Sheet 57 D	09/04/1918	12/04/1918
War Diary	Warluzel 4F 65-70	13/04/1918	18/04/1918
War Diary	Henu D19a 20.65 Sheet 57D	19/04/1918	30/04/1918
Miscellaneous	Strength on April 1st 18 Apps. 7		
Operation(al) Order(s)	172nd Infantry Brigade Operation Order No. 45 Appx 7	01/04/1918	01/04/1918
Miscellaneous	Train Arrangements For Entraining Of 172nd Infantry Bde. Station April 2nd & 3rd 1918		
Miscellaneous	Administrative Arrangements Reference 57th Divisional Order Number 77 Apx 2	31/03/1918	31/03/1918
Miscellaneous	Train Arrangements For Move Of 57th Division Less Artillery.		
Operation(al) Order(s)	172nd Infantry Brigade Order No. 47 Apx 3	12/04/1918	12/04/1918
Miscellaneous	172nd Infantry Brigade March Table For April 12th 1918. (To Accompany Brigade Order No. 47).		
Diagram etc	Sector Of Trenches		
Heading	War Diary of 505th (Wessex) Field Coy R.E From May 1st 1918 To May 31st 1918 Volume 16		
War Diary	Henu D19a20.65 Sheet 57 D	01/05/1918	06/05/1918
War Diary	Gommecourt Wood E28c9870 Sheet 57 D NW	07/05/1918	09/05/1918
War Diary	Gommecourt Wood E28c9870	10/05/1918	30/05/1918
Miscellaneous	505th (Wessex) Field Co R.E.	31/05/1918	31/05/1918

Heading	War Diary Of 505 (Wessex) Field Company RE. From 1st June 1918 to 30th June 1918 volume 17		
War Diary	Gommecourt Wood E28 C9870	31/05/1918	04/06/1918
War Diary	Coigneux 57D NE J3B34	05/06/1918	15/06/1918
War Diary	Gommecourt Wood E28d75.80	16/06/1918	30/06/1918
Miscellaneous	Strength Return Accompanying War Diary Of June 1918	01/06/1918	01/06/1918
Heading	War Diary of the 505th (Wessex) Field Co. R.E. July 1st-July 31st 1918 Vol 18		
War Diary	Warnimont Wood I 24 a Central Intry	01/07/1918	19/07/1918
War Diary	Bois Du Warnimont I24a	20/07/1918	29/07/1918
War Diary	Sombrin (Lensii4F) Etrun (Lensii 3I)	30/07/1918	31/07/1918
Heading	War Diary of 505 Field Co. R.E. Vol 19 August 1918		
Miscellaneous	505th Field Coy RE		
War Diary	St Nicholas (Arras) G16277 (51D NW) 1/10,000	01/08/1918	08/08/1918
War Diary	St Nicholas (Arras) G16277	09/08/1918	18/08/1918
War Diary	La Neuville (W. St. Pol) Lens 11 2F45.25	19/08/1918	21/08/1918
War Diary	Fousseux (W Avesives Le Conte & Barly)	22/08/1918	22/08/1918
War Diary	Bouquemaison	23/08/1918	23/08/1918
War Diary	Bavincourt	24/08/1918	25/08/1918
War Diary	Bellacourt	26/08/1918	26/08/1918
War Diary	Mercatel	27/08/1918	27/08/1918
War Diary	St. Martin. Sur Cojeul (Hindenburg Line)	28/08/1918	31/08/1918
Miscellaneous	Return Of Strength, for War Diary, August 1918. 505th (Wessex) Field Company R.E.	31/08/1918	31/08/1918
Heading	War Diary of the 505th (Wessex) Field Coy. R.E. September 1st-30th 1918 Volume 20		
War Diary	St Martin Sur Cojeul	01/09/1918	03/09/1918
War Diary	Hendicourt	04/09/1918	06/09/1918
War Diary	Between Riencourt & Queant	08/09/1918	15/09/1918
War Diary	Basseux	16/09/1918	25/09/1918
War Diary	Lagnicourt	26/09/1918	26/09/1918
War Diary	Baursies	27/09/1918	27/09/1918
War Diary	Cambrin Road	28/09/1918	28/09/1918
War Diary	Nr Fontaine Notre Dame	29/09/1918	29/09/1918
War Diary	Cambrin Road	29/09/1918	29/09/1918
War Diary	Nr Fontaine Notre Dame	30/09/1918	30/09/1918
Miscellaneous	Strength Return For War Diary.	30/09/1918	30/09/1918
Heading	War Diary Of The 505th (Wessex) Field Company R.E. October 1st 1918 to October 31st 1918. volume 21	31/10/1918	31/10/1918
War Diary	Fontaine Notre Dame	01/10/1918	10/10/1918
War Diary	Boursies	11/10/1918	12/10/1918
War Diary	Vaudricourt	13/10/1918	13/10/1918
War Diary	Fromelles	14/10/1918	16/10/1918
War Diary	Lambersart	17/10/1918	20/10/1918
War Diary	Hellemmes	21/10/1918	21/10/1918
War Diary	Rolingeux	22/10/1918	24/10/1918
War Diary	Blandain	25/10/1918	30/10/1918
War Diary	Blandain St Maurice	31/10/1918	31/10/1918
Miscellaneous	Strength Return-October 1918-For War Diary.		
Heading	War Diary of the 505th (Wessex) Field Coy. R.E. November 1st To November 30th 1918. Volume 22		
War Diary	St. Maurice	01/11/1918	09/11/1918
War Diary	Froyennes Sheet 37 140,000	10/11/1918	18/11/1918
War Diary	Sheet 36 Fives Q. 5d20.70	19/11/1918	30/11/1918
Miscellaneous	Honours And Awards. November 1918		

Miscellaneous	Strength Return For War Diary-November 1918	30/11/1918	30/11/1918
Heading	War Diary of the 505th (Wessex) Field Co. R.E. Dec. 1st To Dec. 31st 1918		
War Diary	Sheet 36 Fives. Q5d20.70	01/12/1918	02/12/1918
War Diary	Lens II 1L30.85	03/12/1918	03/12/1918
War Diary	Lens II 3I60.75	04/12/1918	31/12/1918
Miscellaneous	Strength Return For War Diary. 505th (Wessex) Field Company R.E.	31/12/1918	31/12/1918
Heading	War Diary of the 505th (Wessex) Field Coy. R.E. Jan 1st to Jan 31st 1919 Volume 24		
War Diary	Lens II 1.100.000 Louez 3I.60.75	01/01/1919	31/01/1919
Miscellaneous	Strength Return For War Diary.		
Heading	War Diary of the 505 (Wessex) Field Company RE Feby 1st 1919 To Feby 28th 1919 Volume 25		
War Diary	Lens II. 1.100.000 Louez 3I.60.75	01/02/1919	28/02/1919
Miscellaneous	505th (Wessex) Field Coy. R.E. Arrivals And Departures For Month Of February. 1919		
Heading	War Diary Of 505th (Wessex) Field Coy R.E. From 1/3/19 To 31/3/19 Vol 26		
War Diary	Lens II 1.100.000 3I 67.89	01/03/1919	31/03/1919
Miscellaneous	505th (Wessex) Field Coy. R.E.		
War Diary	War Diary of 505 (Wessex) Field Coy. R.E. From 1st April 1919 To 30th April 1919 Volume 27		
War Diary	Lens II. 1.100.000 3I 67.89	01/04/1919	30/04/1919
Miscellaneous	505th (Wessex) Field Coy. R.E.,	30/04/1919	30/04/1919
War Diary	Lens II. 1.100,000 3I 67.89	01/05/1919	31/05/1919
Miscellaneous	505th (Wessex) Field Co. R.E.		
War Diary	Lens II 1.100.000 3I 67.89	01/06/1919	04/06/1919
War Diary	Dumkirk	05/06/1919	10/06/1919

WO95/2973/2

505 Field Company
Royal Engineers

57TH DIVISION

505TH FIELD COY R.E.
FEB 1917 - JUN 1919

WAR DIARY
~~INTELLIGENCE SUMMARY~~
(Erase heading not required.)

Army Form C. 2118.

Instructions regarding War Diaries and Intelligence Summaries are contained in F.S. Regs., Part II. and the Staff Manual respectively. Title pages will be prepared in manuscript.

Hour, Date, Place	Summary of Events and Information	Remarks and references to Appendices
	WAR DIARY OF THE 505th (WESSEX) FIELD CO R.E. FROM FEBY 13th 1917. TO 28 FEBY 1917. VOLUMN I	

Army Form C. 2118.

WAR DIARY
or
INTELLIGENCE SUMMARY.
(Erase heading not required.)

Instructions regarding War Diaries and Intelligence Summaries are contained in F.S. Regs., Part II and the Staff Manual respectively. Title pages will be prepared in manuscript.

Place	Hour, Date	Summary of Events and Information	Remarks and references to Appendices
HAVRE	Feb 13th 1pm	MANCHESTER IMPORTER, with whole of Transport horses + 143 men including all drivers, arrived at the Docks + commenced disembarking (Both Hartlett + 2nd Green with 67 men arrived earlier by ARCHANGEL and had proceeded ahead to the Rest Camp (Docks) —	
do	Feb 14th	Rest rang at Docks Rest Camp. Paraded 4.30 pm + marched to fine merchandise to entrain — Accident occurred at one of the iron bridges over way to the difference of the iron brightening the mule + one mule broke his leg + had to be shot by V.O. Left station at 9.15 pm	
En Route	Feb 15th	Insufficient halts both for watering horses + to enable troops to use latrines.	
BAILLEUL	Feb 16th ASSR	arrived & disentrained & marched to billets at VIEUX BERQUIN	
VIEUX BERQUIN	Feb 17 to 22	Route marches, Bot Respirator drill + general 'hardening' Training	

(73989) W.4141—463. 400,000. 9/14. H.&J.Ltd. Forms/C. 2118/16.

WAR DIARY
or
INTELLIGENCE SUMMARY.

(Erase heading not required.)

Army Form C. 2118.

Instructions regarding War Diaries and Intelligence Summaries are contained in F. S. Regs., Part II. and the Staff Manual respectively. Title pages will be prepared in manuscript.

Hour, Date, Place		Summary of Events and Information	Remarks and references to Appendices
VIEUX BERQUIN	Feb 23rd	Rec'd orders to move marched out at 3-10 pm to ESTAIRES & were billetted at NOUVEAU MONDE	
NOUVEAU MONDE	Feb 25th	Captain Hartnett with all transport moved to BAC ST MAUR & the FOUR sections with their officers, under self, moved to advanced billets at GRIS POT H18c2.6	
GRIS POT	Feb 26th	All Officers & Section Senior NCOs made reconnaissance of all lines in four parties under guidance of members of the advance party – the Pumps & Dumps were taken over from ANZACS last night.	
	Feb 27th	Indents for stores & working parties sent in for tomorrow – Sections commence work by themselves. As the line is in very bad condition & the Southern must become acquainted with the work before they act the infantry on – Division orders heavily bombard enemy line at 10pm & 12.30 pm.	
	Feb 28th	400 (inclusive of NCO) working party at work under R.E.s on Subsidian line & Com. Trenches.	

WAR DIARY
or
INTELLIGENCE SUMMARY.

Army Form C. 2118.

WAR DIARY
OF
505th (WESSEX) FLD Co R.E.

From March 1st to 31st 1917

Volume II

Mindelmaya
505 (Wx) Fld Co R.E.

WAR DIARY
or
INTELLIGENCE SUMMARY.
(Erase heading not required.)

Army Form C. 2118.

Hour, Date, Place	Summary of Events and Information	Remarks and references to Appendices
In the Field March 1st 1917. Billet H.18.c.3.6. The Corps area I.31.c.7.7 to I.20.d.4.3 Sheet 36	The arrangement of working between RE & the Brigade is as follows - one section of RE under Lieut Ogleby are affiliated with the 172nd Brigade & work only upon the front line & support line, with all avenues forward of the support line. The Brigadier is solely responsible for the upkeep of these lines. The O.C. Field Coy is responsible for the work on the Subsidiary line all avenues, tramways drainage etc. For all stores on front & support lines the Brigade submit indents for, & fetch in their own transport, stores from the R.E. Park direct the indent being franked by the R.E. officer affiliated to the Brigade. For the Subsidiary line & the Remainder of the work, i.e. the Subsidiary line & avenues are divided evenly between the three other Section officers who indent thro' O.C. Field Co & have their stores carted at night to their respective advanced dumps. (3)	

WAR DIARY
or
INTELLIGENCE SUMMARY.
(Erase heading not required.)

Army Form C. 2118.

Hour, Date, Place	Summary of Events and Information	Remarks and references to Appendices
Thiefield Mar. 1st continued	The 'Brigade' R.E. Officer draws his working party from the Corps who inspects trenches where he works. The other Batns. are supplied with working parties from the Battalions in reserve. These at present comprise 400 men daily and 40 permanently detailed men for drainage & tramways.	
March 2nd	Owing to shortage of material Stokes 20 infantry under 2 Sappers salvaging material from the old drained trenches near. Our billet is much to advanced for a Field Coy. Seeking transport under the Captain the distance from our HQrs Section at S.18.d.8.8 means a lot of extra work — The site chosen for Meins billet (being a hut camp) is for foul ideal being surrounded by gun positions for which the Boch continually searches, & at cross roads, & underarms	④

WAR DIARY
or
INTELLIGENCE SUMMARY.

(Erase heading not required.)

Army Form C. 2118.

Hour, Date, Place	Summary of Events and Information	Remarks and references to Appendices

Whitefield War 3rd
of tall trees affording a splendid target for registering on.
The Boch shelled our own advanced dumps & the track beside same leading to the artillery line. This was owing to the Infantry carrying parties not obeying orders & using the communication trench also by, white tapes being easily visible from the enemy's ridge opposite.

March 4
Great difficulty being experienced with the drainage owing to all the bombs falling in with the thaw. Our transport was shrapnelled at night but no casualties.

March 5
Boche dropped nearly 40 shells into the men's field to our billet & his bullets had clear view over our camp, causing great inconvenience in movement. Decided to apply for permission to move billet further from rent. Sent officer out to look for suitable site.

(5)

WAR DIARY
or
INTELLIGENCE SUMMARY.
(Erase heading not required.)

Army Form C. 2118.

Hour, Date, Place	Summary of Events and Information	Remarks and references to Appendices
In the field	From 18 months experience I find it is a great mistake to billet RE Coys within the Hell area as unlike the Infantry they have no turn out of line to rest & consequently it gradually wears the whole Coy down, whether they in turn shrink to feel no sense of security. An advanced section is sometimes necessary but this section can be relieved both in line as usual — practically all return work & drainage but Sappers only, as it is change day.	
March 6	No working parties as a rest day after the change (vide Divisional orders) as Sappers had not all gone. I went to Bailleul by section. The CRE has obtained permission for us to move into H 3 d 3 2, the farm found suitable & vacant by 2 kind Sheen, so moved into same, was joined by Capt Hartnett & the remainder of the Coy.	

(6)

WAR DIARY
or
INTELLIGENCE SUMMARY.

(Erase heading not required.)

Army Form C. 2118.

Hour, Date, Place	Summary of Events and Information	Remarks and references to Appendices
In the Field Mar 7.	Only 2 working parties as enemy was more in area in the air.	
Mar 8	Forward billet just left shelled with shrapnel! Rec'd orders to extend my area to I.16 & 3.7, thus doubling the area that the Coy has to work – Met & took over plans & papers (which were very vague) from the outgoing Coy. Arranged to move on the 15th inst. but shall leave the transport not used here as the billet is on the enemies edge of the town & liable to be shelled. Only 8 officers worked in line as Infantry engaged in the mine.	
Mar. 9"	Moved to new billet at H.6.d & 6.8. Owing to the enormous area under my control asked & obtained permission to cancel the attachment of one officer to the Brigade & divided the line up evenly between the four Section officers, by far the best arrangement. ⑦	

Instructions regarding War Diaries and Intelligence Summaries are contained in F.S. Regs., Part II. and the Staff Manual respectively. Title pages will be prepared in manuscript.

Army Form C. 2118.

WAR DIARY
or
INTELLIGENCE SUMMARY.
(Erase heading not required.)

Hour, Date, Place	Summary of Events and Information	Remarks and references to Appendices
Inniskillen March 10"	Heavy Artillery staff and as the Coy were proceeding in squads (under NCOs guides from the outgoing Coy) matters were rendered rather unpleasant.	
March 11" -	All working parties had come from the Reserve Brigade (excepting those for work on the front & support lines, which are supplied from the Reserve Coy in the Subsidiary line.) The work undertaken with the H.T. Mortar (Minnenwerfer) & did great damage. Also an increased amount of Trenchmortar fire.	
March 12"	1st working parties under Kerrschner in rear area 10 Platoons ie about 250 men. Arranged inaddition 150 men for front line work, i.e. the usual permanent duty of 40 to be increased to 4 Platoons ie 100 men.	
March 13"	Heavy Artillery staff + heavy rain last night - result - chaos in certain parts of the line. Dec the	

WAR DIARY
or
INTELLIGENCE SUMMARY.

(Erase heading not required.)

Army Form C. 2118.

Hour, Date, Place	Summary of Events and Information	Remarks and references to Appendices
In the field	Water is blocked everywhere & the trenches flooded. The area under this Corps contains new Companies not less than 16,800 yards of Communication Trench, and 18,800 yards of firing trench, the total of 35,600 ells i.e. 20 miles!	
March 14th	The trenches were in very bad condition when we took over & the wet + 'drafting' has caused the work to increase appallingly. 9 have 47 Sappers detailed away from their Sections on such jobs as running Pumps. 1/c of Dumps. CRE's Yard etc. So that to see more than one Sapper for ¼ mile is a rare thing but the whole Corps is working splendidly.	
March 15th	More work! Switchline from I7 A 7.1. to F19 A 9.8. to be put into usable condition at once — at present it is absolutely dilapidated & flooded.	
March 16th	Inspected new line — The trench of the 3 Corps working	

WAR DIARY or INTELLIGENCE SUMMARY

Army Form C. 2118.

Hour, Date, Place	Summary of Events and Information	Remarks and references to Appendices
Kemmel	Labour to be diverted into this work. Decided to cut new drains into the R. faces & deepen others before anything else, as it will lessen labour & require no stores such as the wholesale placing of trench boards entails, & raising fall parapets will involve -	
March 17th	New working parties commence work. 300 at early night under Capt. Hirst & 300 at early morning under Lieut. Green, leaving 150 on special wiring by night over the whole area between Suburban & Fulham lines.	
March 18th	Already the water is considerably lowered in the trenches & the rear work by draining - Work to trenches thro' L.Coy working parties practically at a standstill.	
March 19th	Work as usual - Rear work & wiring. (10)	

WAR DIARY
or
INTELLIGENCE SUMMARY.
(Erase heading not required.)

Army Form C. 2118.

Hour, Date, Place	Summary of Events and Information	Remarks and references to Appendices
Wakefield Mar 20	The strong winds was still further work in the slope of hundreds of yards of screens being blown down, the gunners sent S.O.S. messages to R.E. Headqn for Sapper to help but only 1 Sapper for Denton canbe supplied.	
Mar 21st	Work as usual — night parties commence resetting + clearing trenches + sandbagging.	
Mar 22nd	Sapper Coleman wounded by shrapnel — our 2nd casualty. — Considerable trouble being experienced in rear work having to do the repair work by night, with Infantry inexperienced to night work + NCOs who have not yet grasped the fact that they are expected to be pleased with commencing + invaluable for this repair work require little else from them —	

(11)

WAR DIARY
or
INTELLIGENCE SUMMARY.
(Erase heading not required.)

Army Form C. 2118.

Hour, Date, Place	Summary of Events and Information	Remarks and references to Appendices
In the field March 23rd	C.R.E. approved from laying a new tramline down to the support line as at present there is no tramline at all in the left half of our area & great trouble & waste of time occurs thro' the difficulty of getting the stores down line.	
March 24"	The C.R.E. has arranged for the 421st F.C.Co to relieve us of some 1500 yards width of our right area ie up to I 26 c 3.3 - a great relief. A certain number of men rehearsed the demolition of a Bridge at our rear, & have also thrown over the No 2 Pontoon Bridge near - Work as usual.	FRANCE 36. N.W. #4C1.5.
March 25	421st Co took over 1500 yards - from Cromwell to Shaftbury Avenue - Work on line as usual	
March 26	The activity of the trench mortars great additional work in repair of trenches blown in	

(12)

WAR DIARY
or
INTELLIGENCE SUMMARY.
(Erase heading not required.)

Army Form C. 2118.

Hour, Date, Place	Summary of Events and Information	Remarks and references to Appendices
March 27th	The Pioneer Coy to be attached to this unit turns up. They have been formed from men fall units in the Brigade & I cannot but feel that the Battalions have taken advantage of the scheme to get rid of all their undesirables - The officers too are unsuitable yet I could have nominated a dozen suitable officers who have the required initiative & training - Drainage is a great problem within Sector	
March 28th	The Bosch shells the switch line (RUE FLEURIE) almost daily now & I have altered the early morning 300 working party & they will work at night instead. No working parties today owing to change	
March 29th	Rest day for all working parties - The Saxtians	

WAR DIARY
or
INTELLIGENCE SUMMARY.
(Erase heading not required.)

Army Form C. 2118.

Hour, Date, Place	Summary of Events and Information	Remarks and references to Appendices
March 30	Work over the two Pontoon bridges at ERQUINGHEM. alteration must be made to the landing stages as the flow is too great, & the cantilevers also weak.	
	New working parties commence work from Reserve Brigade	
	2 Platoons on RUE FLEURIE switch line	= about 880 men
	6 Platoons on Subsidiary line + CTs " " "	
	4 Platoons wiring " " "	
March 31st	Additional working Parties commence work, drawn from the fifth Corps line, to work on front support line	
	1 Coy = about 120 men	= about 120 men
	Difficulty is being found with the Switchline parties as the RE officers in charge only have 4 NCOs + 12 Sappers between them, + being all spare work of over description, this number of Sappers is insufficient.	TOTAL men 1000 Daily

(14)

R. Udall Major
505th (Wessex) Fld Coy R.E.

Army Form C. 2118.

WAR DIARY
or
INTELLIGENCE SUMMARY

(Erase heading not required.)

Vol 3

1/158/7

Confidential

WAR DIARY
of
505th (Wessex) Field Co. RE
from April 1st to April 30th 1917.
—
Volume 3.

Army Form C. 2118.

WAR DIARY
or
INTELLIGENCE SUMMARY.
(Erase heading not required.)

Hour, Date, Place	Summary of Events and Information	Remarks and references to Appendices
In the field. APRIL 1ST 17. Advanced Billets H6d 8·8 Rear Parties Trenches H3d 2·3 Sheet 36 N.W. FRANCE	Working Parties (as per Appendix "A" attached) of 30 Platoons, from Brigade in Reserve ———— about 750 men from 5th Coy in line ———— about 120 men Per 24 hour Total about 870 men The men supplied by the 5th Coy in line work on the support & Front lines & communication trenches connecting these lines. Of the 30 Reserve Platoons, 20 work by night on the Rue FLEURIE switch line, + 10 Platoons on wiring in front of the subsidiary line.	
April 2nd	Boche aeroplane dropped 2 bombs on the road outside our billet at 9-5 am but beyond smashing the glass in the windows did no material damage. The only casualty was a little girl who had her thigh broken. — Work as usual. (1)	

WAR DIARY
~~INTELLIGENCE SUMMARY.~~

(Erase heading not required.)

Army Form C. 2118.

Hour, Date, Place	Summary of Events and Information	Remarks and references to Appendices
In the field April 3rd	Enemy Artillery is decidedly more active than it was last month & he continues to register on the Rue Flleuve works - The night working parties are by no means satisfactory. The officers & NCOs not realising their responsibility - They are under the impression that as soon as they arrive on the works they hand over their men to the RE officers & sapper & are able to retire to a sheltered spot & do nothing - The Brigade are also handicapped by the work being engaged on 1 officer per Coy - the remainder being engaged on Brigade Convoy & Malmohan.	
April 4th 5th	Heavy snow, no working parties cancelled - working parties as usual but inclement weather made work difficult -	
6th	Work as usual - The shortage of stone supplies to	(2)

WAR DIARY
or
INTELLIGENCE SUMMARY.
(Erase heading not required.)

Army Form C. 2118.

Hour, Date, Place	Summary of Events and Information	Remarks and references to Appendices

Inchyfield

The line is hopelessly short of the amount required & we are hardly able to carry on by salvaging material from disused lines - Part for Shellfrog Machine Gun Dugouts material cannot in this way be secured.

April 7th — For levelling through and by lowering a certain ditch it is possible to divert the surface water round the WINDGATE DUMP Area (I.19.b.3.1) & so do away with the necessity of the motor driven pump at that dump.

Our work on the front support subsidiary lines is now a matter of repair after damage by shell fire only.

The wiring of the Subsidiary lines is proceeding fairly satisfactorily but more wire could be used if available.

The Brigade in line is doing good work in wiring in the front line. A Boche aeroplane dropped three bombs by ammunition station at 11-10 p.m. Work as usual.

April 8th

WAR DIARY
INTELLIGENCE SUMMARY

(Erase heading not required.)

Army Form C. 2118.

Hour, Date, Place	Summary of Events and Information	Remarks and references to Appendices
Rue Fleurie April 9th	The enemy sent a number of well directed shells into our line on Rue Fleurie at 8-30 pm which demolished a small building where a machine gun emplacement was being built but as our parties were not there at night there were no casualties - A party of Pioneers with a Sapper had to go down to the line during the night as shell fire had blocked the drains & water was rapidly rising in the trenches in this area.	
April 10th	Work as usual	
April 11th	Work as usual	
April 12th	Additional new Switch line to be taken in hand running from L'ARMÉE, H1 & central to I1c 5·3 sheet 36 N.W. on inspection found them more or less dilapidated through being unrevetted and water standing in them -	(4)

WAR DIARY
or
INTELLIGENCE SUMMARY
(Erase heading not required.)

Army Form C. 2118.

Hour, Date, Place	Summary of Events and Information	Remarks and references to Appendices
In the field April 13th Hd & S Sheet 36 NW. FRANCE	Work on line at standstill owing to Brigade changing attention. The Battalion worked at many odd jobs however that needed attention.	
April 14th	Bad day for infantry after change, as whole Bay did not go into the line it being the only opportunity for a General Company Parade, Gas helmet drill etc.	
April 15th	The strong winds prevailing continue to blow down the screen everywhere — As screen which has been blown down several times re-erected was in last time re-erected in a different manner — instead of being one continuous line thus ————————— we erected 3 at thus ——— ——— ——— + this screen appears to withstand the present gale, as the wind makes through the gaps — also should a portion blow down it does not as before drag a large portion of adjoining screen down with it.	

(5)

WAR DIARY
or
INTELLIGENCE SUMMARY

(Erase heading not required.)

Army Form C. 2118.

Hour, Date, Place	Summary of Events and Information	Remarks and references to Appendices
In the field April 16th	A new method of working on the rear lines has been tried when by the G. Staff. This refers to the Rue FLEURIE & L'ARMÉE switches before mentioned - a Battalion from the Brigade Reserve on the former work, & one Coy of another Battalion on the latter work, be after being withdrawn over the work in daylight, have undertaken the work as a whole, care to be possible to come into 1 R.E. officers & 10 Sappers to help with advice when necessary. This not only relieves the R.E. proportionately, but tends to make the Platoon Commander take more interest in keeping the men at work, which hitherto has not been done, as they seemed to think that the moment they arrived on the work the R.E. officer "took over". They had nothing to do with the	
April 17.	R.E. stores being very short we have to obtain 50% of the required material & often more, by salvaging from disused trenches - The Principal is good but as extra working parties are not available, it means stopping the parties at refair work to - salvage.	(6)

WAR DIARY
or
INTELLIGENCE SUMMARY

Army Form C. 2118.

Hour, Date, Place	Summary of Events and Information	Remarks and references to Appendices
In the field April 18	Work as usual. — Lieut G.W. Hitfield leaves the Coy. to clearing station as the strain of the P.E. work has caused a breakdown. — Of my three heavy waggons (& two Pontoons + Trestle) only one is usable owing to the 4 wheels (back) being useless — (pneumatics, through green wood being used in construction.) It is over a month since the first wheel was indented for from SA.DOS & there are no spare frames coming up. If we have to move we must leave our Pontoons behind. At least one spare Pontoon wheel should be carried by a Field Coy. as the breakdown of a wheel might might prevent a Division crossing a River. — All the R.S.C. waggon are provided with a spare wheel but on 95 waggon containing valuable Technical stores, is not & if a breakdown occurred on "trek", it would be left on the road until one was secured.	
April 20"	G.O.C. Division inspected officers & men billets & horse lines & expressed his satisfaction at the condition of same. ⑦	

WAR DIARY
INTELLIGENCE SUMMARY.
(Erase heading not required.)

Army Form C. 2118.

Hour, Date, Place	Summary of Events and Information	Remarks and references to Appendices
Ap 20 Cont^d	This is largely owing to the men themselves & I am of the opinion that if once men can be made to realise the difference in effect upon others of respectively a smart & well disciplined Coy, & the contrary, their is no difficulty in keeping the men up to the standard. This especially applies to the cleaning of harness. Revd G.W. HIPPISLEY went owing to breakdown in hearse, to the Ambulance Dressing Station.	
April 21st	Sapper Cruse is ordered to join the 2nd Survey Field Co R.E. It is a serious drawback to a Field Coy for it's Sapper to be transferred to other units, & I cannot but feel that there must be men amongst the numbers at the R.E. Base who could be transferred without handicapping the Field Corp, so in this case I only have two new remaining who can survey, & look are if i corpl, & one is a candidate for an R.E. commission. Officers & NCOs inspected the new further line which we are to take over on the right [deleted]	
April 22nd	Extended our line between No 3015 GRENIER Salient so that we now have 5,500 yards frontage.	

WAR DIARY
or
INTELLIGENCE SUMMARY.

(Erase heading not required.)

Army Form C. 2118.

Hour, Date, Place	Summary of Events and Information	Remarks and references to Appendices
April 23rd	The water in the new sector taken over is a source of great trouble being in places a foot above the duck-boards. The greater portion of the Drainage Pioneers therefore are set to work in this area.	
April 24th	Owing to the large area that each Field Coy is now responsible for, the Field Coys have been put under the orders of the Brigadier. Work as usual. The C R E is inspecting	
April 25th	The working parties are knocking off owing to the change.	
April 26th	The last of the Reserve working parties finish today	
April 27th	We now only have 6 Platoons working party on the two Sectors (Rue du Bois Sector & Bois Grenier Sector) and no parties at all on the rear lines. Our main work just now is the reclaiming of the support line from the extreme left of the Rue du Bois Sector (I 10 c 2-3) to The Orchard I 15 c 7.4. + in the BOIS GRENIER Sector - the reclaiming of the support line from The WHITE CITY I 31 a Central to STANWAY POST I 31 b 2-9 & also SAFETY ALLEY	9

Army Form C. 2118.

WAR DIARY
or
INTELLIGENCE SUMMARY
(Erase heading not required.)

Place	Date	Hour	Summary of Events and Information	Remarks and references to Appendices
Fakefield	April 27th continued		which run from the support line down to the BOIS GRENIER salient, and where one gets sniped daily owing to low parapets	
"	April 28th		Heavy minnie wafer were continues to dugout and the trenches in headrent around CHARDS FARM I 16 central and I understand it is under consideration to abandon the salient altogether. The Advanced Brigade Dugouts in RUE FLEURIE proceed satisfactorily but slowly owing to delay a few men here are able to work under the camouflage, the site being under direct observation	
"	29th		The enemy put 60 odd shots into + totally destroy an "Cottage" dump - I 19 c 4 . 2 about 36	
"	30		Nothing unusual - only refers to damaged trenches is done now no new work being possible without working parties	

P. Tindan
Major
505" (Wemen) Field Co RE

(10)

Vol 4

Confidential

War Diary
of the
505th (Wessex) Field Coy R.E.
from May 1st to 31st 1917.

(Volume 4)

R. Tindall Major
O.C. 505th (Wessex) Field Coy R.E.

WAR DIARY
or
INTELLIGENCE SUMMARY

(Erase heading not required.)

Army Form C. 2118.

Place	Date	Hour	Summary of Events and Information	Remarks and references to Appendices
Ypres field Billets H6d 8.8 Sheet 36.	May 1st 1917		The enemy put three shells into our CROMBALOT DUMP. H30a 6 3 - Shortly the same rec{-}hard{-} recurred at our COTTAGE DUMP - at album Dumps, H + L.T.M ammunition has been dumped + quantities of Infantry stores also such as Very lights SAA + Bombs + I have written the G.O.C. 172nd Bde requesting that all these explosives be moved away at once as they are liable to give away our dump. This happened on the 29th ulto. When the enemy put two shells into the Farm the second exploded about 4 VERY lights resulting in flares going off in all directions - within 10 minutes over 50 shells fell into the Farm totally destroying all our stores there also our tools - The weather now being typical spring weather I have stopped all revetting except to actual fireboys as the ground is drying hard, + stores + working parties being almost nil, all work not absolutely necessary must be left -	
"	2nd		The Rue delalottre heavily shelled with 4 to 5 in shells the road was hit 5 large shell hole stopping all transport - a Sapper + 12 Pioneers went down at night + repaired damage by filling in with sandbags -	
"	3rd		Rue delalottre shell holes about Canteen Farm H 23 a 8.8 sheet 36 - finished off with broken brick obtained last night -	

Army Form C. 2118.

WAR DIARY
or
INTELLIGENCE SUMMARY
(Erase heading not required.)

Instructions regarding War Diaries and Intelligence Summaries are contained in F.S. Regs., Part II. and the Staff Manual respectively. Title Pages will be prepared in manuscript.

Place	Date	Hour	Summary of Events and Information	Remarks and references to Appendices
Steenwerck	4th		2Lieut H.T. Trotman reported for duty having come from the 508th (Wessex) Res. Field Coy. — Two of the shellproof Machine gun dugouts in the Rue PLEURIE about I13 b.d.; are now completed & 4 more are well in hand. — The Brigade battle Hqrs are also well in hand at I13 d.2.9. but Interpmn is behind owing to only few men being able to work under camouflage.	Sheet 36 France
	5th		2Lieut R.H. Speedy who was due back from leave this morning has obtained leave until the 11th from the WAR OFFICE.	"
	6th		A working party of 6 men commence digging up the disused water supply pipe from BOIS GRENIER BREWERY with view to repair. Nos 1 & 2 Sections practise the demolition of BAC ST MAUR bridge at G.18.b.9.1. & also threw Pontoon bridge over, reforming.	
	7th		No 3 Section commenced to practise demolition of BAC ST MAUR bridge. When the enemy opened fire upon it with heavy guns — 5 shells exploded immediately near the bridge one setting a cottage on fire close to the ammunition store — GAS alarm circulated at 8th pm but as our guns were "strafing"	"

2449 Wt. W14957/M90 750,000 1/16 J.B.C. & A. Forms/C.2118/12.

WAR DIARY
or
INTELLIGENCE SUMMARY

Army Form C. 2118.

Place	Date	Hour	Summary of Events and Information	Remarks and references to Appendices
Nieppe Erquinghem	7th cont'd		Hostility he caused alarm were gas shells - Boch retaliation continued up to about 3 am on Armentières - The nearest shell to our billet was 150 yards away killing 2 mules & wounding three men.	
		1.30pm	Pte Corpl H.J. Hawkins 506233 of this unit was seriously wounded while returning from the front line where he had been in charge of a party of infantry repairing a breech in the parapet	
	8th		Worked as usual - Conference at CRE's	
	9th		L/Cpl Hawkins died from wounds received on 7th inst. Worked usual in line	
	10th		Pte Cpl Hawkins buried at ERQUINGHEM. Worked as usual	
	11th 12th 13th		Worked as usual - nothing of importance occurred. 2nd Lieut R.H. Baglehole have extended by W.O. to July 9th in order that he may of the enemy anti-aircraft shells a considerable number are duds not answer. These explode on contact with the ground - a large number of these have fallen in this area lately. Inspected works round Armentières town. Known as locality - Our Section taken in the ERQUINGHEM RD locality about # 6a 1.9 Sheet 36 NW	

WAR DIARY or INTELLIGENCE SUMMARY

Army Form C. 2118.

Place	Date	Hour	Summary of Events and Information	Remarks and references to Appendices
White Fm.	13th contd		Rue MARIE locality H 6 c 9 2 (about) & LILLE Rd locality about I 1 d 7.3	Sheet 36 NW.
	14th		Went G E Edams goes on leave. (15th to 25th.) Work as usual.	
	15th		The G.O.C. inspected the Coy. Horses expressed his satisfaction.	
	16th		The Enemy fired a number of rounds attempting to destroy several of the screens in this area but the Pioneers renewed same at nightfall.	
	17th		Work as usual - mostly repair of wire damage - our working parties consisting of only 10 platoons (there always weak in strength) on the whole feature.	
	18th		The enemy shelled the new trench "LLOYDS WALK" & damaged it considerably.	
	19th		The Sappers are mostly working on in the Support line as owing to the scattered area the infantry would never get the trench into a usable condition.	
	20th		Two new trench mortar emplacements commenced - at I 31 a 5.5 & I 31 a 2.7	

WAR DIARY
INTELLIGENCE SUMMARY
(Erase heading not required.)

Army Form C. 2118.

Place	Date	Hour	Summary of Events and Information	Remarks and references to Appendices
#6d 68 Sheet 36. France	21st		Floyd Walk repaired during yesterday & last night again damaged. This trench runs from I 21a 1-2 to I 27a 4-4.	Sheet 36 France
	22nd		The under & the eight machine gun dugouts on the RUE FLEURIE I 13 b 10·1 to I 7 b 8·1 are now completed and three emplacements are now nearing completion &	
	23rd		The Brigade HQrs. dugouts at I 13 c 9·5 are now ready for the concrete burster layer. Work as usual.	
	24th		The C.R.E. inspected this Corps trench area & called at our Coy billet aftn. Found a derived motor engine at CHARD FARM I 16a 8·2 covered with debris but whole so it is being recovered & removed.	
	25th		As the Southern are to leave the Support line under to carry on with their work. Toward dumps were established. The stores roughly stored handed over to the Infantry.	
	26th		Lt. Kent & E. Eden return from leave with the exception of the relaying of the support line where it passes round the orchard I 15 c 10·5, the Southern finish up all work in their [signature]	

WAR DIARY
or
INTELLIGENCE SUMMARY

Army Form C. 2118.

Place	Date	Hour	Summary of Events and Information	Remarks and references to Appendices
Whitefield H Gabes Shed 36.	27th		Wire & trenches as far as revetting & ordinary work is concerned the Infantry will carry out by themselves. Sappers commence work on Subsidiary line, on return to HQ Pontoon bridge fatigue, water supplies, machine gun & trench mortar emplacement trenching in & Artillery Emplts, Signals Dugout, New Coy HQrs (I 20 b 96) Safety alley again blown in, & repaired day & night work.	
	28th		The Three Pioneer Officers have been replaced by three good men 2 Lieut W.S. HALL 2/5th South Lancs Regt in command, 2 Lieut W.H. FLETCHER 2/10th Kings Liverpool Regt, & 2 Lieut P.O. PLATTS, 2/4th South Lancs Regt - (The officers who have returned to their battalions are Capt F.H. PREEDY, 2/4th South Lancs Regt (in command), 2 Lieut J.D. EASTON 2/10th Kings Liverpool Regt, & 2 Lieut A.A. NIMMO, 2/5th South Lancs Regt - I reported on these latter officers recently as being quite unsuited for their work as Pioneer Officers & the three officers who have now taken over will I think be three excellent men & will make a great difference to the utility of the 172nd Pioneer Coy.	

Pw

WAR DIARY
or
INTELLIGENCE SUMMARY

Army Form C. 2118.

Place	Date	Hour	Summary of Events and Information	Remarks and references to Appendices
Inchfield	29th		Owing to there only being two skilled draughtsmen in this Coy, & both of these being ii Corps & engaged always with their sections, & with the fact in view that they may leave any day for a Cadet Training College or have been accepted as candidates to R.E. Commissions & the other will probably be accepted, a few likely men have been chosen from the Sections and are now under a course of instruction by these two N.C.Os. in order that there will be some men left to us to do the various survey revels that are necessary. The course has lasted 14 days & the result w very satisfactory on the whole. Conference with G.O.C. 172nd Brigade as to employment of the R.E.	
	30th 31st		in case of the enemy retiring from his present line — Arranged matter (as per letter Appx A). Conference of all C.Os (vide to Saturday next.	
	1st	9-10 pm	An enemy aeroplane after three attacks has had destroyed our air sausage balloon near B.E. 505" (nearest) F.H.Co R.E	

B. Tindall Major

Appendix A

505th (Wessex) Field Co. R.E.

Strength on 1st May 1917 ;- 7 Officers, 211 O. R.

ARRIVALS

2/Lieut. H. T. Trotman joined Company		4th May 1917.
164981. Sapper H. Williams joined Company		4th May 1917.
488588. Sapper A. Walker " ")		
540760. " E. Divall " ")		12th May 1917.
199476 Driver H. Clark " ")		
522829 Sapper J. Allen " ")		
400684 " C. Souter " ")		16th May 1917.
550982 " F. Tilford. " ")		
199338 Driver A. E. Groves " "		23rd May 1917.

TOTAL;- 1 Officer, 8 O. R.

DEPARTURES.

508233. L/Cpl. H. J. Hawkins, died of wounds,	9th May 1917.
508188. Sapper W. Deane, admitted Hospital,	11th may 1917.
508064. " H. C. Hunt, " "	25th May 1917

TOTAL;- 3 O. R.

Strength on 31st May, 1917;-   8 Officers, 216 O. R.

31st May 1917.

Major.
Commanding 505th (Wessex) Field Co.R.E.

Headquarters. Appendix B

172nd Infantry Brigade.

Regarding my interview with the G.O.C. this afternoon, in the event of the enemy making certain movements, I propose to base my orders for this Company as follows:-

No R.E.'s or Pioneers will be available to assist in the consolidation of the captured trench, their main tasks being:-

(1) The preliminary arrangements for the stocking of advance Dumps.

(2) The supervision of working parties to construct 2 Communication Trenches across No Mans Land and the selection of the position of same.

(3) The selection of two routes across No Mans Land for Pack Mules.

(4) The marking with Sign-boards of the enemy's trenches.

(5) Searching for enemy's Mines and other ruses.

(6) Searching for, and opening up water supplies.

(7) Construction of Trench Tramways as far as material, time, and labour permits.

(8) Alteration of trucks to take stretchers.

(9) Creation of R.E. Dumps in the captured lines.

(10) Construction of bridges over the River Laies and drains to allow Field Guns to advance if necessary, O.C. Centre Group R.A. to select routes.

I shall be glad if you will kindly confirm these matters please, so that I can proceed accordingly,

Tindall Major.

31/5/17.   Commanding. 505th (Wessex) Field Co. R.E.

Vol 5

Confidential

WAR DIARY

of the

505th (Wessex) Field Company R.E.

June 1st to June 30th
1917

Volume 5

[signature] Capt
for O.C. 505 (Wessex) Field Co. R.E.
(absent on leave)

30th June 1917.

Army Form C. 2118.

WAR DIARY
or
INTELLIGENCE SUMMARY
(Erase heading not required.)

Instructions regarding War Diaries and Intelligence Summaries are contained in F. S. Regs., Part II. and the Staff Manual respectively. Title Pages will be prepared in manuscript.

Place	Date	Hour	Summary of Events and Information	Remarks and references to Appendices
Whitefield #bd 88 Sheet 36 France	JUNE 1st		Work on the line as usual & repair of damage by shelling — The three new officers of the Pioneer Coy are excellent men, and I am able to use them for individual work, more so to Pork, & survey of a minor description; which relieves the strain on the RE officers	
	2nd		All work in drainage is stopped since the hot weather is drying all the drains up & there is a lot of repair work for the Pioneer	
	3rd		Put on Conference of G.O.C. 172nd Brigade with OCs Battalions, RE etc. Work as usual — Hostile heavy shelling in neighbourhood	H6b 3.4
	4th		Enemy shelled our billet, I believe by accident, as I think he was really after the junction of the La Gorgue – ARMENTIERES line with the BAILLEUL – ARMENTIERES line just at the back of the men's billet, but all wires went to Camp were got away safely — 3 shells fell actually in the billet & many immediately adjoining —	
	5th		The enemy again shelled the Billet & neighbourhood — Casualties	P—

WAR DIARY or INTELLIGENCE SUMMARY

Army Form C. 2118.

Place	Date	Hour	Summary of Events and Information	Remarks and references to Appendices
Millefds	6th		1 Pioneer wounded, 1 Horse slightly wounded. Inspected ERQUINGHEM Baths. – These were heavily shelled nearly destroyed a week or so ago. Owing to heavy gas shell fire & being discovered. The 172nd Brigade have have to go to SAILLY BATHS – 9 between 5 & 6 miles off. – 2 Lieut S.G.R SHUNDERS reported for duty from the reserve Coy. – To G.O.C. B 172nd INF. BRIGADE turn informed of the situation.	9.176 central
	7th		The enemy withdrawing to the lines on RIDGE – was informed that [crossed out] to before Aachens including the continuation of two communication trenches (one to each Battalion front). Enemy shelled our billet but only one shell hit anywhere tho' a dozen flew everywhere. Some hundreds of 5.9 shell fell from 8 PM to within ¾ mile Radius – The shells came from our direct enemy front i.e. S.E., but from S.S.W, presumably AUBERS. Staffed order for this Corps work in the event of a move forward taking place. Appx A. Interview with G.O.C re same. Work as usual, preparatory work commenced for move forward.	B.

WAR DIARY or INTELLIGENCE SUMMARY

Army Form C. 2118.

Place	Date	Hour	Summary of Events and Information	Remarks and references to Appendices
In the field H6d 8.8 Sheet 36.	7th	contd	At 3.10 am Heavy Bombardment on left, with mine explosions, opened up the attack by us on MESSINES. Heard during the day that the British captured the MESSINE- WYTSCHAETE RIDGE.	
	8th		Lieut R.M. FINCH ordered to proceed to ENGLAND to R.E. Commission - Work in Moparata & forward mine saw occupies most of the Sappers Pioneers. The Chief Engineer inspected the trenches.	
	9th		The Bosch shelled round our billet with heavy HE from 1pm to 5pm - Lt Col. F. Vie (508264) was badly wounded in billet died soon after. P.Col. F. Vie (508264) was badly wounded in billet died soon after. 508191 Sergt C Wagg & 508273 Sergt F.L. Evered received congratulations from the G.O.C 57th Division on their Gallant Cordial Devotion to Duty - appendix B.	
	10th		505470. 2. Boyle R.M. Finch left the unit for England to take up an R.E. Commission - Billet area shelled 2pm to 6pm regain about midnight when Gas shells were also sent over. Capt N.C. Harbutt proceeds to Corps School 1 Signalled at MERVILLE as R.E. Instructor.	
	11th		The presence of a Heavy Gun near our billet results in the enemy sending over a considerable number of heavy HE was any many & all our animals have bivouaced but over a twice each day have to stand in the fields for three stretch. Enemy did this today from 6 pm to 3 am.	

WAR DIARY or INTELLIGENCE SUMMARY

Army Form C. 2118.

Place	Date	Hour	Summary of Events and Information	Remarks and references to Appendices
	11th		2nd Lieut G.E. proceeded to WIMEREUX for course in Camouflage.	
	12th		Enemy again shelled billet from 8am to 11am - 2 Lieut H.T Trotman proceeds to 502nd Field Coy to assist them for a time. The weather for the last month has been kept summer weather.	
	13th		The CRE order transfer 2 Lieut H.T Trotman to the 502 nd Coy Enemy shelled Armentières as usual. Work in trenches now mostly in preparation for moving forward - The Portuguese are taking turn in our trenches. Annual 4 Transport returns forwarded - Enemy shelled heavily - work as usual - ERQUINGHEM as well came within reach of shells just outside billet & burst outside but we had just bolted into the dugout. C.S.M. Cameron - gone to Ambulance. RE	H307.5.
	14th 15th		The Portuguese here cause trouble - They take the stores out of the emergency dumps in spite of notices in Portuguese & wherever nightly with the Batho engine pump. 2nd Lieut G.E. Edm returned from Camouflage Course.	
	17th		Work in preparation with more forward will in hand. Bridges are being constructed where trenches cut through the roads, & dumps stocked.	
	19th		Rain fell - Thunderstorm - Work as usual.	

WAR DIARY or INTELLIGENCE SUMMARY

Army Form C. 2118.

Place	Date	Hour	Summary of Events and Information	Remarks and references to Appendices
Whitfield Hd Qs Sheet 36	19th		Major J.E. Tindeel proceeded on leave from 20th to 30th inst. More Rain.	
	20th		To Brigade H.Q for conference on Operation Order. Work in trenches as usual. Pontoon equipment moved to transport lines. Dump stocking continued. Notification from O.C. XIC RS that CSM Cameron had been evacuated to 5A CCS. Rain in the evening.	
	21st		Work in trenches as usual. Notification from Dvnl H.Q. that Lieutenant General Broadwood died of wounds. Some shelling round billets about 10 am and again from 11.30 – 12.30 am.	
	22nd		Work in trenches as usual. Sedan Officer and NCO's speak very well of the Portuguese working parties, especially the way they dig. Lt J.W. Long attended funeral of G.O.C at G 22. C.2.6. Heard from C.R.E that 172 Inf. Bde has command of Bangalore Torpedoes and Stokes Shells Shells arranged to instruct and promised Sappers to help.	
	23rd		1 Infantry Batman came over from 172 Inf. Bde. to get details on use of B. Torpedoes. 1 NCO. and 10. OR detached to rear union. Attached 502 (Wessex) Field Co RE for rations. Work in trenches as usual. Some shell my round billet. 4-15 – 4.45 a.m.	
	24th		Lieut H.H. Forsyth reported for duty.	
	25th		Work in trenches as usual except at Safety alley, where the Pioneer party was shelled out in the morning and changed to night work.	/K.

Army Form C. 2118.

WAR DIARY
or
INTELLIGENCE SUMMARY
(Erase heading not required.)

Instructions regarding War Diaries and Intelligence Summaries are contained in F. S. Regs., Part II. and the Staff Manual respectively. Title Pages will be prepared in manuscript.

Place	Date	Hour	Summary of Events and Information	Remarks and references to Appendices
In the field	25th (cont.)		Enemy shelled woods and surrounding district from 8.30 pm – 12.0 midnight. Transport held up in ERQUINGHEM. Rain at night.	
	26th		Work in trenches as usual. Lieut. J. W. LLOYD given acting rank of Captain to date from JUNE 11th 1917.	
	27th		Conference of officers of the Company on work to be done in the event of withdrawal by the enemy. Interview with C.R.E. who approved material for Tunnel Bridges. To 172 Inf. Bde H.Q. and settled work in connection with Gotzen operation.	
	28th		Work in trenches as usual. Enemy shelled district from 9.0 pm – 4.0 am 29th. The left half company had very little sleep as the shelling was very close to their new billets. Heavy rain from 9.0 pm.	
	29th		Work in trenches as usual. Interview with C.R.E. re sappers for special work in Gotzen Operation. Enemy shelled district from 10-30 pm – 12.0 midnight.	
	30th.		Work in trenches as usual.	
			Strength of Company.) Casualties during month attached	Appendix C

SECRET

SPECIAL OPERATION ORDERS
ISSUED BY
MAJOR J.E.TINDALL, M.C.,"
Commanding
505th (Wessex) Field Co. R.E.

These orders will take effect on any date, without any further
special orders being issued, and preparation as stated hereunder
will be commenced immediately.
The time may be notified by the Section Officers or may be ~~reported~~
notified by Infantry.
No R.E's. or Pioneers will be available to assist in the consolidation
of the captured trenches.
Section Detail Orders will be issued by the Section Officers.

The Duties of the R.E. are as follows:-

1. All preliminary arrangements for the stocking of Advance Dumps.

2. The siting, setting out of, and construction of, two Communication
   Trenches. Infantry Parties who will undertake this work will report
   at the Rendezvous given hereafter.

3. The opening up of communication trenches in main routes from
   support line to present front line to freely admit stretchers

4. The opening up and marking of pack mule routes.

5. The marking with sign boards of the enemy's trench, according
   to the nomenclature of same on the Official Maps.

6. Searching for enemy's mines and other ruses, and destroying same
   where possible, or where not destroyed, erecting a DANGER board.

7. Searching for, and opening up, water supply

8. Construction of Trench Tramways as far as material, time, and
   labour permit.

9. Alteration of treucks for stretchers.

10. Creation of R. E. Dumps in the captured lines.

11. Construction of bridges over the River Laies and drains, to
    for Field Guns to advance if necessary.

    The R.E.Sections will work forward from their present Sector
    Boundaries as follows:-

No.1 Section.   (Right   I.31.C.0.0.15 forward to I.a.20.95
2/Lieut.F.A.Sheen (Left }   Shaftesbury Av. forward to INCONSISTENT Trench
                             in a line with La Motte Houssain Farm (I.32c 1.6)
No.2 Section   (Right }   Park Row I.20.d.45.20 forward to junction of
2/Lieut.Trotman   (Left }   INCOME TRENCH and INCOME LANE I.26.b.85. 70
                             Hotel I.27.c.8.9.
No.3 Section   (Right }
2/Lieut.Saunders (Left }   Wine Street forward across INCLEMENT Trench,and
                             Support in straight line to bend in Distillery
                         }   Road at I.28.a.5.10.
No.4 Section   (Right }
2/Lieut.G.E.Edson (Left   Pear Tree Farm toward I.16.d.5.0 and along ditch
                             to Q.17.c.35.10 to I.17.c.2.0 along ditch to
                             I.23.b.05.95.

If the order is given for the Infantry to advance during the time that the R.E. and Pioneers are in the trenches, all ranks of both R.E. and Pioneers will at once concentrate at their R.E. Section Dump, viz.;-

        No.1 Section at Crombalot Dump.
        " 2 " " Windygate Farm.
        " 3 " " Wine Avenue
        " 4 " " Leith Walk Dump.

Special care must be taken to move towards the rendezvous in not more larger groups than 10 men, and all ranks on arrival will at once take cover in case of hostile fire being opened and to avoid observation by aircraft. The N.C.O's. and men allotted to special tasks will await the arrival of the Infantry working parties, at the appointed hours, and having secured the necessary stores and tools, will proceed to their tasks without further orders, and act in accordance with further separate instructions issued.

INFANTRY WORKING PARTIES.

      The two companies of the Right Reserve Battalion who are detailed to dig a communication trench across No Man's Land will rendezvous at Windygate Farm I.19.b.2.1, and will approach the Dump in Platoons at not less than 100 yds. interval, preferably by the Subsidiary Line. They will be met there by 2/Lieut. Trotman, who will conduct them to the site of the work
      The one Company from the Left Reserve Battalion which is detailed to dig a communication trench across No Man's Land will rendezvous in the Subsidiary Line at R.E.Dump at Wine Avenue where Lieut. Lloyd, R.E. will meet them. The Coy. will be kept under cover, and will draw tools by Platoons. Each man of both parties will take a shovel and every second man will take in addition a pick. These trenches must be completed to the satisfaction of the R.E.Officers during the night. R. E. Officers will endeavour to get the new communication trenches set out by daylight. Orders in writing will be sent by the O.C.505th (Wessex) Field Co.R.E.to the C.O's. Reserve Battalions stating the hour of rendezvous of these working parties.

PIONEERS.

      2/Lieut. Hood (Pioneers) will proceed at 8.0 p.m. with one section of Pioneers to the R.E.Dump at Tramway Avenue near the Support Line (I.26.a.5.3) and will take tools at the rate of 1 shovel per man, and 1 pick in addition each second man, and will cut through the enemy parapet where the new C.T.will join up, and will continue the trench through the delapidated portion of INCOMPLETE trench from I.26.d.2.5 to the commencement of INCOMPLETE avenue I.26.d.6.5.
      2/Lieut. Platts will proceed with one section of Pioneers assisted by 4 Sappers, and will search for, and open up, all wells in the captured lines. Specimens of water will be taken for analysis, which must be carefully numbered, and a board erected at the well, notifying that the water is poisonous, and will be numbered to correspond with the number of specimen of water.
      2/Lieut. Platts will also be the Pioneer Officer in charge of 63 men of a Middlesex Labour Battn.who will lay a double duckboard track across from the Rue du Bois to the captured INCLUDE trench. A sergeant and another N.C.O. must be detailed to meet the party at R.E.Coy.Headquarters to conduct them to the R.E.Dump, and a Sapper will assist.
      1 Section Pioneers will work with Nos. 1 & 2 Sections R.E. and 1 Section Pioneers will work with Sections 3 & 4 R.E. in removing Barricades.

MARKING OF TRENCHES.

Each R. E. Officer will personally supervise the marking of the captured trenches, and will be held personally responsible that the boards are correctly placed and labelled. This will be done as soon as the consolidation is well in hand, but must not be allowed to interfere with the assistance of the working parties

TRAMWAY.

The railway line of Tramway Avenue will be continued down to our present front line. If possible the Cowgate Avenue Tramway will be continued to the front line.

INFANTRY DUMPS.

Special Dumps will be formed as follows.:-
One under Front Line parapet at
1. Bois Grenier Salient about I.31.c.9.5.
2. Near Junction of Kiwi Rd. and Front Line at I.26 c.7.9.
3. Rue due Bois Salient I.21.c.9.9.
4. Chard Farm Salient about I.16 central.

Special Reserve Dumps will be formed at:-
1. White City about I.31.a.5.6.
2. Tramway Avenue near Support Line adjoining present R.E.Dump
I.26.a.4
3. Queen St. adjoining Railway I.21.a.05.65
4. On Leith Walk, site not definitely settled.

Material for these Dumps may be indented for through the Brigade on the schedule hereafter, and must under no circumstances be taken for any other purpose than for work in this advance.

R.E. ADVANCE DUMPS.

Special Dumps for the advance will be made at :-

1. White City about I.31.a.4.6.
2. At present R.E.Dump at Tramway Avenue I.26 a.4.7.
3. Queen St. under Railway Arch I.21.a.15.55
4. Leith Walk - site not definitely chosen.

These Stores must not be touched by the Infantry.

R. E. DUMPS IN NEW LINES.

As soon as possible, the R. E. Officers will choose sites suitable for Dumps of R. E. Material, and fix boards.

BARRICADES.

R. E. Officers will see that as soon as possible at dusk the barricades on the various roads are opened up to permit traffic to pass through.

SHELL HOLES.

A Sapper N.C.O. to each R.E.Sector will be specially detailed to see that all shell holes of the advanced roads are filled up as soon as possible after dusk

MINES AND RUSES.

Each R.E.Section Officer will detail an N.C.O. and 10 Sappers to carefully examine every part of the captured trenches at the earliest possible moment to search out and destroy all mines, ruses, etc. and where not possible to destroy, a danger board must be erected. If a timed mine is expected, boards must be erected at a safe distance and the approach barred.

MAJOR,
O.C. 555TH (WESSEX) FIELD COY. R.E.

S E C R E T.

AFTER ORDER NO.1.

Labour

The 03 men of the 4th Infantry Middlesex/Bn.th. will report for, and work on, laying a double duckboard track across No Man's Land and will be in charge of 2/Lieut. Platts, 1/2nd Bde. Pioneer Co. The site of the track will be from Burnt Farm (I.20.d.3.6) to Income Trench (approx I.26.b.9.7.) They will be provided with a special dump, and the following stores will be provided:-

600 Duckboards. Bridge about 10 ft in length and 3'6 wide for crossing the Courant. A certain number of trestles and spare timber. 40 shovels. 20 picks. 2 Mauls. 4 Hammers. 1 cwt nails. 2 Saws.

A Sergeant of the Pioneer Co. will be detailed and will meet the Middlesex Labour Co. party at the 172 Bde. Hqrs. and will conduct them to the allotted billets in CHAPELLE D'ARMENTIERES. Another Pioneers N.C.O. must be detailed to assist the party, without assistance from the R. E.

The Sergeant above mentioned will be responsible that the above Stores are stored at the Dump.

AFTER ORDER NO.2.

The main road from Grigpot through Bois Grenier into Radinghem will be made fit for lorry traffic.

One Section of the Pioneers will take in hand the whole of the barricade work of other roads, so as to free one Section, who will be detailed to work entirely upon this road.

———————————————

Signed:- J. E. TINDALL, Major
Commanding 505th (Wessex) Field Co. R.E.

12/6/17.

SECRET   7/6/17.

    To.;-   O. C.   Battalion.

In accordance with 172nd Brigade Operation Order No.4 Para 5
please instruct the TWO Companies detailed to dig the Communication Trench across NO MAN'S Land, to report to 2nd Lieut.
Trotman, R.E. at Windygates Dump, I.19.b.2.1. at   p.m. on
the   instant.

The Comapnies will approach the rendezvous under cover by
the Subsidiary Line, by Platoons at intervals of not less than
100 yards, and will draw tools at the rate of 1 shovel per
man and in addition each second man will take a pick. Material
will also be supplied by the R. E.

                                                            Major.
............1917.   O/C. 505th (Wessex) Field Co.R.E.

SECRET.   7/6/17.

         To   O. C. .   Battalion.

In accordance with 172nd Brigade Operation Order No. 4, para 5,
please instruct the ONE Company detailed to dig the Communication
trench across NO MAN's LAND to report to Lieut. Lloyd,R.E., at
WINE AVENUE DUMP I.14.b.8.5.

The Company will approach the rendezvous under cover by the
Subsidiary Line, by platoons at intervals of not less than 100 yds
and will draw tools at the rate of 1 shovel per man and in addition
each second man will take a pick.
Material will also be supplied by the R. E.

                                                            Major.
.... 1917.   O. C. 505th (Wessex) Field Co. R. E.

INFANTRY ADVANCE DUMPS.

Materials.	1 Coy.	2 Coy.	3 Coy.	4 Coy.	5 Coy.	6 Coy.	Total.	Remarks.
Bags. Sand.	2,000	2,000	2,000	2,000	2,000	2,000	12,000	Drawn from Leith Wlk.
Pickets. Angle Iron. 3' 6"	160	160	160	160	160	160	960	
do 5' 0"	60	60	60	60	60	60	360	
Posts screw. 4' 6"	20	20	20	20	20	20	120	
do 1' 6"	-	-	-	-	-	-	-	Nil in stock.
Wire, barbed, coild.	50	50	50	50	50	50	300	
Wire, French, coils.	5	5	5	5	5	5	30	
Wirecutters.	2	2	2	2	2	2	12	6 from RE Park. 6 in present Inf Dumps.
Mauls.	2	2	2	2	2	2	12	6 from RE Park. 6 in present Inf Dumps.
Picks, head	30	30	30	30	30	30	180	
" helves.	30	30	30	30	30	30	180	
Shovels.	60	60	60	60	60	60	360	300 from RE Park. 150 are at present in Inf Dumps & will cover balance.

INFANTRY RESERVE DUMPS.

Material.	No.1. White City.	No.2. Tramway Av.	No.3. Rue du Bois.	No.4. Leith Walk.	Total.	Remarks.
Boxes, water, lined. 10 gall.	1	1	1	1	4	
Bridges trench. 9' to 12'.	6	6	6	6	24	Not yet available.
Corr. Iron sheets.	24	24	24	24	96	
Duckwalks.	50	50	50	50	200	
"A" Frames. 3' 0"	25	25	25	25	100	
Frames, folding, breastwork.	50	50	50	50	200	
Hurdles revetting wood.	25	25	25	25	100	Only 50 available at R.E. Pk. Remainder to be salved.
Panels revetting, light.	25	25	25	25	100	Not yet available.
Pickets, wood. 6' 0"	25	25	25	25	100	
" " 3' 0"	170	170	170	170	680	Not yet available.
" angle iron 5' 0"	35	35	35	35	140	
Screens, Canvas.	-	-	-	-	-	To be supplied by Field Coy.
Windles.	50	50	50	50	200	
Wire, barbed coils.	50	50	50	50	200	

BRIGADE RESERVE DUMP.

Material.	No.
Bags, sand.	20,000
Bricks, broken in bags.	200
Corr. Iron. sheets.	60
Duckboards.	200
" Trestles.	-
Gravel in bags, tons.	4
Loopholes, wood	12
Lewis Gun traversing	-
Frames.	10
Pickets, 3' 0"	500
Posts, screw. 4'6"	240
Plates, loophole.	20
Props, pit, 6"	50
Sand in bags, tons.	4
Screens, brushwood, 6 yd rolls	4
Wire barbed, coils.	100
Windles.	200
Wire, French, coils.	10
do concertina) barbed) lengths.	50
Axes, hand.	6
Crowbars.	4
Hammers, hand	5
do sledge.	2
Hooks, bill.	6
Measuring rods, 6'	1
Saws, hand.	4

R. E. RESERVE DUMPS.

Material	1 Sec.	2 Sec.	3 Sec.	4 Sec.	H.Q.	Each of the Rear Dumps	Total	Remarks
Bridges, trench 2' to 12'	5	5	5	5	-	-	20	
Baby Elephants complete	4	4	4	4	4	-	20	
Boards, notice, black	20	20	20	20	20	-	100	
Burster blocks					40	40	200	
Canvas, rolls					3		3	
Cement, barrels					4	4	20	
C.I.Sheets 6 ft	48	48	48	48	48		240	
Dogs, sawyers					10		10	
Duckboards	20	20	170	20	100		330	
Duckboard trestles	40	40	240	40	40		400	Not yet available
Fmes. folding breastwork	40	40	40	40	40		200	
X.P.M.Sheets	20	20	20	20	20		100	
Girders 10 ft RSJ					20		20	
Hop Poles					100		100	
Nails 6" lbs.	20	20	20	20	20		100	
4"	20	20	20	20	20		100	
3"	20	20	20	20	20		100	
Paint white lbs					10		10	
" green "					10		10	
" red "					10		10	Not yet avai
Pickets wood 3'					50		50	
Props pit 6'					20		20	
Rails steel 18'					20		20	
" " 9'					2		2	
Spun yarn coils					400		400	
Tape tracing yds					100		100	
Windles					2		10	
Wire plain coils	2	2	2	2			8	
Wire netting rolls	2	2	2	2	2		8	
Axes hand					2		4	
Measuring rods 6'	1	1	1	1			4	
Saws hand	1	1	1	1			4	
Pump trench with one length suction and 2 lengths delivery hose	-	-	-	-	1		1	

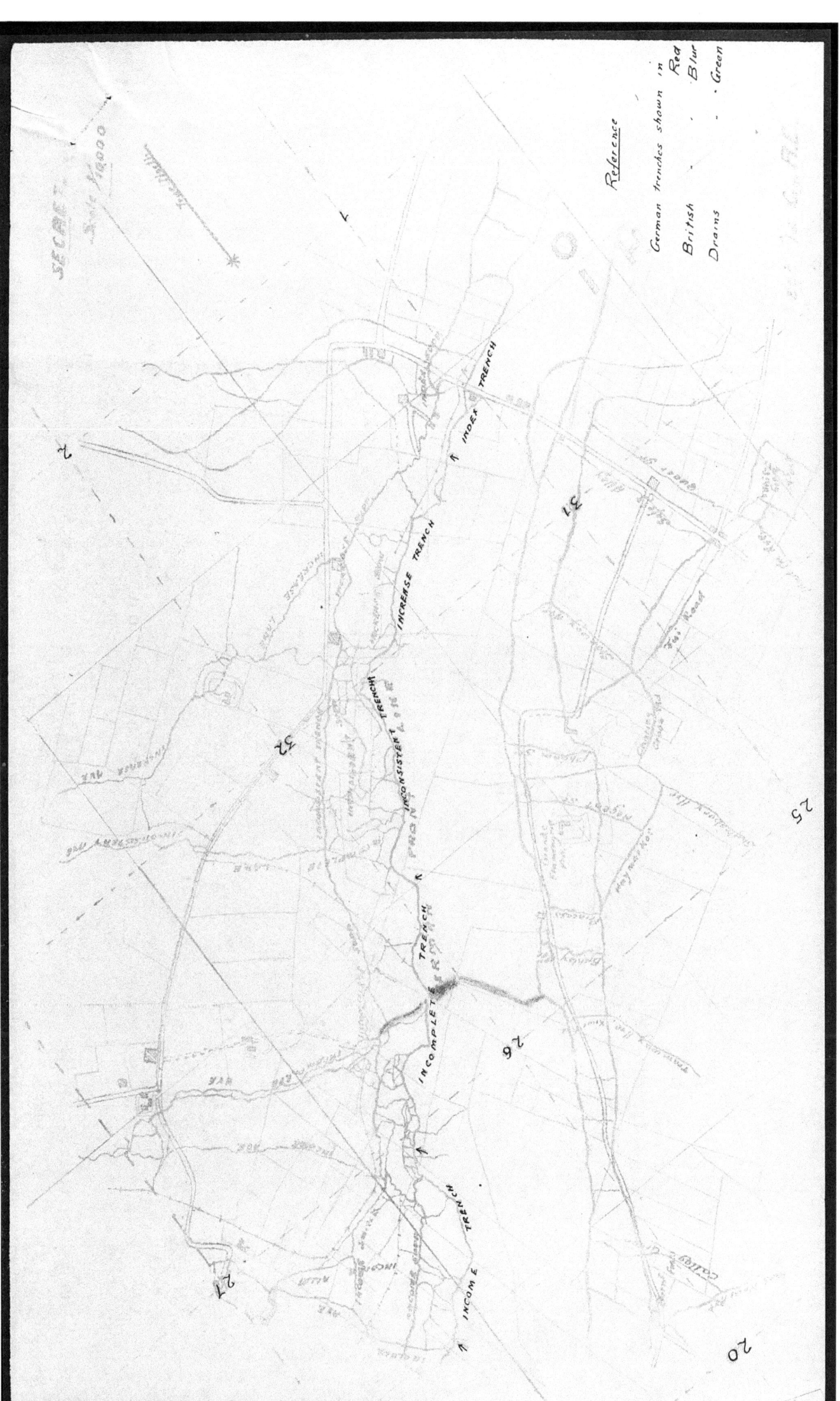

Appx B

The following is a copy of communication sent to the undermentioned N.C.O's. of this Company:-

" I have read with great pleasure the reports of your Commanding
" Officer and Brigade Commander, and congratulate you on your

GALLANT CONDUCT AND DEVOTION TO DUTY
" in the Field.

Signed:- R. G. BROADWOOD, Lieut.Genl.

Commanding the Division.

The C.R.E. also wished that his congratulations be given to N. C. O's.

The Reports referred to above were as follows:-

No.508845. Sergt.F.L.Evered, 505th (Wessex) Field Co. R. E.

On June 7th 1917, the enemy shelled the Company Billet at Rue Marle with heavy high explosive. As the first shells fell over the Railway, men in the billet were ordered to cover. When one of the shells however fell into the building adjoining one of the stables I ordered the mounted section to get the mules away at once. Sergt. Evered came up to me of his own accord, to see if there was anything to be done, and, on seeing that the Tool Carts containing our explosives and tools were in danger, he ran and collected up most of the Sappers, and in spite of further shells falling in the immediate area, by skilfully manoeuvring his men in rushes, he got all the toolcarts and wagons removed to a safe spot.

By his coolness and determination, he set a splendid example to the men, and it was only by the skill and initiative shown by him that the movement was carried out without a casualty.

No.508181. Sergt. C. Maggs. 505th (Wessex) Field Co. R. E.

On the 7th May while Lieut. J.W.Lloyd and No.3 Section of this Unit were rehearsing the demolition of a certain bridge, the enemy opened fire, and five of the shells fell in the immediate vicinity to where the men were working. Lieut.Lloyd who was under the Bridge in a boat full of explosive, gave the order to disconnect the charges on the bridge. Sergt. Maggs at once set the men to work and by his coolness and determination got the whole of the charges disconnected and removed to the explosive store, and although one of the shells burst within 5 yards, he personally attended to the packing away of the whole of the explosive, and stayed to check same to ensure that all had been removed before he took cover.

Had this work not been done skillfully and promptly, and a fragment of shell had struck on of the detonators, serious damage would probably have been done to the bridge.

Signed:- J. C. TINDALL, Major

Commanding 505th (Wessex) Field Co.R.E.

10/6/17.

Appendix C

505th (Wessex) Field Co. R. E.

Strength on 31st May 1917.   ;-   8 Officers   216 O.R.

ARRIVALS.

2/Lieut. S.J.R. Saunders	joined Company	6/6/17.
Lieut. H. H. Lowther	"	"	24/6/17
508453. 2/Corpl. Mogg	"	"	25/6/17.

DEPARTURES

508246. Sapper A. Reynolds	admitted Hospital	1/6/17
508163. Driver G. Palmer	" "	1/6/17
508189. Sapper F. Rutty	" "	8/6/17.
508264. L/Cpl. F. Vile	died of wounds	9/6/17.
508470. 2/Corpl. R. Finch	To U.K. for Commission	11/6/17.
Lieut. H.T. Trotman	Posted to 502nd (Wessex) Field Coy. R. E.	11/6/17.
508439. Sapper R. Ley	admitted Hospital	12/6/17
508255. Driver W. Allen	" "	12/6/17.
508027. " T.A. Bailey	" "	12/6/17.
1957. C.S.M. C.R. Cameron	" "	14/6/17.
427576. Sapper P. Foy	" "	22/6/17.
508186. " T.R. Bailey	" -"	23/6/17.
508274. L/Cpl. W. H. Smith	" "	24/6/17.

Strength on 30/6/17 ;-   9 Officers   206 O. R.

Confidential
9566

WAR DIARY
of the
505th (Wessex) Field Co. RE

from 1st to 31st July 1917

Volume 6

31st July 1917

Tindall Major
505 (Wessex) Field Co RE

Army Form C. 2118.

WAR DIARY
or
INTELLIGENCE SUMMARY
(Erase heading not required.)

Place	Date	Hour	Summary of Events and Information	Remarks and references to Appendices
H 6 d 8.8 Sheet 36. FRANCE	JULY 1st	3 pm 5 pm	MAJOR J.E. TINDALL returned from leave in England. Two shells fell in mens billet (schoolroom) to which they have only just moved owing to being shelled out of the last billet across the road in RUE MARLE. No casualties but equipment destroyed.	
"	2nd		Work as usual on line, ie repair of old fire bays & construction of Trench mortar & Machine gun emplacements. Billets heavily shelled but no direct hits.	
"	3rd		Work as usual - Men are showing considerable signs of strain owing to the heavy shelling around billets keeping them awake & in anxiety. Another heavy gun came up which this morning so arranged with parapade as to make billets to BATHS billet as even so the men returned from the trenches we moved to H 5 a 3.6	
H 5 a 3.6	4th		Work as usual. Area greater (Rue Marle) shelled heavily.	
"	5th		Work as usual - Trouble is being experienced with water supply. Many wells drying up - water supply is being laid on from the BREWERY BOIS GRENIER (H 30 b 5.8) along ditch beside BRIDOUX ROAD to Battalion Headqrs at Culvert Farm (I 25 c 3.4) thence left along RUE LAYES to Gordon Bridge at I 25 d 3.8, continuing along ditch to Tramway Avenue I 26 a 3.4. This will	APDX I. Sheet 36

Army Form C. 2118.

WAR DIARY
or
INTELLIGENCE SUMMARY
(Erase heading not required.)

Place	Date	Hour	Summary of Events and Information	Remarks and references to Appendices
H5a 3.6	6th		The supply water to be front lines by hose avenues & will be ready for extension should any forward movement be made. Work as usual but our Transports were unable to go down at night owing to bombardment. Our horse lines at H3 c 8.5 were bombed by a Boche aeroplane flying very low - 1 horse killed & 3 men & 3 mules injured.	
"	7th		Several thousand yards of trench badly damaged in our Brigade sector & much of it comes to be put in a trench. Several trench mortar emplacements where we were carrying on, are also blown away.	
	8th		Repair of rear billets & Transport lines ordered to be put in hand in addition to three new R.A. observation posts. - Work as usual.	
	9th		Inspected Artillery O.Ps. Several good well built O.Ps are put out of use owing to foliage of trees in front. These O.Ps were evidently chosen in the winter & summer foliage overlooked. As many further O.Ps as it is possible to have are being concentrated on cutting away through, for communication, the smashed up trenches.	
	10th		Orders received to attend to rear billet repairs & have standings for	

Army Form C. 2118.

WAR DIARY
or
INTELLIGENCE SUMMARY

(Erase heading not required.)

Instructions regarding War Diaries and Intelligence Summaries are contained in F. S. Regs., Part II. and the Staff Manual respectively. Title Pages will be prepared in manuscript.

Place	Date	Hour	Summary of Events and Information	Remarks and references to Appendices
H5a 3.6			the coming winter -	Sheet 36 France
	11th		Work as usual - Repair work -	
	12th		Sites chosen for new T.M. emplacements to replace those rendered useless by recent bombardment. Work as usual.	
	13th		The damaged lines are receiving first attention & the whole of the communication are now tested & are being reformed & checkworked.	
	14th		Our daily working parties comprise no seldom more than 3 Platoons over the whole front for all work there.	
	15th		Work as usual	
	16th		" " "	
	17th		" " "	
	18th		Lieut R.H. Oglesby struck off the strength of the unit, he having resigned his commission -	
	19th		Work as usual - Inspected other gunner O.P.'s & arranged with O.C. centre	

2449 Wt. W14957/Mgo 750,000 1/16 J.B.C. & A. Forms/C.2118/12.

WAR DIARY or INTELLIGENCE SUMMARY

Army Form C. 2118.

Place	Date	Hour	Summary of Events and Information	Remarks and references to Appendices
Whitfield	Sept 20th		Gun fire to which OPs' bivouacked hutch remote towers to be built. Enemy heavily bombarded with gas shell 4.5 shells HE Rue Fleurie from bellevue I 19 a 95.80 to Sandbag Corner I 14.7 + apparently reaching to batteries. 2 Lieut F.A. Sheen went on leave, 31st to 31st inst.	
	21st		Work as usual.	
	22nd		Clearing & repairing walled dockin from I 19 B 9.5 completed. Which will help to relieve the pressure on few remaining wells not damaged by enemy rifle fire. Heavy bombardment by enemy from Rear Billets. Lieut H.H. Lawther slightly wounded. Company of Portuguese having been shelled out of billets rated here for the night. Enemy bombard ARMENTIERES heavily.	
	23rd		The Brigade having arranged with me to give 2 lectures to the officers + NCOs each course the first lecture was given today, and Lieut LLOYD will instead of a lecture will give a demonstration on how to. (4)	

2449 Wt. W14957/M90 750,000 1/16 J.B.C. & A. Forms/C.2118/12.

WAR DIARY
or
INTELLIGENCE SUMMARY

Army Form C. 2118.

Place	Date	Hour	Summary of Events and Information	Remarks and references to Appendices
			and How not to - revet a trench in trench in the various materials. These lectures + the following Demonstration will I hope do much to train me Infantry to their responsibilities in Trench repair.	
	25th		Work as usual - a Water Supply from the Brewery (see Page 1) to RUN being completed.	
	26		Heut Floyd's demonstration at Trimple School. Work on clearing bricks for new O.P. GLENFIELD (I 9 c central) Commenced but as 25,000 are required, it means a long job.	
	27"		Enemy put 15 heavy shells at Bridge B 29 c 7.7 but failed to obtain hit. at 3.30 pm & another 12 shells at 2 A.M. Armentières heavily shelled.	
	28"		Armentières heavily shelled very much with heavy HE - "POISON" gas. 5 Sappers were gassed at night not recognising the gas being new.	
	29"		Armentières heavily shelled all day & night - Also HE & Poison gas.	
	30"		do do do	
	31st		do do do Work as usual	

Work as usual

F. Tindall Moyo
50th (Wessex) Field Co. RE.

505th (Wessex) Field Co. R.E.

Strength on 1st July 1917 :- 9 Offs. 206 O.R.

Arrivals.

209005. Driver J. Whittaker	}	Transferred to this Coy from 7th Reinforcement Co. R.E., & taken on the strength of this Coy. as and from 3/7/17.
209315 " S. Saunderson		
202906 " W.D. Ward		
536320 Sapper A.M. Read	}	Transferred to this Coy. from 7th Reinforcement Co. R.E. & taken on the strength of this Coy. as and from 11/7/17.
203359 " S. Hart		
542010 " W.E. Crew		
508189 " F. Rutty		Reported to this Coy for duty on 30/7/17 from No. 2 Wing, R.E. Base Depot.
2/Lieut. R.B. Paul.		Attached to this Unit as and from 30/7/17.

Departures.

508544. Sapper A.E. Jones.	Admitted Hospital	5/7/17.
Capt. N.C. Harbutt.	Transferred to XI Corps School.	1/7/17.
508202. Sapper L. Adams.	Admitted Hospital	7/7/17
508217 Driver R. Nicholls	" "	7/7/17.
508201 Sergt. C. Greenway	" "	9/7/17
508592 Sapper A. Macklin	" "	13/7/17
508275 Corpl. W.J. Webber	" "	13/7/17.
508153. Driver H. Aldridge	Transferred XI Corps School.	9/7/17.
Lieut. G.W. Hippisley	Proceeded to England & struck off strength of Coy. as and from 23/6/17.	
508251. Sapper W. Passmore	} Admitted Hospital	16/7/17
508245 " L.A. Taylor		
508178 " R. Hargreaves	" "	13/7/17
2/Lieut. R.H. Oglesby	Struck off strength of this Coy as & from 18/7/17.	
508219 Sapper R. Shedden	Admitted Hospital	23/7/17
~~508~~ " ~~P.~~	— —	~~~~
92936 Sapper F. Nicholls	Admitted Hospital	24/7/17.
508223. " S. Holder	" "	24/7/17
508467 " A. Pullinger	" "	25/7/17
508211 " R. Corrak	" "	25/7/17
508206 " A. Chidgey.	Transferred to 350th (E. & W.) Field Co. R.E.	30/7/17.

Strength on 30th July 1917 :- 7 Officers 197 O.R.

T. May Maj/R.E.
O/C. 505th (Wessex) Fd. Co. R.E.

CONFIDENTIAL

WAR DIARY
Vol 7
of the
505th (WESSEX) FIELD COY. R.E.
from
AUGUST 1st to 31st 1917

Volume SEVEN

R. Buckingham
O.C. 505th (Wessex) Field Coy RE

August 31st 1917

Army Form C. 2118.

WAR DIARY
or
INTELLIGENCE SUMMARY

(Erase heading not required.)

Month: **AUGUST**

Place	Date	Hour	Summary of Events and Information	Remarks and references to Appendices
H5a 3.6	August 1st	1 A.M.	Two R.E. N° 508595 2/Cpl. G.F. Thompson & 508626 Sapper J.S. Barrett of this unit took part in raid enemy's trenches. Sapper Barrett was killed on the enemy wire. Thompson did splendid work to report on enemy wire. Weather - wet & cold. Work much as usual.	Appx 1
	2nd		After consultation with the O.C. 172nd Brigade, it was decided to hand over the whole of the working parties of the Brigade to be under the control of this unit as unless they are under the organization & supervision of the R.E., little, if any, work is done.	
	3rd		Work as usual, no repairs to trenches. New Flank work to be attended to - The wiring trench to be repaired running from H 30 d 5.0 off Greatwood Avenue to Brigade Boundary in direction of Canyon H 36 a central, called OLD CUT - wiring in front of trench also triangle in front to be done.	
	4th		Work started WM 6" Co on right of Brigade area (Right Battalion) on OLD CUT WIRING, & MM 6" Coy of LEFT Battalion carrying was	Pl —

WAR DIARY
or
INTELLIGENCE SUMMARY

Army Form C. 2118.

Place	Date	Hour	Summary of Events and Information	Remarks and references to Appendices
	5th		Continued in conjunction with Tem(?)man Medium Trench Mortar emplacements in front line at abt I 16 c 2-6 to right of CHAPEL FARM	
	6th		Very Wet - Work as usual. Two of the new Trench mortar emplacements just completed destroyed by the fire	
	7th		Work as usual. In spite of all efforts the destruction of Front support line is gaining the ascendancy over the amount of repair work we can do.	
	8th		With O.C. Division Brigade round rear defences in 4 ARMIES area H 18 & Central	Sheet 36 France
	9th		Work increased considerably by wet which has caused many of the dugouts to collapse.	
	10th		Severe Thunderstorm. Round left sector front line from Clark Farm to Baedu. Bros with O.C. Durham Brigade.	
	11th		Severe Thunderstorm. The enemy do further severe damage to front line support line & special posts are reinforced tonight. The repair bresbre communication - Camouflage screens are to be erected tonight & the two 6th Corps (from both Brittalian) are to turn up enough earth to give cover. Before communicating	[2]

2449 Wt. W14957/M90 750,000 1/16 J.B.C. & A. Forms/C.2118/12.

WAR DIARY
or
INTELLIGENCE SUMMARY
(Erase heading not required.)

Army Form C. 2118.

Place	Date	Hour	Summary of Events and Information	Remarks and references to Appendices
Whitefield H5a 3.6.	12th		Owing to rearrangement of battalions the few men at our disposal as working party are now stopped - severe thunderstorm floods the trenches.	
	13th		Party elephants dugouts are being supplied frame parts etc of by week to replace old sandbag shelters now collapsed in trenches. The Advance Brigade Dugouts are now completed & camouflaged, after numerous delays.	
	14th		Experiments at D.H.Q. to ascertain the best method of making proof transport to carry Trench Mortar Ammunition, Rifles etc. A light wood frame case, sides & bottom of padded metal was decided upon.	
	15th		Work as usual.	
	16th		" " "	
	17th		" " "	
	18th		" " "	
	19th		" " "	

(3)

WAR DIARY or INTELLIGENCE SUMMARY

Army Form C. 2118.

Place	Date	Hour	Summary of Events and Information	Remarks and references to Appendices
	20th		Capt J.W. Allard returns from leave in England.	
	21.0		Really working parties available & engaged at front wiring - The Sappers are employed on erection of Brizances T.M. Portals, R.T. OP.s, Emergency Roads, Repair work, Screens, the truth of the Pioneers are on Drainage work as usual.	
	22nd		Heavy rain floods trenches - Drainage m/n pumps started at work again - Pioneers ready also on Drainage work.	
	23rd			
	24th		Heavy rain continues on + off	
	25th		No working parties from to-day	
	26		Met CRE by appt. at OLD CUT H.30.d.4.0 - work in this area has been stopped by the Brig'r - but CRE advises completion before we hand over to Tracking or Division.	
	27th		With S.O.C. round Brigade round new Rest area South of BONY 1/2 miles South of STOKER - 2Lieut G.H. BUTLER reports for duty with unit	

Army Form C. 2118.

WAR DIARY
or
INTELLIGENCE SUMMARY
(Erase heading not required.)

Instructions regarding War Diaries and Intelligence Summaries are contained in F. S. Regs., Part II. and the Staff Manual respectively. Title Pages will be prepared in manuscript.

Place	Date	Hour	Summary of Events and Information	Remarks and references to Appendices
Whotele	28th		2/Lieut N. Dixon reports for duty	LISBOURG sheet 5A France Hazebrook Y/0000
	29th		2/Lieut FASHEEN reports with motor lorries into this section to report for duty in advance (6.C.6.1.) - Musketry range; Bayonet fighting course + latrines being first works to be put in hand.	
			OLD CUT to be completed before handing over to the 6th Coy in line we are ordered it again to working party at night + work resumed in wiring left (east) side of Heathwood Avenue.	
	30th		Work as usual. Rain each day continues	
	31st		Work as usual. Two new H.T.M. Emplacements commenced	
			① HULL RD I 16 a 6.4 + WHITE CTY I 31 a 1.6.	

(5)

R. Mitchell
Major
OC. 505th (Wessex) Field Co. R.E.

505th Wessex Field Co R.E.

Strength on 1st August 1917: — 7 officers, 198 other ranks.

ARRIVALS

~~505189 Spr F.Rutty (Transferred) to this Co. from No 2 Wing Depot Rouen~~

155164 Spr G. Handman transferred to this Co. from No 10 Reinforcement Camp 2.8.17.

508464 Spr A. Legg returned from 1st Army Rest Camp 2.8.17
508067 Spr. J. Merricks
508219 Spr. R. Stedder discharged from Corps Rest Station. taken on strength 4.8.17.
508245 Sapper S.H Taylor discharged from No 4. Stationary Hospl. taken on strength 6.8.17.
508488 2/Cpl O.E Beard discharged from Hospl. taken on strength 7.8.17.
508172 Sgt F. Duddridge returned to Unit from Section in Reserve 7.8.17.

428672 Sapper W.G. Pain ⎫
428676 " W. Rogers ⎪ Reported from 7th Reinforcement
428678 " J. Runham ⎬ Co. taken on our strength
428645 " C. Shaw. ⎪ 6.8.17
428668 " A. Murrell. ⎪
513901 " A.C. Boulger ⎭

504749 Driver S. Potter reported to this Co from Base 7.8.17.
476039 Sgt J.W. Castle reported to this Co from Base 8.8.17.
564516 A/L.Cpl T. Smith do do do 8.8.17
506224 Spr H. Hasell returned from leave in U.K. 7.8.17
164273 Spr G.T. Thornton ⎫ Reported to this Company from
176876 " J.M. Wheatley ⎬ 7th Reinforcement Camp RE & taken
217077 " J.W. Grainger ⎪ on strength 16.8.17.
522805 " A. Read ⎪
217688 " A. Mynard ⎭

16010 Sgt H. Street reported to this Co from Base & taken on strength 13.8.17.

508458 L/Cpl Ch. W.E. Chappell ⎫ Returned from 1st Army Rest
506631 Spr H Smith ⎬ Camp. 13.8.17
508258 Driver J.H Cridland ⎭

2 Lieut S.J.R. Saunders returned from Gas Course 14.8.17.
19938 Drvr H.E Groves discharged from Hospital 16.8.17.
508608 Spr R.C. Tiddall do 20.8.17.
508506 L/Cpl J. Gregory do 20.8.17.
508453 2/Cpl E.M Ogg returned from Gas Course 19.8.17.
Capt J. LLOYD returned from leave in U.K. 20.8.17.
2 Lieut L.C BUTLER reported to this Unit for duty 27.8.17.
2 Lieut MYLES DIXON " " " " 28.8.17.
508170 Sapper W.J Talbot returned from leave in U.K. 27.8.17.
508275 Cpl W.J. Webber discharged from Hospital 29.8.17.

2.

DEPARTURES.

508468	1/Cpl D.E. Beard admitted to hospital	1.8.17
508455	L/Cpl A.V.E. Chubbell	
508628	Sapper J.S. Barrett posted as missing	1.8.17.
508501	1/Cpl E.J. Broadway proceeded to England to take Commission, & struck off strength	5.8.17
508201	Sgt C. Greenway transferred to 508 Wessex Reserve Field Co. as from 17.7.17. (In hospital Chatham).	
426576	Sapper P. Foy transferred to 426 West Lancs Reserve Field Co. as from 18.7.17	
508253	Sapper G. Mutton admitted to hospital	6.8.17.
508275	Corpl W.J. Webber admitted hospital	6.8.17.
2/Lieut	S.R.J. Saunders proceeded on Gas Course	10.8.17.
508139	L/Cpl L. Mills " "	10.8.17
508170	Sapper W.J. Talbot proceeded on leave to UK	15.8.17.
508253	Sapper G. Mutton evacuated to 54th C.C.S.	7.8.17.
508608	Sapper R.C. Tidball admitted hospital	12.8.17
199338	Driver A.E. Groves " "	13.8.17
508506	L/Cpl F. Gregory " "	14.8.17.
508453	1/Cpl E. Mogg proceeded on Gas Course	16.8.17.
508186	Sapper T.R. Bailey transferred to 508 Wessex Field Co. R.E. 25.7.17.	25.8.17
508592	Sapper A. Macklin do do	25.7.17
508594	Sapper P. Crossman evacuated from Divisional area	19.8.17
	1 NCO 10 men proceeded to Section in Reserve	25.8.17
508457	1/Cpl H. Montacute proceeded on Gas Course	27.8.17.
508191	Sgt C. Maggs on leave to U.K.	
92936	Sapper F. Nicholls transferred to R.E.T.C. Newark as from 6.8.17	
508544	Sapper A.E. Jones transferred 508 Wessex Field Co. R.E.	19.8.17
508211	Sapper R. Corrick " " "	19.8.17
	1 Officer 35 O.R. proceeded to B.O.M.Y. Training Centre as Advance party	28.8.17.

SECRET.

FOX TROT.

Special Operation Orders by Major J.E.Tindall, M.C.
O/C. 505th (Wessex) Field Co. R. E.
for
Lance Corporal Thompson and Sapper Barrett, attached
to the 2/4th S. L. R. for raid.

The Sappers will be attached to "D" Coy. 2/4th S.L.R. for instruction and training.

(1) O/C. 505th (Wessex) Field Co. R. E. will provide Tools, and Mobile Charges for (a) The two Sappers to blow in Dugout door, to free Machine Gun if secured, or to destroy the Gun if it cannot be released. (b) Mobile Charges for Infantry Party to blow in doors of Dugouts. (3 charges of six slabs with primers, detonators, fuse and lighter)

(2) These Sappers will be provided with the following by O/C. Raid,
    Revolver and ammunition.   Electric Torch.
    Watch.   Bombs.
    Anti-Gas Appliances

(3) O.C. 505th (Wessex) Field Company will provide Sappers with Mobile Charges (2 charges of 6 slabs with fuse, detonator, and lighter complete, and spare fuse)
    Hand Axe 1.   Large Adjustable Spanner 2.
    Wire Cutters 1,   Fitters Hammer 1
    Cold chisels 2   Side cutting pliers 1.

(4) <u>Duties.</u> The Sappers duties will be;-

    1. To remove the M.G. if possible, or to destroy it in position.
    2. To place spare charges if any in position to damage enemy dugouts
    3. To leave E.F.L. with the M.G. and make their way to our F.L. by way of a flank, and report to O.C. Raid, immediately on their return.

(5) <u>Training.</u> O/C. 505th (Wessex) Field Co. R. E. will train Sappers in duties stated above. Sappers will train the Infantrymen detailed by O.C. Raid in the placing and detonating of the Mobile Charges.

(6) The actual movement, and position of Sappers in the assault will be arranged by O.C. Raid, who will detail one man to assist and to carry spare charges. The Sappers will be inspected by O.C. Raid for identity marks, etc., and will be provided by him with special equipment if required beyond that shown as being provided by O.C. 505th (Wessex) Field Co. R. E.

(7) Sappers will return as soon as their task is successfully accomplished, and report to O.C. Raid.

                                                  Major.
29/7/17.   Commanding 505th (Wessex) Field Co. R. E.

Army Form W. 3121.

Brigade.	Division.	Corps.	Date of Recommendation.
172nd	57th	XI	August 4th 1917

Regtl. No.	Rank and Name (Christian names must be stated)	Unit	Action for which commended (Date and place of action must be stated)	Recommended by	Honour or Reward	(To be left blank)
508595	Acting-Lance Corporal George Francis THOMPSON	505th (Wessex) Field Co. R.E.	On the night 31st July /1st August, he took part with a Sapper and an Infantryman to assist, in a raid on the enemy trenches - was rendered unconscious by a bursting shell and thrown into the enemy's wire. Proceeding alone he came across four men partially buried, and helped them out, leaving them to carry on. After shooting a German and seeing him fall, he found the position where the Machine Gun Emplacement was thought to be, and the Sapper having been killed and the Infantry -man separated, he salved a spare charge dropped by one of the party, demolished the dugout built of concrete, waiting until the explosion took place. Finding and Officer, Lt. Mearne, alone, he stayed with him until the time for return. In N.M.L. coming across several of the party, and one becoming wounded he helped him into our trenches. L/Cpl. Thompson volunteered for this raid, and his action in proceeding alone throughout the enemy trenches, and executing his task with- out his assistants and in spite of difficulties, shows a splendid discipline, and devotion to duty. Position. I.22/.3.9.5	O.C. 505th (Wessex) Field Co. R.E.(T.F)	Military Medal.	Not awarded

CONFIDENTIAL

WAR DIARY
of the
505th (WESSEX) FIELD CO. R.E.
from
SEPTEMBER 1st to 30th 1917

VOLUME EIGHT

P. Tyndall Major
OC 505th (Wessex) Field Co. RE

SEPTEMBER

WAR DIARY
or
INTELLIGENCE SUMMARY

Army Form C. 2118.

Place	Date	Hour	Summary of Events and Information	Remarks and references to Appendices
H5a 3-6 Sheet 36 France	1st		Owing to the approaching moon of the Division every effort is being made to complete all wire warm weather	
	2nd		Old Cut Trench, which is to act as flank defence between the centre & right brigades H 30 d 5.1 to H 36 a 5.8. is being received wired to GREATWOOD AVENUE, round H 30 central, is to be wired on the left (east) side; this avenue having first been firestepped on both sides. RUE PLEURIE SWITCH LINE wiring also commenced tonight, from I 19 central to I 1 d 8.8. & Working parties will continue on these works until completed.	
	3rd		Head Patrons & section returns from HOUPLINES as the Division will not now move to this area.	
	4th		Court Martial (F.G.) on N/ Mgr R. Locke, 50 8259. West Yorks. Court sentenced for taking property from houses in ARMENTIERES belonging to civilians (in abandoned houses).	
	5th		with G.O.C. Division reco. round RUE PLEURIE SWITCH WIRING	

WAR DIARY or INTELLIGENCE SUMMARY

Army Form C. 2118.

(Erase heading not required.)

Place	Date	Hour	Summary of Events and Information	Remarks and references to Appendices
	6th		2nd Lieut G.E. EDSON on leave (7th to 17th) - Work as usual.	
	7th		The powerful winds of the last week together with counter battery shellfire have wrecked many of the screens in this area & have got to be replaced before moving.	
	8th		Work as usual.	
	9th		Divn. Pickets centenance of 72 days F.P. not confirmed	
	10th		2nd Lieut F.A. BROWN goes with GOC 2nd Lieut INGRAMto new Road area. Work as usual, opened office in empwall to get all wiring completed to rear line.	
	11th		2nd Lieut SHEEN proceeds to FRECAIN in charge of 100 men (34 Sappers, remainder Pioneers) under 2nd Lieut P.O. PLATTS	Sheet 5th HAZEBROUCK FRANCE
	12th		Work as usual.	
	13th			
	14th		2 officers. 2nd Lieut LLOYD & 2nd Lieut TONG of the 123rd Field Coy arrive to take over - Keyfare 1A Sappers with them.	(1) F.

Army Form C. 2118.

WAR DIARY
or
INTELLIGENCE SUMMARY

(Erase heading not required.)

Place	Date	Hour	Summary of Events and Information	Remarks and references to Appendices
Asn 3.6 fleet 3.6	15th	3.6 -	Handing over all works to 123rd Fdd Co RE.	
	16th		Handed no an papers etc etc to 123rd B. advance officer	
	17th		At 3 pm March off to ESTAIRES arriving there about 6·30 p.m. Billeted in STEENWERK ROAD –	Hazebrouck SA FRANCE 1/10,000
	18th		Rest day.	
	19th		Marched off at 9·30am traced starting point as ordered by Brigade orders at 10·15 am LA GORGUE – Route NESTREM – PARADIS – cross roads H 5·6·1, HINGES, + billeted at LE CAUROY H 6·3·8 arriving there at 4 pm.	
	20th		Marched off at 8·45am to pass STARTING POINT cross roads 9·6. 05·65 at 11·15 am – Inspected by GOC 17nd ? Brigade at railway crossing in LILLARS F 6·7·8. Then by road running south of ST HILAIRE continued march through AUCHY au BOIS & WESTERHEM – leaving main road at D 6·95·40 through FEBIN-PALFART to LAIRES D 6.1.5 where we are billeted – arrived complete in good trim not one man nor a vehicle having fallen en route. arrived at 5·30 pm – Total trek ARMENTIERES TO LAIRES 39½ miles.	

(2)

WAR DIARY
or
INTELLIGENCE SUMMARY
(Erase heading not required.)

Army Form C. 2118.

Place	Date	Hour	Summary of Events and Information	Remarks and references to Appendices
LAIRES	Sept 21st		Fitting up Coy billets.	Reel 5th HAZEBROUCK 6D1·5·
	22nd 23rd		REST. No 2, 3 r 4 Sections arriving infantry unit billets & finishing off Ranges etc.	
	24th		Sections commence Training – Mornings from 9 am to 1pm	
	25th		do	
	26th		Route march.	
	27th		Coy. Training.	
	28th		No 2 & 3 Sections to ENGUINEGATTE to form bo targets with job to Marken & to flan 100 metres Ab, on the Divisional manoeuvre area. – No 1 Section making targets, erecting baths in Brigade area, No 4 training in 28th	5a sheet 5D 20/25
	29th 30th		No 4 Section moved on 29th to MATRINGHAM to form new Musketry Camp.	5a sheet 6B9/6
	30th		from 9 to 12.30, 30 men of No 1 Section erected a hang room	

(3)

In competition with other RE Corps in Division.

Promotion of 2nd Lieut. on completing 18 months service under G.R.O. 2032 dated 22-9-17 the G.O.C. 57th Division sanctions the wearing of badges of rank of Lieutenant by

2nd Lieut. G.E. EDSON
" " F.A. SHEEN
" " S.J.R. SAUNDERS
" " L.C. BUTLER.

30/9/17.

(signed)
OC "505" (Wessex) Field Co. RE

Strength of Company on 1st September 1917.   8 Officers,
---   213 O.R.

INS.

    508253. Sapper G. Mutton – Rejoined this Company from
                                      X1. Corps Rest. Camp, & taken
                                      on strength 8/9/17.

OUTS.

    504620. Sapper J. Ayles – admitted Hospital (sick) 8/9/17.
                                              Evacuated   9/9/17

    508465.   "   V.E.Lucas – admitted Hospital (sick) 17/9/17.
                                              Evacuated   17/9/17.

    508453. 2/Corpl. E.Mogg. – Admitted Hospl.(acc.inj.) 22/9/17.
                                              Evacuated   23/9/17.

1 officer, 36 men left Laires for Mahingham on R.E. works 29/9/17.

Strength on 30th September,1917;-   8 Officers, 211 O. R.

                                                                             Major.

30/9/17.   Commanding 505th (Wessex) Field Co. R. E.

CONFIDENTIAL

WAR DIARY.
of the
505th (WESSEX) FIELD COY R.E.
from
OCTOBER 1st to 31st. 1917.

VOLUME NINE.

W19

R Wall Major
OC 505 (Wessex) Fld Co RE

WAR DIARY or INTELLIGENCE SUMMARY

Army Form C. 2118.

OCTOBER

Place	Date	Hour	Summary of Events and Information	Remarks and references to Appendices
AIRES sheet 5A HAZEBROOK 6D 1·5·	OCT 1st		THE G.OC'S DIVISION, 170th BRIGADE & 172nd BRIGADE inspected the work done by the two Sections during the last two days which comprises:- 60 lifting targets stands made, carted & erected - 60 butts trips, 75 cub. ft. framework prepared in construction - 96 shelters 8 ft long × 3 ft deep dawn - & expressed their great satisfaction. Spray baths erected at HONENGHEM (sheet 36A) S 27 c 0.7 -	
	2nd		15 men (RE) augmented 100 Infantry working party in Manoeuvre, & constructed 60 pits for men representing barrage, each of 62½ cub. ft, & also flew up 40 shell hles round the starting points. R.E Dixd Spots at RELY, T2c2.7 · (sheet 36A) Received orders to move remainder of Coy to MATRINGHEM on R.E Services.	
	3rd		Fired weekly competition. Coy arrived at 5pm to MATRINGHEM (sheet 5A) 6B 92.58.	
MATRINGHEM	4th		The works to be taken in hand comprises 2 large NISSON HUT camps	

(1)

WAR DIARY or INTELLIGENCE SUMMARY

Army Form C. 2118.

Place	Date	Hour	Summary of Events and Information	Remarks and references to Appendices
MAYRINGHEM 6 Sq. 58 Shed 5a Ruysbroek	5th		Miniature range + a 1000 yard range - CRE 1st Army Troops inspected Work expressed satisfaction at the progress in the works in hand. 90 men of the 55th Labour Battalion + 1 officer report for duty.	
	6th		Heavy rain - Drafted men off work at 11. a.m. - worked in evening instead	
	7th		Heavy gale + being Sunday did not work men. Labour party ordered to return in evening.	
	8th		13 lorry loads of huts for No 2 (Officers) Camp arrived here. Owing to storm party having returned to their unit last night the whole Coy were unloading all the morning.	
	9th		Do	
	10th		Work at No 1 Camp (Nos 1 + 2) proceeding well.	
	11th		Do. Major J.F. Tindall proceeded on leave to England (12th to 22nd). 508177 Sgt C.G. Tyler left to report to War Office in accordance with War Office letter 160/Engineers/H44 (SDs) dated 4/10/17, orders issued by A.G. 1924. Work in both Camps going well	JL

2

WAR DIARY or INTELLIGENCE SUMMARY

Army Form C. 2118.

Place	Date	Hour	Summary of Events and Information	Remarks and references to Appendices
MATRINGHEM 6.B. 92.58 Sheet 5a HAZEBROUCK	12th		1 Officer and 137 O.R. reported for work on the Camp & were billeted in the huts already completed. Party from 30th Labour Battn. under Lt. Downer.	
	13th		Work handed over to Lt Downer in accordance with 172nd Bgde Operation O. No 6. Sappers and Labour party at work on camp. Movement subsequently cancelled. Weather conditions very bad.	
	14th		Sappers continued with works. Cement standing found for horses in sheep stalls. Horses moved. Work going well in spite of rough weather.	
	15th		Mules moved to finish picket lines on hard ground above quarry. Orders recd. to set out 1,000 yd range.	
	16th		Work proceeding as usual. 30 yd range 1000 yd range set out and checked. Shrank in hand.	
	17th		68th Fd Co. R.E. reported to take over work, and moved into huts in the camp huts. C.R.E. 1st Army and 2nd i/c XIV Corps musketry School inspected works and decided upon a timber framed firing point for 30 yd range. Sappers engaged in afternoon upon cleaning up and broken up to prepare to move in accordance with orders from 172nd Inf Bde.	

JL

WAR DIARY
or
INTELLIGENCE SUMMARY

Army Form C. 2118.

OCTOBER

Place	Date	Hour	Summary of Events and Information	Remarks and references to Appendices
MATRINGHEM G.B.90.58 Sht 5a HAZEBROUCK	18th		Company moved from Matringhem to rejoin 172nd Inf Bn in RENESCURE area. March via. RECLINGHEM – COYECQUE – THEROUANNE to CAMPAGNE Lt L.G. BUTLER and advance party preceded by bus to PROVEN area where 172nd Inf Bn were. Unit rejoined 172nd Inf Bn Group upon arrival in RENESCURE area.	
	19th		Transport under Lt G.E. EDSON proceeded to PROVEN area with Bn Group transport. Remainder of Company entrained at RENESCURE and proceeded to PROVEN via HAZEBROUCK – STEENVOORDE – WINNEZEELE – WATOU. Detrained S of PROVEN and marched to billets at PORTSDOWN CAMP X 25. a. 7.3. Transport rejoined Company at PROVEN. Company complete, neither horse nor men fell out. Strength 7 Off. 203 O.R. General clean up and inspection of men & horses. Number of boots have worn badly and there are some that had for continuance.	
	20th			
	21st		Lt W.S. Hall & 103 O.R. reported as attached infantry and were billeted to improve shelters erected in the Camp. Conference at H.Q. 57th Divn R.E. Present C.R.E. & O.S.C. 421st 502nd & 505th Fd Cos. To 172nd Inf Bde H.Q. GOC 57th Div. approved M.A. team going stand. Arranged to make 64 of these for Bde L.G.O. JL	

WAR DIARY
INTELLIGENCE SUMMARY

(Erase heading not required.)

Army Form C. 2118.

OCTOBER

Place	Date	Hour	Summary of Events and Information	Remarks and references to Appendices
	22nd		Lt F.A. SHEEN & 6 O.R. proceeded to take over from 208th Fd Co R.E. at C.19.a.0.2. 1/Lt K.L.GORDON reported to attached infantry & Cpl Walker proceeded to XI Corps reinforcement camp to act as instructor. 64 A.A. Lewis Gun stands made and delivered to 172nd Tun Coy HQ.	
	23rd		Lt Capt Chappel 5 Sappers and 6 attached infantry proceeded to C.19.a.0.2 to take over dumps. Transport moved off at 7:30 a.m. under Lt G.E.Edom. 1/Lt MYLES DIXON & proceeded to B.24.c.0.2. Remainder of Company moved off at 12:45 p.m., entrained at PROVEN Station at 1:45 p.m. detrained at BOESINGHE at 3:0 p.m. and marched into billets at C.19.a.0.2. and took over from 208th Fd Co R.E. Major J.E.TINDALL returned from leave in the U.K. and took over	

Army Form C. 2118.

WAR DIARY
or
INTELLIGENCE SUMMARY
(Erase heading not required.)

Instructions regarding War Diaries and Intelligence Summaries are contained in F.S. Regs., Part II. and the Staff Manual respectively. Title Pages will be prepared in manuscript.

Place	Date	Hour	Summary of Events and Information	Remarks and references to Appendices
BELGIUM Sheet 28 NW B24.6.95-80	24th		Stores carted up to advance dumps at (WEEDON DUMP U 28 7·6) sheet 20 SW Carrying party of 150 men + 100 Pioneers carried Duckboards + pickets from there after dark & continued Track A which runs from the CANAL L'YSER at C 13 a 3-4 in North Easterly direction parallel with & about 600 yds distant from the Railway line to THOUROUT, & passes through the South edge of LANGEMARCK. Hence on to the present British front line in vicinity of Poelcapelle. — 3 Pioneers machine & still more personal dump at LANGEMARCK U 23 c 3-1, (sheet 20 S.W) 1 Sapper & 3 attached Infantry were wounded last night & 2 horses wounded —	
	25th			
	26th		Work proceeded on mdr but enemy fire delayed considerably. 170th Inf. Brigade attacked enemy position early morning but were not very successful, only first objective being gained one half of our line - consequently the posts which had to be taped out for guidance from new line back to existing duckboard track was not done by R.E.	
	27th		Laying of LANGEMARCK TRACK continued being held but work was	

WAR DIARY or INTELLIGENCE SUMMARY

Army Form C. 2118.

Place	Date	Hour	Summary of Events and Information	Remarks and references to Appendices
Belgium sheet 28NW B24 & 6520	29th		The Infantry working party of 110 were scattered by enemy shellfire which was very intense & sustained caused casualties. The PdHeirs suffered 7 casualties. 43 Sappers engaged in repair by rear portion of Track A. CRE instructed that a new siding be made at HAYMARKET C 13 c 50.15 sheet 28 NW adjoins the Ygel railway will facilitate delivery to R.E. stores. 9 Sapper & 15 Infantry engaged in levelling etc of stores forward. G.S.O's dugouts required wiring to partial collapse. Various repairs to G.O.C. & G.S.O's dugouts required owing to partial collapse.	sheet 28 NW
	29th		LANGEMARCK TRACK pushed forward by inpt & Rn broken up & repaired by Rm. Various R.E. services at rear. 150 working party asked for man reduced to 70 men.	
	30th		As usual - but the working party of 150 further reduced to 61 men.	
	31st		As usual - Enemy totally demolished the bridge over the STEENBEEK 20 SW 4. Used 2.5 wheel camel Track A track. The Enemy bombs ran killed & dumps round ELVERDINGE almost nightly.	

R. Findlay Major
to 505/ WD Fields RE

Strength of Company on 1st October 1917:- Officers 8.
O.R. 211.

In.

414705 Sapper J. Fleming, transferred to
this Unit from R.E. Base Depot   12/10/17.

522221 Sapper W. Childs, transferred to
this Unit from R.E. Base Depot   12/10/17.

2 Officers, 103 O.R. Infantry attached to this Unit.   21/10/17.

Out.

550982. Sapper J. Pifford evacuated to 58 C.C.S.
(sick) 28/9/17.

508187 Sapper H. Cox evacuated to 58 C.C.S.
(sick) 29/9/17.

217677. Sapper W. Grainger evacuated to 58 C.C.S.
(sick) 8/10/17.

508170. Sapper W. Talbot evacuated to 58 C.C.S.
(sick). 10/10/17.

508465. Sapper V. Lucas evacuated to 58 C.C.S.
(sick) 10/10/17.

508177. Sergt. C. Tyler proceeded to England to
undergo training preparatory to taking Commission
11/10/17. (Authority W.O. Letter Engineers/H.44 (SD.3) 4/10/17)

508266. Sapper W. Cray evacuated to C.C.S. (sick) 26/10/17.

508595 L/Cpl. G.L. Thompson — G.S Wound 26/10/17 —
evacuated to C.C.S. 27/10/17.

Strength on 31st October 1917:-   8 Officers.
                                   205 O.R.
Attached Infantry   2.Offs. 103 O.R.

31/10/17.

O/c 505th (Wessex) Field Co. R.E.   Major.

Report of Work done for 24 hours ending 6.0 am 1/4/17

Place or Map Reference	Infantry Working Parties.			no of R.E.	Name of O/c. Party or Work.	Percentage Progress	Description of work.
	Number agreed for.	Number actually employed	Number of hours at work.				
Canal Bank				6.	Capt. LLOYD	100%	Billet 22.
do				6	do.	100%	G.O.C. Billet.
do.				2.	do.	30%	Nissen Huts
do.				4	do.	75%	Notice Boards
do.				2.	do.	100%	Fixing Stoves.
HAYMARKET.	15	15	3¾ hrs. (1st party withdrawn)	6.	Lt. PAUL.	10%	Laying Roadway
STRAY. FM. Locality				4 11.	do.	31 new dklbds laid. 24 raised & relaid. 12 repaired	General repairs to TRACK "A"
LANGEMARCK TRACK.	150. 80 (attached Infantry)	68. 22* 49	4 hrs.		Lt. BUTLER	90 yds. track laid	Laying track.
TRAFALGAR SQ.				2.	Lt. PAUL.	100%	Painting Pickets
CANAL BANK.				3	Capt. LLOYD.	3%	Repairing dklds.

* Senior N.C.O's & Stretcher bearers.

MAJOR,
O.C. 505TH (WESSEX) FIELD COY. R.E.

WAR DIARY
INTELLIGENCE SUMMARY

Army Form C. 2118.

Vol 10

Confidential

War Diary
of the
505th (Wessex) Field Coy R.E.

from
NOVEMBER 1st to 30th 1917

Volume TEN

Lindsay Major
OC 505 Field Coy RE

Army Form C. 2118.

WAR DIARY
or
INTELLIGENCE SUMMARY

(Erase heading not required.)

NOVEMBER

Place	Date	Hour	Summary of Events and Information	Remarks and references to Appendices
BELGIUM 28 N.W. B.24.6.95.20	Nov 1st		Works as usual - The LANGEMARCK TRACK is now at V 7 C 95.20. Recd N.S Half 2/5 the attached infantry. Evacuated Sgt Metcalf of Gas. 2/5 S^th Lanc Regt. recd slight (gun) injuries new trench (at night)	Sheet 20 SE Belgium
	2nd		Works as usual - Lieut K.L. GORDON attached from the 2/4th S.L. Regt injured his knee by falling into a shellhole last night	
	3rd		Lieut K.L. GORDON evacuated - Affiliate CRE for two new trenches for the attached infantry.	
			LIEUT F.J. FRODSHAM 2/5 S Lancs Regt + 2/Lt MOLYNEUX of the 2/4th South Lancs Regt reported for duty with attached infantry.	
	4th		Instructions received from CRE to take over tramway from 92nd Field Co. RE further along the Canal Bank at C.13.a.3.9. + Smac tramcar -	28. N.W.
	5th		Moved took over billets from 92 M.F.C RE at C.13.a.4.4.	
	6th		Endeavoured to find 157 Brigade RFA tracers when Sam detailed for in laying artillery feeder tramlines but they have moved - The 2/50 Brigade whose country their portion served required the line.	

WAR DIARY
or
INTELLIGENCE SUMMARY

Army Form C. 2118.

Place	Date	Hour	Summary of Events and Information	Remarks and references to Appendices
Sheet 28 NW C13a 2.4	7th		The Right Centre, Left Group RA electorate that they do not require the feeder line - Constructed bridge for 18 pdr across the STEENBECQUE at U.28.d.2.5.	
	8th		CRA Left Group RA at am interview this morning instructed me to lay new feeder from existing tramline at about U.21 b central to U.22.b.0.8. Wired CE XIX accordingly. In evening received wire instructing me to take no further orders from R.A. & to take in hand erection of Nissen Huts tramlining Huts at B12.d.5~2. & new tram lines at A18.d.4.9. Reconnoitred new camp site, interviewed CRE 50th Div. who has the hub & will deliver tomorrow morning. 1 Nissan hut completed & 2 nearly completed - 1 cook house & 2 latrines nearly erected, + 3 Armstrong huts erected. 2 forge wheels filed in at U28.c.8.3 to allow guns to move & road in place made to them with fascines - shelter new horselines at A18.d.4.9 inspected - does not moderate.	57th Division to get 6 R.B? but at the usual manner in course.
	9th			
	10th		Camp at B12.d.5 completed - work in Horselines at A18.d.4.9 continues. Lt Butler proceed to course at FINECOURT.	Belgium 28 NW

WAR DIARY
or
INTELLIGENCE SUMMARY
(Erase heading not required.)

Army Form C. 2118.

Place	Date	Hour	Summary of Events and Information	Remarks and references to Appendices
Sht 28 C13a 9-4	7th		Instructed by CRE 57 Div to establish Indep 9r STEEN BECQUE U28d25-53 & commenced work	20 SW
	8th		Lieut R.B. PAUL 2/S. South Lancs Regt. attached this unit for instrum. proceeded on leave. Late arrive received from CRE 57 Div that Lieut Paul was to proceed to England to S.M. E. DECANWY for corpse. GOC RA left orders wired us to callupon him that he wished us instructed us to lay new artillery feeder line about CANNE'S FARM U22a 3-3. Bridge over Steenbeque completed. 57th Div move out of line	20 SW
	9th		Three Nissen Huts + 3 Armstrong Huts put in hand for erection for Camp Commandant B rd S-2	25 NW
	10th		Lieut L.G. Porter proceeds to FLIXECOURT for monthe Stawin Corpse Stabling for 350 horses put in hand for 33rd Res. Park A118d 49	28 NW
	11th 12 13		Instln in standlum in allen work in Camp Camelts huts completed with antitank standing	well done

(B)

(2)

Place	Date	Hour	Summary of Events and Information	Remarks and references to Appendices
Sheet 28NW Belgium C.13.a.4.4	14th		New entrance track commenced on am hoarding at Lang 5. Other work as usual.	
	15		Work as usual.	
	16		2/Cpl F.W. Breedy 508155 awarded Military Medal to date 8/4/17. Sergt F. Duddridge 508172 awarded Distinguished Conduct Medal - 2/4/17. 2/Corp G. Fortacre 508430 awarded Military Medal to date 15/4/17. Sapper W. Snowdon 506610 awarded Military Cross to date 15/4/17.	
	17		Work as usual - Inspected remains of Motor car at C.W.D.S. B22 b 8.3. Also site for Motor new car standing there. Pearl J.W. Lgd on leave 18th to 1/5/April. Horse standing for 33rd Res Park completed but are require standing for further 20 tyres. Inspected site for new standing for 72 Heavy Draft +5 Riders for the 5th Army Auxilary Horse Transport No 2 Section at B22 a 8.5. Also inspected Cemetary approach at B24d 2-9 which requires from road surface level	28 NW

P.

WAR DIARY or INTELLIGENCE SUMMARY

Army Form C. 2118.

Place	Date	Hour	Summary of Events and Information	Remarks and references to Appendices
28 NW C13a4.4	19"		Arrangts to Atorage motors, Coy haveis Rest day + Baths. Drying Room erected at our Horse lines	
	20"		Interviewed OC 7 Field Co RE + arranged to loan services of two sections of the unit for work on lines of No 2 Gen Sec at B16a 1.9 + D Bty 251 Bgde RFA at B10d 60 95. Work commenced on 5th army AHT lines + on new Wells (2) 33 Res Pk	
	21		Work as above — 2 Sections Commence work under 7 Field Co RE.	
	22 23 24 25 26 27 28		Work as above. Stabling being erected for RA 50th Division + AEC + several Nissen Huts	Apx ①
			25th Lieut F.A. SHEEN & 2 Lieut M. DIXON awarded the Military Cross	
	29		Notice from CRE XIX Corps to take over work of 7th Field Co RE of similar nature in addition to our own work	
	30"		Took over 7 Field Corps work so that we now have to erect stabling to the whole of the 50th Div RA CASC	

Rundall Major
OC 505 Fld Co RE

Strength of Coy. on 1/11/17 : 8 Offs. 207 O.R.

Outs.

508155.	2/Cpl. F. W. Breedy	Evacuated thro' C.C.S.	29/10/17
542010	Sapper W. E. Green	" "	29/10/17
508387.	Sapper R. C. Williams	" "	29/10/17
508196.	Sapper E. Francis	" "	31/10/17
508263	" E. Sweet	" "	3/11/17

Lieut. R. B. Paul (2/5th S.L.R.) attached. Ceased to be attached to this Unit on proceeding to England to undertake Commission 8/11/17.

242020 Rfn. W. Stockley (2/5 S.L.R.) Returned to his battalion on ceasing to act as Batman to Lieut. Paul 8/11/17.

508158.	Driver R. P. Seeley	Evacuated thro' C.C.S.	10/11/17
508464	Sapper W. Padfield	" "	11/11/17
522221.	" W. Childs	" "	15/11/17
209005	Driver J. Whittaker	" "	28/11/17

Ins.

450150.	2/Cpl. J. Jenkins	reported from No. 7 Reinforcement Coy.	6/11/17
526108	Sapper. J. Viney	reported from Base	10/11/17.
213526.	Driver W. Russell	" " "	17/11/17.
426634.	Sapper W. King	" " Calais	29/11/17.
472022	Sergt. G. Bulcraig	" " Base	29/11/17.
231343	Sapper J. S. Welsh	" " "	29/11/17.
187566.	" G. Blackmore	" " "	29/11/17.

Strength of Coy. 30/11/17. 7 Officers 204 O.R.

Honours and Awards.

Divisional Routine Order 1754 dated 27th November 1917

Honours and Awards.

Under authority granted by His Majesty the King, the Field Marshal Commanding-in-Chief, has awarded the MILITARY CROSS to the undermentioned for gallantry and devotion to duty in action :- { Authority XIX Corps Routine Order 935. 24/11/17.

2nd Lieut. F. A. SHEEN.   505th (Wessex) Field Co. R.E.

Near LANGEMARCK during the nights Oct. 23rd-24th, 24th-25th and 26th-27th showed great devotion to duty. He has led large working parties through several barrages, and succeeded in carrying out his work in spite of greatest difficulties. On one occasion, after having completed a day's work in forward area under shell fire, he voluntarily took the place of another Officer in charge of night work also in forward area, and succeeded in carrying out his work though subjected to heavy shell fire. His conduct on these occasions has set a splendid example to those under him.

2nd Lieut. M. DIXON.   505th (Wessex) Field Co. R.E.

Near LANGEMARCK on the night 28th-29th Oct. this Officer was in charge of a working party near the Front Line, when the enemy opened a heavy barrage interspersed with gas. In spite of this he completed the work, having nine casualties. He then proceeded on a reconnaissance accompanied by a Sergeant and returning found four more wounded Pioneers in shell holes. Two of these being severely wounded, he and the Sergeant carried them back nearly two miles to the dressing station. His conduct and devotion to duty, after an exceptionally arduous night's work, was exemplary.

The G.O.C. 57th Division congratulates the above mentioned on the receipt of the reward for their gallantry.

Major
O/c. 505th (Wessex) Field Co. R.E.

D.R.O. 1712. 17/11/17.

MILITARY MEDAL. (Authy. XIX Corps I.R. 17/1773.) Date of award 15/11/17

508430 2/Corpl. G. Louracre, 505 (Wessex) Field Co. R.E. (T.F.)

hear on the night 25th/26th October, 1917, this N.C.O. was in charge of a large party carrying duckboards to the Front Line. When near the Front the enemy opened a heavy barrage, which owing to the fatigued condition of the men, and the inclement weather, caused considerable disorganization. 2/Corpl. Louracre showed great skill, coolness and courage in rallying the party and proceeding with the work.

D.R.O. 1712. 17/11/17.

MILITARY MEDAL. (Authy. XIX. Corps. I.R. 17/1773). Date of award 15/11/17

508610 Sapper. W. Snowden, 505 (Wessex) Field Co. R.E. (T.F.)

hear on the night of the 24th/25th October, 1917, this man was one of a working party engaged in carrying forward duckboard tracks, when the enemy opened a heavy barrage, and four men were wounded. Although wounded himself, Sapper Snowden rallied his party and carried on with his work for six hours until same was completed. By his coolness under fire and devotion to duty, he set a splendid example to those under him.

The G.O.C. 59th Division congratulates the above mentioned N.C.O's and men on the receipt of the award for their gallantry

B. Tindall Major
Commanding 505th (Wessex) Field Co. R.E.

19/11/17

Honours and Awards

D.R.O. 1686. 12/7.

MILITARY MEDAL. (Authy: XIX Corps. I.R. 76/1724/52. Date of award 8/7)

No. 508155 2/Corpl. Frederick Walter Creedy. 505 (Wessex) Field Co. R.E. (T.F.)

at ——— on the night 23rd/24th October, when in charge of a working party, who scattered under heavy barrage, showed conspicuous bravery and great devotion to duty in rallying them, and, though not entirely successful, he returned with a few, and, by his personal efforts, succeeded in getting the work carried out for which he had been detailed.

D.R.O. 1710. 16/7. (Authy: I.M.C. in C.) Date of award 2/7.

Distinguished Conduct Medal

508172 Sergeant Frank Duddridge, 505 (Wessex) Field Co. R.E. (T.F.)

Near ——— on the night 28th/29th October 1917, having completed the night's work laying a track to the Front Line, during which 10% were casualties, he accompanied his Section Officer on a reconnaissance. Returning, they found a badly wounded Pioneer, and whilst 2/Lieut. Dixon applied first aid, Sergt. Duddridge searched the neighbouring area in spite of enemy shells and found three more Pioneers wounded, in shell holes, one being badly wounded. With 2/Lieut. Dixon he carried the two badly wounded men nearly two miles to the nearest Dressing Station on duckboards, it being dawn before the last one was got in. His disregard of danger and devotion to duty have set a splendid example to the men under him.

Army Form C. 2118.

WAR DIARY
or
INTELLIGENCE SUMMARY

(Erase heading not required.)

Original

Confidential

War Diary of the
505th (Wessex) Field Co. RE.

December 1st to 31st 1917

Volume Eleven

31/12/17

B. Riddell
O.C. 505 Fd Co RE.

Army Form C. 2118.

WAR DIARY
or
INTELLIGENCE SUMMARY
(Erase heading not required.)

December 1917

Place	Date	Hour	Summary of Events and Information	Remarks and references to Appendices
28 N.W. C.13a 4.4	1st to 6th		Work as usual - erecting Stabling Nissen Huts for 50th Divisional Ammn. Column & Reserve Parks A6C	
	4th		3rd Field S.P. SAUNDERS to Bridging Course at AIRE. 2nd Capt J.W. FLOYD returns from leave	
	7th		Lieut MYLES-DIXON MC proceeds on leave - 8th to 22nd. Received order that we were to be relieved by the 502 (Wessex) F.W. Co.R.E. a.Division commence moving up today.	
	8th		Enemy aeroplane drop bombs round area west of the Yser Canal every night but so far have not actually hit the Canal Bank. Weather, far from being fine trying lately. Work as usual - Weather wet.	
	9th		No turned wet. Finishing up work on many of the huts/lines today & performing handing over notes & others not complete.	
	10th		Moved to PROVEN Area	

Army Form C. 2118.

WAR DIARY
or
INTELLIGENCE SUMMARY

(Erase heading not required.)

Instructions regarding War Diaries and Intelligence Summaries are contained in F. S. Regs., Part II. and the Staff Manual respectively. Title Pages will be prepared in manuscript.

Place	Date	Hour	Summary of Events and Information	Remarks and references to Appendices
Sheet 27. F.14.c.8.6	11th		Major J.E. TINDALL M.C. proceeds to ROUSBRUGGE. (57th Divn RE.HQ) as A/C.R.E. Instructions to prepare scheme for Spray Baths	
"	12th		Lt G.E. EDSON and 3 O.R. to ELVERDINGHE Chateau as advance party. Company Nof-stores checked	
	13th		Reptthy routine no features. Scheme for Spray Baths completed.	
	14th			
	15th		Preparation to move into line	
Sheet 28 N.W. B.11.a.3.4.	16th		Transport under Lt F.A. SHEEN by road from F.14.c.8.6 to A.11.a.9.G. Sappers under Capt J.W. LLOYD by train from PROVEN to BOESINGHE. s by road to HAMPTON Camp B.11.a.3.4. Relieved 92nd Fld Coy R.E. Work handed over is mainly Decauville Track, with fosston to Battery Positions dummy stations etc. Area appears much quieter, but an enemy shell fell and are firing hostile roads. Neighbourhood of BOESINGHE dump shelled heavily from 6 to 7.0 pm.	

Army Form C. 2118.

WAR DIARY
or
INTELLIGENCE SUMMARY
(Erase heading not required.)

Instructions regarding War Diaries and Intelligence Summaries are contained in F. S. Regs., Part II. and the Staff Manual respectively. Title Pages will be prepared in manuscript.

Place	Date	Hour	Summary of Events and Information	Remarks and references to Appendices
Sheet 28 NW B.11 a 3.4	17th		Maintenance party commence work. Working party table received, further work in road maintenance, duckboard track and wiring of Corps line to proceed with. Working parties from 170th Inf Bde. Remainder of work and reconnaissance of position, stores etc. Lt L.G BUTIER returns from course	
	18th		Attached in party from 172nd Inf Bde. reports for duty. Lt HOLLAND 2/5 S. Lanc R. O.C 1 Lt D TOMLINSON 2/9 KLR 1 Lt E.W.W. BROWN 2/4 S.L.R 102 O.R. Lt S.J.R SAUNDERS returns from bridging course at AIRE. Infantry working parties working very well. Sharp frost makes delay the work in the morning for a delay the train, and the ground is hard for excavating. Thaw does not suffice to weaken as the frost lasts in driving pickets in ground in the camping and wiring along the wire.	
	19th		Arranged with D.T.O to carry on maintenance of decauville track. Instructions to prepare BROENBEKE bridge for signal cable and M.G. dugout in Corps line. Reconnaissance of position with D.M.G.O. Instructions to erect screens in V.20.	

WAR DIARY or INTELLIGENCE SUMMARY

Army Form C. 2118.

Place	Date	Hour	Summary of Events and Information	Remarks and references to Appendices
Sheet 28 NW B11a 3.4.	20th		Position of forces reconnoitred. Search extended to MG dugout. Instructions to prepare scheme for destroying BROENBEKE bridges in case of destruction in Enemy attack. Fire instructions to posts and O.C. patrols occupied by artillery. 1/5 HOLLAND 2/5 SLR relieved by 1/5 LeMARE an O.C. attached infantry. Attached infantry 3 O/c 102 O.R. left to be attached to 502 Fd Co RE. Parties rearranged to suit.	
	21st		Pill boxes and set up new plates in Bluewell track reconnoitred & cam. nets set. Instructions to support R.A.P.s and A.D. Station.	
	22nd		Work commenced on M.G. dugouts. Front still holding. Artillery active on both sides from 4.20 pm – 5.0 pm. Working parties passed through the lean fire with no casualties. Lt. L.G. BUTLER left for 14 days leave to U.K.	
	23rd		Work proceeding suit. patrols. Scheme for securing bridges over BROENBEKE discussed with a/CRE. Dump of trestles & chalk boards decided upon. E.A. bomb raid from S.O. to 5.20 pm. in neighbourhood of camp. Night very bright and moonlight. Wind half windy and brisk E on the evening up. No casualties. ma(w)SET will proceed onward onstream from Sewing Acting CRE. ...	

Army Form C. 2118.

WAR DIARY
or
INTELLIGENCE SUMMARY
(Erase heading not required.)

Instructions regarding War Diaries and Intelligence Summaries are contained in F. S. Regs., Part II. and the Staff Manual respectively. Title Pages will be prepared in manuscript.

Place	Date	Hour	Summary of Events and Information	Remarks and references to Appendices
POTSINGHE B11 a 3 4 Sheet 28 NW	24th		Order from CRE to put 2 further belts of double apron fence wiring across Corps line front - arranged for additional parties accordingly. Work as usual	Frost & snow. Clear moonlight nights.
	25th		Snowfall - Rest day	
	26th		New wiring commenced - also kept shelter for infantry in REKRUIT Dugout across U.16.a.t. Sheet 20 S.W. All stores and apparently wagons etc. are taken up on light railway by pushing trucks. NYDENDRIFT U.21 Central	
	27th		Work as usual - 90 men from 172nd Inf. Brigade under instruction commenced erecting shelters on the Corps line at KOEKUIT.	
	28th		Work as above - men lying - forty bright nights. Orders to move and re 3rd Army received the 92nd Fd Co relieving us which the 80th Fd Co meant	
	29th		No working parties - damage done to road by enemy fire repaired.	
	30th		Working parties from incoming 53rd Brigade - snowstorm lies firm	
	31st		Handing over papers etc. Was prepared for relief by 80th Fd Co RE.	

R. Randall Major
505 Field Co RE

Strength on 1/7. Offs. 7, O.R. 204.

Ins.

518350 Sapper J. Sirdan reported from Base 3/12/17.
508191. Sergt. C. Maggs
85666. 2/Cpl. J. McKay
28461 Driver J. Simpson
136750.   "   J. Spraggon   } Reported from Base
203896 Sapper J. Lingwood   } 6/12/17.
412784   "   W. Little
536037.   "   J. Lucas
143601.   "   J. Crading
99818.   "   G. Cornes
434344. 2/Cpl. R. Rowbottom reported from Base 20/12/17.

Outs.

526108 Sapper J. Nivey evacuated through C.C.S. 29/11/17
508272 Sapper J. Roaber evacuated through C.C.S. 26/11/17
506496. Sapper E. L. Jones   "   "   "   16/12/17
506610 Sapper W. Snowden, M.M. "   "   "   28/12/17
505247 Corpl. S. P. Taylor transferred to 508th (Wessex) Res.
           Field Co. R.E. 20/12/17.
508171. 2/Cpl. A. D. Jones evacuated through C.C.S. 28/12/17

Strength on 31/12/17. 7 Offs. 209 O.R.

31/12/17

Tindall Major
O/C. 505th (Wessex) Field Co. R.E.

WAR DIARY
OR
INTELLIGENCE SUMMARY

JANY. 1916.

Army Form C. 2118.

Place	Date	Hour	Summary of Events and Information	Remarks and references to Appendices
BOESINGHE Hampton Camp K 2 14-75	1st		Handed over work as directed by CRE to 80th Field Co RE advance officer, but as no men of that unit were available for work I had to carry on with the working parties as usual and in addition had to render officer & 1 section RE to send to infantry to work sector V 12 a as the inf. already had failed to carry out the work, the two previous nights the RE Co in line moved yesterday — the relieving Coy have not yet arrived.	Sheet 5A Hazebrouck Sheet 20 SW
	2nd		Unit moved from BOESINGHE at 10 a.m. handing billets over to the 92nd Field Co RE. The Roads were covered with ice & I had to leave behind all the extra usual stores, trappage, that a Field Coy has to carry, in order to run the waggons light — We arrived without a hitch at LA CLYTTE J 3 54-59 at 3 p.m. only to find that the billet allotted to us was occupied by a Canadian RE Co. so far to find a billet for twelve. — Cold intense. — Route via ELVERDINGHE — V-VLAMERTINGHE — RENINGHELST.	APX 1
LACLYTTE J3 54-59	3rd		Moved out at 10 a.m. & by route LOCRE — BAILLEUL marched to ARMENTIÈRES arriving at Horseliens allotted LA HAYES FARM K 4 - 18-21 only to find it occupied by a 12th Divn Full Co RE — again march was to be made for nights shelter — on arrival at the new billet THE BLUE BLIND FACTORY K 4/45-21 it was found that the billet comprises one large room the factory will the glass blown out — an unsuitable place to warm the officers billet was occupied by the 70 Field co who however had to move out —	Sheet 5A APX 2 & 3 (1) J.T.

WAR DIARY
or
INTELLIGENCE SUMMARY

Army Form C. 2118.

Place	Date	Hour	Summary of Events and Information	Remarks and references to Appendices
ARMENTIERES B30d 05.65 Sheet 36	4th		Made Reconnaissance of Houplines N°5 with regard to providing 5.9 front cellar accommodation - Interview with Town Major re obtaining Timber from buildings 5 O.R. reported to ERQUINGHEM DUMP H.4 c.6.4 sheet 36.	
	5th		Moved to better billet at PONT MEPPE B.23 d.3-9 (new billet) Held an hour on main road B.23 b.4-1. - Homelnis B.23 c 6.3. The new billet is badly damaged by shellfire but can be repaired, & only accommodates & works for 30 horses whereas our strength is 75 animals. Rejected Timber merchants' premises in Armentieres with Town Major. Lieut DIXON.M. evacuated to Hospital. - 1 NCO v 30 O.R. of attached Infantry sent to ERQUINGHEM + BAC ST MAUR DUMPS	
	6		Wiring from WEST YORKS POST C.27 d central NE ward to River top commenced with Pioneers - shelter at Homelines also commenced - all available men are engaged in salvaging material in ruined buildings of Armentieres suitable for strutting up cellars, & iron for reinforced concrete. Transport carting same to local dumps near proposed works. Lieut MYLES DIXON evacuated to CCS Reconnaissance made of all bridges over River, & minor & Pontoon. Permanent Pontoon. Roads very bad repair with ice making work difficult.	RT

Army Form C. 2118.

WAR DIARY
or
INTELLIGENCE SUMMARY

(Erase heading not required.)

Instructions regarding War Diaries and Intelligence Summaries are contained in F. S. Regs., Part II. and the Staff Manual respectively. Title Pages will be prepared in manuscript.

Place	Date	Hour	Summary of Events and Information	Remarks and references to Appendices
Pont Nieppe B23 b 4-1	7th		All work to in ARMENTIERES town to be stopped and whole Company to be concentrated on Hoplines asylum & areas – Reconnaissance accordingly.	
	8th		Detailed Reconnaissance of Cellar master areas –	
	9th		Area again changed this unit is to concentrate on the Hoplines Sector. N°45 Army Troops Coy, R.E. coming up to take the ASYLUM area.	
	10th		Reconnaissance & rewriting. Pt 9.E.E. down proceed in lorries to 11" to 25". Peplanka & plans – entering of trench stores – our works include the wiring scheme above mentioned include	
	11th		(1) a double belt of wire to be made from Rue L75 at C21 b 2·7 westward to C.19 b central	
			(2) Rendering 5·9 shellproof M.G. team dugouts + emplacements	Third 3b
			at FARM POST C 21 d 60·45 HERRING CORNER C21 b 95·10	
			DUBLIN CASTLE C22 c 2·6 JAMES CORNER C21 d 9·2	
			FISHERS HOLE C27 b 8·7 KENNETHS PRIDE C27 & 70·35	
			LEOS RETREAT C27 b 60·35 ALLANS POSSE C27 c 8·7	

(3)

Place	Date	Hour	Summary of Events and Information	Remarks and references to Appendices
Port Neuffe B25 b4	11th		Casth. 3 Infantry Wounded in wiring tonight in party Hortimer. Cement is coming up but Sand is so far rare.	
	12th		Work commenced on fire proofing all Machine gunner Dugouts, reinforcements & shellproofing commenced on FISHER'S HOLE C 27 b 8 7 & DURHAM CASTLE C 22 b 2 6. Concrete Materials are drawn from FROUVIGHEM in the morning & taken down to the Coy Rear Dump at C 26 d 07.57 - afternoon The buffers unload then pick up salvaged material in the town & take it to the same dump.	
	13th		The waggons again collect wiring material from Equingham dump in the afternoon & take it onward to the forward dump at C 21 d 75 - 27, then returning to the rear dump & carting concrete material from there to the forward dump. Snow makes work difficult & given away by tractor, all horses & tracks used.	(4)

WAR DIARY or INTELLIGENCE SUMMARY

Army Form C. 2118.

Place: Nieppe / Bisbey(?)

Date	Hour	Summary of Events and Information	Remarks and references to Appendices
13th		Continued. Working parties let out snow today only as wiring party of 158 has been working - snow continues -	Apx.
14th		2 Lieut J.T.S. FREEMAN returns to duty from S.O.S. (Nieuw) Res. FLECRE. THAW set in with strong wind - Carpenter to SEELE Pettinado in Armentieres to inspect signal dugouts - work employed.	
15th		Two houses 84 Rue de Lille, & 36 Rue de 12 ARMISTRES, Armentieres demolished by explosive as they were in dangerous condition. Signals Dugouts Resp. Pettinado Armentieres & Pontet. Wind damage the Rurd Pont d'Ate & 2 Sappers at Plain rue B25a2 Reinforcement Camp at Steenwerck, A18a5,9 needs trucking & Carpenter sent to commence work.	Wet + THAW.
16		Explosives at the various bridges over the Lys in Armentieres (which in case of need would have to be demolished) Tested -	
17		Baths doing considerably in Lys when in flooding adjoining area. Field Paths at ERQUINGHEM attended to - Boom across river at C 26 a 61 attended to but return unfavourable owing to flood.	Apx.

(5)

Army Form C. 2118.

WAR DIARY
or
INTELLIGENCE SUMMARY
(Erase heading not required.)

Place	Date	Hour	Summary of Events and Information	Remarks and references to Appendices
Pont Nieppe	17th		Battery Headqrs at C.26a in Colefour Cowditz & Sappers were sent at once to save & strengthen same - Gunners invariably ignore all instructions in making new places of habitation, in this case 4 feet of stone & brick were placed over the first floor over a room 16 × 14 with a vain attempt at strutting up the floor above. The Thaw has brought down the walls of all the new communication trenches where not revetted.	
	18th		Flood still rising & Notices from billets are under water - also several of the works i.e. M.G. Dugouts.	
	19th		Flood still rising - at PONT NIEPPE it is 13½" only below the record flood mark of NOV. 1894 - working parties nearly all failed to turn up as they got their feet wet en route to the rendezvous!	
	20th		Flood fell 3 in. - Floor of Concrete, reinforced, 12" thick laid to FISHERS HOLE C.27.b.80.65 -	
	21st		Work as usual. Concrete dugout C.27.C.87. (ALLAN'S POSTE) repaired & made fit for use. Other work as usual.	

(6)

R.

WAR DIARY or INTELLIGENCE SUMMARY

Army Form C. 2118.

Place	Date	Hour	Summary of Events and Information	Remarks and references to Appendices
Pont Nieppe B23 c.4.1 Sheet 36	22nd		Flood still high but subsiding. Two Coy to be forward, in the event of the enemy attacking & attacking ARMENTIERES, to demolishing 11 bridges & for erecting & putting bridges all between the bank PONT NIEPPE B24 c.0.9. Sheet 36 and C21 d 4.4. – O.C. Coy & C Stonework inspected with regard to stones being filled safely in accordance with letter from Division re prevention of fires. Artillery OP at BRENTWOOD C 26 d 3.9 inspected – There was a chimney on left of observation – came repaired by 2 Sappers.	Sheet 36
	24th		Conference with C.R.E., O Coy Commanders at Armentieres in 421 Field Coy billet.	
	25 26th		CRE inspected M.G. Dugouts & emplacements at FISHERS HOLE & DURHAM CASTLE. The flood dropped sharply during night & the two barrel pier bridges were found to be stranded on land & had to be cleared by the working party. We were found for the purpose.	
	27th 28th		Both as usual on the two Pultroys (at Lamorche Dugouts) The order to go proof all hutted in Armentières unable to be complied with.	

(7)

WAR DIARY
or
INTELLIGENCE SUMMARY

Army Form C. 2118.

Place	Date	Hour	Summary of Events and Information	Remarks and references to Appendices
	29th		Arrangements made to [prepare?] canvas roof being a small lt.g. Lieut G.E. EATON returned from leave (27th). Previous on Pillbox now templates into draft re 7 am to 12 noon	
	30th	12 noon to 5 pm	Weather fine. Lieut S.J.R. SAUNDERS proceed to UK on leave 12/7/17 to 17/7/17 owing to pressure of work at Houplines it is impossible with working parties to ensure to have a section off to rehearse bridge demolition on 3 NCOs & 3 Sappers from each section rehearse daily. be parties changing each two days when all ratings have been rehearsed	
	31st		R.E. drawing giving level section of Railway embankment at C 27a 15.99 to CRE is being prepared to control column engats here.	

R. [signature] Major
C.O. 555 R.E. C.S.R.E.

(8)

SECRET.   53rd. Inf. Bde. No. G.914   APX 1

Norf. R.
Suff. R.
Essex R.
R. Berks R.

1.   The 18th. Div. Engineers are to relieve 57th. Div. Engineers as follows :-

   (a) 79th. Fd. Coy.R.E. to relieve 502nd. Fd. Coy.R.E. on Jan 1 st.
   (b) 80th. Fd. Coy.R.E. to relieve 505th. Fd. Coy.R.E. on Jan 1 st.
   (c) 92nd. Fd. Coy.R.E. to relieve 421st. Fd. Coy.R.E. on Jan.2nd.

   In consequence of the above reliefs, 53rd. Inf. Brigade will not be required to provide Serial Nos. 2, 6, and 8 on January 1st. These parties will recommence on January 2nd.

2.   Attached Infantry Platoons as when the Brigade was last in the line, will rejoin the 79th. Field Coy. R.E. on January 2nd., by 12 noon.
   Camp of 79th. Field Coy. R. E. is at BORSINGHE CAMP.

   Reference this office No. B. M. 210 dated 31st. August, 1917. 6th. R. Berks R. will detail an officer in relief of :-

   2nd. Lieut. R. H. TOTTMAN, 10th. Essex R.

   (name to be reported to this office).

   Acknowledge.

29th. Dec. 1917.   Captain,
                                    Brigade Major, 53rd. Inf. Brigade.

Copies to :-   79th. Fd. Coy. R.E.
               C. R. E. 18th. Div.
               502nd. Fd. Coy. R.E.
               505th. Fd. Coy. R.E.

SECRET.   Copy No......3......

57th DIVISION.

C.R.E's. OPERATION ORDER No. 14.

Map reference:-
HAZEBROUCK 5a, 1/100,000.   Headquarters, R.E.,
SHEET 20 S.W., 20 S.E., 28 N.W., 1/20,000.   29th December, 1917.

1. The 57th Divisional Engineers will be relieved by the 18th Divisional Engineers in the Forward Area as follows :-

    (a) The 421 Field Company R.E. will be replaced at CANAL BANK (B.6.c.8.2.) by the 80th Field Company R.E., on January 1st, 1918. The work being done in Line by the 421 Field Coy. R.E. will be taken over by the 92nd Field Company R.E. Advance Parties from this Company reporting to 421 Field Company R.E. on December 30th, 1917.

    (b) The 502 Field Company R.E. will be relieved by the 79th Field Company R.E. on January 1st, 1918.

    (c) The 505 Field Company R.E. will be replaced at HAMPTON CAMP (B.11.a.2.3.) by the 92nd Field Company R.E. on January 2nd, 1918. The work being done by the 505 Field Coy. R.E. will be taken over by the 80th Field Coy. R.E.

2. (a) The R.E. Personnel at BOESINGHE DUMP will be replaced by 18th Divisional R.E. on January 1st, 1918.

    (b) The 20 Other Ranks at BOESINGHE DUMP will rejoin their respective Units on night of December 30th, 1917.

3. (a) R.S.M. Cook, R.E., will be relieved at ONDANK R.E. DUMP on January 2nd, 1918.

    (b) The R.E. Personnel at ONDANK DUMP of 57th Divisional R.E. will rejoin their Units the day prior to the move of their respective Companies.

    (c) The 2 O.R. at ONDANK DUMP will rejoin their respective Units on night of December 30th, 1917.

4. (a) Movements in connection with the Relief will be carried out in accordance with attached March Table.

    (b) The attached Infantry will move with the Field Companies.

5. On Relief the 57th Divisional R.E. will be transferred to the 1st Anzac Corps.

6. Completion of Moves will be notified to this Office daily.

7. All Plans, Papers, etc., relating to the Sector will be handed over to the incoming Companies and receipts obtained.

8. C.R.E's Office will close at ELVERDINGHE CHATEAU 10 a.m. on January 3rd, 1918, and reopen at a place which will be notified later.

9. ACKNOWLEDGE.

                                                    Athole Campbell
                                                         Lieut.-Colonel,
Issued at 3 p.m.   C.R.E., 57th Division.

D I S T R I B U T I O N :-

Copy No. 1 - O.C. 421 Field Company R.E.
        2 - O.C. 502   - do -
        3 - O.C. 505   - do -
        4 - C.R.E., 18th Division.
        5 - "G" 57th Div.
        6 - "A & Q" 57th Div.
        7 - 170th Infantry Brigade.
        8 - 171st   - do -
        9 - 172nd   - do -
       10 - 57th Divl. Sig. Coy. R.E.
       11 - 57th Div. Train.
       12 - R.S.M. Cook, R.E.
       13 - War Diary.
       14 -   -do-
       15 - File.
       16 - Spare.

MARCH TABLE ISSUED WITH C.R.E'S OPERATION ORDER No. 14.

1. Serial No.	2. Date.	3. Unit.	4. From.	5. To.	6. Bus, Train, or Road.	7. Route.	8. Remarks.
1.	1st Jany. 1918.	421 Fld. Coy. with attached Infantry.	CANAL BANK.	GODE AREA.	Road.	To join the surplus transport of 170th Inf. Brigade and march with them under orders of G.O.C. 170th Inf. Brigade.	Billets in GODE AREA will be allotted by Staff Captain 170th Inf. Bde. 1 3 cwt lorry will report to carry surplus kit of attached Infty. Reach POPERINGHE Switch Rd., at 10.15 a.m.
2.	1st Jany. 1918.	502 Fld. Coy. Personnel.	BOESINGHE AREA.	PROOSDY AREA.	Road.	F.l.o. & d.	Clear INTERNATIONAL CORNER at 10.45 a.m.
3.	1st Jany. 1918.	502 Fld. Coy. Transport.	- do -	GODE AREA.	Road.	POPERINGHE SWITCH ROAD, ABEELE.	To join 170th Brigade surplus Transport at POPERINGHE Switch Rd, at 10.15 a.m.
4.	2nd Jany. 1918.	421 Fld. Coy. & Attd. Infantry.	GODE AREA.	LA HAYS AREA.	Road.	Via BAILLEUL.	Motor lorry to return to Unit on arrival at LA HAYS.
5.	2nd Jany. 1918.	502 Fld. Coy. Personnel.	PROOSDY AREA.	BAILLEUL WEST by train thence to LA HAYS by road.	Road, Rail, Road.		Entrain at PROVEN under Brigade arrangements. (Sufficient Camp kettles to be taken by Unit.)
6.	2nd Jany. 1918.	502 Fld. Coy. Transport.	GODE AREA.	LA HAYS.	Road.	BAILLEUL.	Move with 421 Fld. Coy. and surplus Transport 170 Bde.

1. Serial No.	2. Date.	3. Unit.	4. From.	5. To.	6. Bus, Train or Road.	7. Route.	8. Remarks.
7.	2nd Jany. 1918.	505 Fld.Coy. & Attd.Infantry.	BOESINGHE AREA.	WESTOUTRE.	Road.	VLAMERTINGHE, OUDERDOM & RENINGHELST.	Billets to be obtained from Town Major. arrive WESTOUTRE between 3 & 4 p.m.
8.	3rd Jany. 1918.	505 Fld.Coy. & Attd.Infantry.	WESTOUTRE	LA HAYS AREA.	Road.	LOCRE & BAILLEUL.	13 cwt. Motor lorry will report to carry surplus kit of attd.Infty. on Jany. 2nd & 3rd.
9.	3rd Jany. 1918.	421 Fld.Coy.with Attd.Infantry.	LA HAYS AREA.	To billets of 3rd /ust.Div. Fld.Coy. ANENITIES.	Road.	Any.	Application to be made to train Coy. at STEENWERCK for G.S. wagons required to carry surplus kit of Attached Infantry with 505 and 421 Coys.
10.	3rd Jany. 1918.	502 Field Coy.	L. HAYS	- do -	Road.	Any.	
11.	4th Jany. 1918.	505 Field Coy. with /ttd. Infantry.	L. HAYS	To billets of 3rd Aust.Div. R.E.	Road.	Any.	Orders with regard to Reliefs of Aust. Field Coys. will be issued later.

SECRET.   Copy No....3....

57th DIVISION.

C.R.E's. OPERATION ORDER No. 15.

Map reference:-
HAZEBROUCK 5a, 1/100,000.   Headquarters, R.E.,
SHEET 20 S.W., 20 S.E., 28 N.W., 1/20,000.   30th December, 1917.

1. On arrival in the 1st Anzac Corps Area, 57th Division will relieve 3rd Australian Division in Line.

2. The 57th Divisional Engineers will relieve the 3rd Australian Divisional Engineers.

   (a) The 421 Field Company R.E. relieving the 9th Australian Field Coy. R.E. on January 2nd, 1918.

   (b) The 502 Field Company R.E. relieving the 11th Australian Field Coy. R.E. on January 3rd, 1918.

3. Officers Commanding concerned will arrange details of take-over direct and will occupy billets vacated by outgoing Companies.

   All documents, plans, etc., relating to their Sector will be taken over.

4. Advance Parties consisting of 1 Officer, 2 N.C.O's. and 2 Sappers from the 421 and 502 Field Companies will proceed on January 1st, 1918, by cycles, reporting same day to 9th and 11th Australian Field Companies respectively.

5. The March Table issued with C.R.E's Operation Order No. 14, of 28th December, 1917, will be modified as attached.

6. **MOVEMENTS BY TRAIN.**

   (a) Two personnel and 1 transport train will be allotted to 170th Infantry Brigade on 2nd January. Time Tables will be issued in due course.

   (b) Troops and Transport must be clear of trains within 30 minutes of arrival at destination.

7. **MOVEMENT BY ROAD.**

   (a) Transport moving by road of Brigade Groups going by train will march under orders of O.C. Affiliated Company of Divisional Train.

   (b) An Officer will be detailed to proceed in advance in sufficient time to arrange billets and horse lines.

8. The following minimum distances will be maintained between Units on the march :-

Between Companies	100 yards.
,, Unit & its Transport...	100 ,,
,, Battalions	500 ,,
,, Transport of Units when Brigaded	100 ,,

   In addition, vehicles of all kinds, whether mechanical or horse must leave gaps of 25 yards between each section of 6 vehicles, and 50 yards between columns to enable traffic to pass.

9. Columns of troops and transport will not be allowed to halt in the following sections of road :-
   (A) Roads in BAILLEUL.
   (B) BAILLEUL - LOCRE - ECHERPENBERG - LA GLYTTE - DICKSBUSCH - CAFE BEIGE ROAD.
   (C) Roads through POPERINGHE.
   (D) POPERINGHE Switch Road.

10. ACKNOWLEDGE.

                                              A La Tobe Campbell
                                              Lieut.-Colonel,
                                     C.R.E., 57th Division.

Issued at 8 0 a.m.

DISTRIBUTION:-

Copy No. 1. - O.C. 421 Field Coy. R.E.
       2. - O.C. 502   - do -
       3. - O.C. 505   - do -
       4. - ~~C.R.E., 18th Division.~~ MO.RE
       5. - "G" 57th Division.
       6. - "A" and "Q" 57th Division.
       7. - 170 Brigade.
       8. - 171 - do -
       9. - 172 - do -
      10. - 57th Divl. Signal Coy. R.E.
      11. - 57th Divl. Train.
      12. - R.S.M., Cook, R.E.
      13. - War Diary.
      14. - - do -
      15. - File.
      16. - Spare.
      17. - C.R.E., 3rd Australian Division.

MARCH TABLE issued with C.R.E's. OPERATION ORDER No. 15.

1. Serial No.	2. Date.	3. Unit.	4. From.	5. To.	6. Bus, train or road.	7. Route.	8. Remarks.
4.	2nd Jany. 1918.	421 Fld.Co.R.E. with Attd.Infty.	GODE AREA.	Billets in ARMEN-TIERES, Rue Sadi CARNOT, C.25.c.30.30. Transport LA HAYS, B.28.b.05.65.	Road.	BAILLEUL, NIEPPE.	To relieve 9th Australian Field Company R.E., in Left Sector. Motor lorry to return to D.S.C. at once.
5.	2nd Jany. 1918.	502 Fld.Co.R.E. Personnel.	PROOSDY AREA.	To LA HAYS FARM, B.28.d.7.9.	Road, Rail, Road.	BAILLEUL, Pont de NIEPPE, les 3 Tilleuls.	Company to billet in LA HAYS FARM for the night.
6.	2nd Jany. 1918.	502 Fld.Co.R.E. Transport.	GODE.	LA HAYS FARM AREA.	Road.	BAILLEUL, Pont de NIEPPE.	Horse Lines at B.28.b.3.7.
7.	2nd Jany. 1918.	505 Fld.Co.R.E. & Attd.Infantry.	BOESINGHE AREA.	WESTOUTRE AREA.	Road.	RENINGHELST LA CLYTTE.	Billets will be at LA CLYTTE Sheet 28, M.12.d.3.4.
8.	3rd Jany. 1918.	505 Fld.Co.R.E. & Attd.Infantry.	LA CLYTTE.	ARMENTIERES. to Billets.	Road.	LOCRE, BAILLEUL, NIEPPE.	Billets for Company and attached Infantry in BLUE BLIND Factory, ARMENTIERES, B.30.a.7.0. Horse Lines will be notified later. Motor lorry to return to D.S.C.
10.	3rd Jany. 1918.	502 Fld.Co.R.E.	LA HAYS FARM.	ARMENTIERES. Billets of 11th Aust. Field Co.R.E.	Road.	Any.	Billets in Jute Factory, ARMEN-TIERES, C.29.b.5.2. Horse Lines to remain at B.28.b.3.7.

APX 4

WAR DIARY. Jan. 1918.

Strength on Jan 1st 1918. Offs. 7 O.R. 208.

INS.

~~508171 L/Cpl A. W. Jones~~

438695 Driver C. Baguley reported to this Unit from Base 15/8

2/Lieut J.T.S. Freeman (508th (Wessex) Reserve Fd Co. R.E.) reported to this Unit for duty 14/8.

141167 Driver H. Guttridge reported to this Unit from Base 22/8.

OUTS.

508171 L/Cpl A.W. Jones — Evacuated through 63 C.C.S. 28/12/17.
476039 Sergt J.W. Castle — Evacuated to Base & struck off strength
508590 Corpl J.C. Bray.   "   "   "   "   "
2/Lieut M. Dixon M.C. Evacuated through No. 2 C.C.S. 6/1/18.
414705 Sapper T. Fleming Evacuated through 54 C.C.S. 13/8
504641 Sapper W. Bowditch   "   "   "   9/8
508164   "   E. Small   "   "   "   6/8
508241 A/Lce Corpl. A. H. Coombes "   "   "   2/8
136750 Driver L. Spraggins   "   "   "   13/8

Strength on Jan 31st 1918. Offs. 7 O.R. 202

31st Jan. 1918.

B. Tyndall Major.
O/c 505th (Wessex) Field Co. R.E.

Confidential
Vol 13

WAR DIARY
OF THE
505th (WESSEX) FIELD Co R.E.
from
FEBRUARY 1st to 28th 1916

VOLUME THIRTEEN

P. Tindall
Major
OC 505 (W) Fld Co RE

WAR DIARY or INTELLIGENCE SUMMARY

Army Form C. 2118.

FEBY 1918

Place	Date	Hour	Summary of Events and Information	Remarks and references to Appendices
PONT de NIEPPE B.23.b.4.1 Sheet 36	Feb. 1		Major JE TINDALL left for STEENWERCK Reinforcement camp to act as O.C. XV Corps leave party, & proceed on leave U.K. from 4th-18th inst. Platoon posts at CROSS CUT I.3.c.1.3. – C.27.b.4.4 to be put in hand. FISHERS HOLE pill box completed. This to be provided with a splinter proof covered way, strong enough to withstand shock of falling walls of the house to shelter entrance.	
	2		CROSS CUT reconnoitred with C.R.E. for position of platoon posts. No working parties, sappers employed on rehearsal of bridge and general repairs to schemes.	
	3		Leave allotment increased from 1 per week to 4 per week. C.R.E.'s conference with O.C. Pn Corps at 505 billet. Rearrangement of work discussed and method of allotting. Training & working Pioneer Bath in EPINETTE sub sect 505 Company to take over work in line from 421 Company (from I.16.b.4.5 – C.29.c.2.3.) Bridges Nos 17 & 18 to be taken over by 421 Company & No 11,12,19, & 21 to be rehearsed by 421 Company & taken over 8-2-18.	
	4		CROSS CUT position reconnoitred. Recce and scheme for Bridges Nos 11,12,19, & 21 handed over to 421 Company. Wiring of West York - Houplines locality handed over to 421 Company. Work in line reconnoitred for taking over	

WAR DIARY or INTELLIGENCE SUMMARY

Army Form C. 2118.

(Erase heading not required.)

Place	Date	Hour	Summary of Events and Information	Remarks and references to Appendices
	5th		All Inf. made up to 100 men – 38 O.R. from 9th K.L.R & 2/4th K.L.R. Lt. I. G. BUTLER with No 3 Section to forward NUCC in RUE DE LA CRECHE. for work in line	
	6th		Conference with Brig Gen C. 172nd Inf Bde as to friendly of work in line, and working parties. Drainage & maintenance to own front. 1st Lt H. GUY and 1st Lt S. REED with 4 O.R. reported for attachment for instruction. Arranged that one officer with 1st team and one Sergeant is attached for both line & defence work. These officers will be attached for ten days and will exchange duties at the fifth day.	
	7th		Work continues each periodic on new arrangement. Incinerators commenced at A 23 b 15.	
	8th		DURHAM CASTLE pill box completed.	
	9th		B.E shelters to be provided for platoon front in CROSS CUT. Position settled and work commenced.	
	10th		New defence line behind CROSS CUT reconnoitred, and site for proposed dugout in rail way embankment at HOUPLINES STATION.	
	11th		New defence line commenced	
	12th		This day completes the units first years service overseas. Of the original company casualties from all causes have accounted for 3 Officers & 66 O.R. leaving 150 all ranks still serving with the unit. 9 casualties among O.R. have returned to the Company from base depots, and drafts have supplied casualties of 3 Officers and 12 O.R. Total for the year 6 Officers & 87 O.R.	

JL

Army Form C. 2118.

WAR DIARY
or
INTELLIGENCE SUMMARY
(Erase heading not required.)

Instructions regarding War Diaries and Intelligence Summaries are contained in F. S. Regs., Part II. and the Staff Manual respectively. Title Pages will be prepared in manuscript.

Place	Date	Hour	Summary of Events and Information	Remarks and references to Appendices
	13th		Advance party from 123 Fld Coy RE reconnoitred work preparatory to taking over on the 15th inst in accordance with CRE 38th Divn RE Operation order, and Lieut G.E. EDSON and 5 O.R. reconnoitered work of 123 Fld Coy RE in accordance with CRE 57th Divn Operation order.	
	14th		The covered way & bunks in FISHERS HOLE were completed and the work handed over ready for occupation.	
	15th		Relief between 123 Fld Coy RE & 505 Fld Coy RE completed at 11.45 a.m. and Company settled in new billet at LA HAYS FARM. B 28 b 75.05 Sheet 36 N.N. with transport at Ferme Plouc. Work consists of MG shelters and wiring in battle zone. The MG shelter is commenced in accordance with XV Corps design, at H 16 a 35.15 and and of the material is on site. Wiring is mainly in H.17 from Divn boundary to RUE des ACQUETS, north of the RUE de LETTREES	
	16th		Work continued. The MG shelter is carried on in two shifts working from dawn to dusk, but owing to heavy frost concrete has to be held up somewhat and the opportunity is taken to camouflage stores & mixing platforms which are very exposed at present. Lieut REED & GUY with party attached for instruction returned to their unit.	

2449 Wt. W14957/M90 750,000 1/16 J.B.C. & A. Forms/C.2118/12.

Army Form C. 2118.

WAR DIARY
or
INTELLIGENCE SUMMARY

(Erase heading not required.)

Instructions regarding War Diaries and Intelligence Summaries are contained in F. S. Regs., Part II. and the Staff Manual respectively. Title Pages will be prepared in manuscript.

Place	Date	Hour	Summary of Events and Information	Remarks and references to Appendices
	17th		Lieuts. P.J. SKINNER and B. TAYLOR with 4 O.R. reported for 10 days instruction. Lieut. S.J.R. SAUNDERS returned from leave in U.K.	
	18th		2 Lieut. J.T. FREEMAN to A.D.S. and evacuated to C.C.S. sick.	
	19th		Work is at present arranged as follows :- One Section RE with HQ 4th Div. Inf. work the two shifts on M.G. shelter. Three Section RE with 30 atta. Inf. working one RE & 12 Inf. Inf. fatigue party, for Shew. Major J.E. TINDALL returned from leave in U.K.	
	20th		Two M.G. reinforced concrete order at H.16.d.3-1 now well in hand. As is also the wiring before mentioned.	Sheet 36
	21st to 26th		Work as usual, on M.G. shelter & wiring	
	27th		M.G. shelter at H.16.d.3-1 completed - new position for similar shelter reconnoitred at H.33.c.4.9. Croix Blanche Post and H.27.d.35-40 S.g. #1 EURBAIX Sheet 36	
	28th		Camouflaging put in hand to new M.G. shelter at H.33.c.4.9. The wiring to new line now practically completed	

R. Indemann
RE SOS (NA) Field Co RE

Strength on 1st Feb 1918 Offrs. 7   O.R. 202.

INS.

52099 Driver R. Sloane, reported to this Coy. from Base 8/2/18
508496 Sapper H. T. Jones
508510   "   A. Marsh
185504   "   T. J. Masterson
488851   "   G. A. Barker   } Reported to this Unit
179926   "   W. Woods   } from Base
176872   "   H. A. Turner   } 13/2/18
169483   "   A. N. Webber

OUTS.

508626 L/Cpl E. J. Pollard — admitted Hospl. (sick) & evacuated 24/2/18
508277   "   A. Derham   —   "   "   "   "   30/2/18
508194 Sapper B. Weeks   "   "   "   "   1/2/18
508462   "   J. Mico   "   "   "   "   6/2/18
508464   "   A. Legg   "   "   "   "   8/2/18
281343   "   W. Welsh   "   "   "   "   14/2/18
508228   "   J. W. Williams   "   "   "   "   10/2/18

Strength on 1st March 1918 :- Offrs. 7 O.R. 203.

CONFIDENTIAL

WO 14

WAR DIARY
OF THE
505TH (WESSEX) FIELD COY. R.E.
From
MARCH 1st to 31st. 1918

VOLUME FOURTEEN.

R. Meldrum Major
OC 505 Field Coy R.E.

31/3/18

… March 1915.

Army Form C. 2118.

WAR DIARY
or
INTELLIGENCE SUMMARY.

(Erase heading not required.)

Hour, Date, Place	Summary of Events and Information	Remarks and references to Appendices
A Long Farm near ARMENTIERES D.29 & 6505 Sheet 36	1st to 5th — 11 lieuts P.J. SKINNER & BTAYLOR r+o R return to 2/5 LNL (Pioneers) are replaced by 2 Lieuts ER ALFORD & HW CORNER r+ O.R. for instruction. Works in hand — New M.G. shelter at CROIX BLANCHE POST H33 c 4.9. } Site camouflaged by wattled store carted. New M.G. shelter South of THE BATH at H 27d 35-40 } Deconville Track capped & being laid. Site being camouflaged. Wiring round H.17. Gaps being cut rebuilding of fire wade & carried trench. Work on shelters in two shifts, 6 hours each. Total men employed 1 Fd Co. & 100 attd Infantry.	Sheet 36.

WAR DIARY or INTELLIGENCE SUMMARY

Army Form C. 2118.

Place	Date	Hour	Summary of Events and Information	Remarks and references to Appendices
B29 b 65.08 Sheet 36	6th		Floor of concrete reinforced with steel rods commenced to M.G. shelter at H33 c 4.9. CAPT J.W. LLOYD proceeded on leave to UK for 14 days (7th to 21st)	
	7th		Reconnoitred bridges over Rivers LAWE & LYS from LESTREM to ESTAIRES in connection with 57th Div entrenchment scheme	Sheet 36A
	NOUVEAU MONDE			
	8		Work as usual but transport convoys that arrived by night shelled by hostile aircraft in store. 2 Bgmr S/R SAUNDERS slightly wounded in hand by shell splinter.	
	9		2 Lieut Frank SKINNER reported for duty to this unit from No Irene	
	9 to 12		Work as usual. New floor of shelter at H33 c 4.9 being finished. No more concrete work to be done until all stores have been collected. Work south of PLEURBAIX similarly hanging up.	
	13th		Warning from CRE 57 Div that 67th Div will probably relieve 12 Div & this unit to relieve the 69th Field Coy RE - not the 85 as "WE ARE" to relieve matters over. With a shelter started army to lack of stores.- Weather fine but cold.- Bombardment continues on both sides	

(2)

WAR DIARY or INTELLIGENCE SUMMARY

Army Form C. 2118.

Place	Date	Hour	Summary of Events and Information	Remarks and references to Appendices
B.29 & 65-05 Sheet 36	13 Cont'd		Weather fine & sunny. Heavy artillery bombardments on both sides.	
	14		One day's supply now off line. Heavy bombardment continues on front line – 2 shells fell in Eloy trench & work & several round the shelters south of Fleurbaix.	
	15		Roads damaged by artillery – making water transport difficult	
	16		Enemy shells Decoy road near Croix Bacquerot & South of Fleurbaix which increases our line. Loaded with gravel round for renewing the work. Enemy shot our road traffic again available we are filling here in undertram in much during daytime.	
	17		Tunwell fell in Croix Blanche work again yesterday but no casualties, one was destroyed the sandbag by the Work S. of Fleurbaix during night. Work fell in the works during the day but no casualties.	
	18		Lieut. J. E. BUTLER to 1 day course on Concrete at AIRE. Am making dugouts at H.16d 3.5-15, H.23a 2-1 & H.23b 2.8 complete 36 my extra framing etc. but no antigas material is available for curtains	

3

WAR DIARY
or
INTELLIGENCE SUMMARY.
(Erase heading not required.)

Army Form C. 2118.

Place	Date	Hour	Summary of Events and Information	Remarks and references to Appendices
b.28.b.5.d.	19th		Billet Noller 12 tpt with Hqrs & Pioneer Sqns. Shrapnel but only one man wounded in ear. M/O Lt Tindall attended 1 days Gas Course.	Pioneer
H.13.b.36	20.		March and relieved No 62 E.d. of C.R.E. - Billet at H.13.b.3-b and Huts between at S.10.a.9.5. Drew wood quantity of SAA during WM 20/21	APX 1
	21st		Work carried - a new front Snifal & Reserve line being dug at rear of present supports. & wiring forward from FLEURBAIX to GRISPOT #21 to #24 - Working parties 800 men.	Sheet 36
	22.		Int. CRE round this Corps area of work.	
	23.		Round the three Corps area with them to relieving the CRE on the 25th when he goes on special leave.	
	24.		All leave except special leave stopped owing to Irish South. M/o Lt Tindall to Corps HQ here as acting CRE from 25th but returned to unit as all leave stopped. CRE nursing cold.	R—
	25.		Usual - Lieut Butler's party of 100 works on the new Front line running South of the Rue Delettre & Lieut Skinners party on the Suffolk line which runs just North of the same Road - The Reserve	

WAR DIARY
or
INTELLIGENCE SUMMARY.
(Erase heading not required.)

Army Form C. 2118.

Place	Date	Hour	Summary of Events and Information	Remarks and references to Appendices
Fov Rompu H13 b 3 6	25 cont'd		Line at present only skirlocked 1ft deep	
	26		The G.O.C having arranged that one Coy of the Pioneers (7/5 L.N.L Regt) shall work in the area of each Field Coy, the O.C. D.C.O reported today re work. I arranged that he should take over the new Support line – Lt Skinny's Avenue were forward to the Front line – New Brigade Hdqrs are to be constructed & reinforced caverts at BARLET FARM H 26 a 4.5. & drawings are being prepared.	
	27"		Pioneer Coy mentioned above are changed for "A" Co. – O.C.E. approves plan of New Brigade Headqrs at H 26 a.4.5. Work will be commenced forthwith – Anti Tank obstacle being formed at cross roads I 31 a.6.2. Inspected proposed site of New Battalion HQ at H 29 b.15.25. – Arranged with Brigade	
	28"		HQ working parties, also parties to retain & screen in Dry areas which are badly muddied. Old Trench South East of FLEURBAIX from H22 c 2.2 to H 22 c 6.9 are to be either widened or new trench dug in front.	
	29.		H16 d 1.3 to H23 c central men stated or wire etchgra H21 central to H 21 d 9.6 and from Communication Trenches ditched from Communications Trenches Men Brigade Scheme are available	

WAR DIARY
or
INTELLIGENCE SUMMARY.

Army Form C. 2118.

Place	Date	Hour	Summary of Events and Information	Remarks and references to Appendices
H3.6.3.6	29	contd.	The enemy tank attack at trench cross I 31 a 6.2 was anticipated formed by artillery at 3·30 a.m. this morning. Two 50 lb charges & one 100 lb charge were used. Two 20 ft & 1 29 ft craters being formed 8' deep. Weather which has been fine for at least week or more has suddenly turned to wet & gales. Warning of likely move of the Division. Preparation made to hand over to the 40th Div. — Refer wire red. from O.R.E. to proceed to DOULIEU Reel 5th 1/4/65.18 to interview OC 224" Field C.R.E who would take over from me, Marybrook (?) after reaching area & roads to NEUF BERQUIN & MERVILLE was unable to find War Coy.	
"	31	"	Moved at 10 a.m. to trenches A J 29-12 & entered Estaires at 4 a.m. arriving at billets at NEUF BERQUIN 5 I 35-90 at 4-40 p.m. — orders received to move tomorrow to STEEN BECQUE 4 F 8-1 where we draw have to our new area under the orders of the 172nd Brigade.	4

[signature]

Strength on March 1st 1918 = Offrs. 7   O.R. 203.

INS:

546727 Sapper. J. Vanbrook reported to this Unit from Base Depot 5/3/18

Lieut. J. Skinner reported to this Unit from Base 9/3/18

OUTS:

546727 Sapper. J. Vanbrook } Evacuated through 54 C.C.S 9/3/18
199338 Driver A. E. Groves
508266 Sapper W. Gray   "   "   "   "   7/3/18

Strength on March 31st 1918 = Offrs. 7   O.R. 202.

31/3/18

Ry Tindall Major
O/c 505th (Wessex) Field Co. R.E.

SECRET.   Copy No. 4

57th DIVISION.

C.R.E's. OPERATION ORDER No. 18.

Map reference - Sheet 36 N.W.

1. The Field Companies R.E. of 57th Division, and attached Infantry, will relieve the Field Companies R.E., of 12th Division, and attached Infantry, on 20th March, 1918, as follows :-

57th Divn. Unit.		12th Divn. Unit.	Headquarters.	Horse Lines.
421 Coy.	relieves	70 Coy.	G.18.b.8.8.	G.18.b.8.8.
502 ,,	,,	87 ,,	H.13.c.60.90.	G.5.b.central.
505 ,,	,,	69 ,,	H.13.b.3.6.	G.10.b.9.5.

2. Field Companies 57th Division will come temporarily under the orders of C.R.E., 12th Division, till C.R.E., 57th Division takes over.

3. Officers concerned will arrange details direct, and will take over all work in hand, documents, plans, &c., relating to the same, together with all bridging schemes and demolition schemes.

4. Lists of all Area Stores and numbers of all Secret Maps taken over will be submitted, in duplicate, to this Office by 22nd instant.

5. O.C. 421 Field Company will hand over all gum boots received for work on LYS Line to O.C. 70th Field Company and receipt for same will be sent to this Office. O.C. 421 Field Company will send to this Office a statement showing number of barrows, tools, etc., taken over from 38th Division, number since drawn from Corps Park, and numbers actually handed over to O.C. 70th Field Company.

6. The relief of 421 Field Company R.E. by 70th Field Coy. R.E. will not take place until the afternoon of the 20th inst., so that work may be carried on as usual on the LYS Line.

7. **Main Divisional Dump.** (G.11.c.3.0.)

    Personnel for this Dump will be as follows :-

H.Q.R.E.	9471,	R.S.M.	Cook, W.F.	i/c Dump.
	241864,	Pte.	Jones, S.	Clerk. (2/5 K.O.R.L.R)
	21842,	,,	Jones, P.	Painter. (2/7 K.L.R.)
	203728,	,,	Buckley, J.	Carpenter.(- do -)
	48303,	,,	Morris, T.	- do - (- do -)
421 Fd.Co.	430066,	L/Cpl.	Wood, H.	Clerk.
	430024,	Sapper	Bower, W.L.	Painter.
	430089,	,,	Hughes, E.	Fitter.
	430187,	,,	Simms, C.	Tinsmith.
	67097,	,,	Sharp, W.D.	Carpenter.
		,,	Riley, J.	Signwriter.

    502 Fd.Co. One Serjeant or Senior Corporal - Carpenter.
    508368, L/Cpl. Cottrell, W. Checker.
    508401, Sapper Littlejohn, A. Carpenter.
    508034,   ,,   Hatcher, W.H. Sawyer.
    508425,   ,,   Pearce, W.J.B. Signwriter.
    One Sapper Engine Driver (Oil).

- 2 -

505 Fld.Co.	508234,	Sapper	Giles, F.G.
	508573,	,,	Dayman, S.
	508559,	,,	Clarke, R.J.
	508189,	,,	Rutty, F.
	508299,	,,	Chappell, P.

Handwritten annotations: Gillard C, Morgan S C

421 Fld.Co.R.E. Attd. Infantry	- 1 Serjt.	14 O.R.
502 ,, ,, ,, ,,	- 1 Corpl.	14 O.R.
505 ,, ,, ,, ,,	- 1 ,,	14 O.R.

8.   The above Personnel will report at the Dump at 2 p.m. on 20th instant.

9.   Rations for 20th and 21st inst., will be carried by all ranks.
       421 Field Company R.E. will provide Rations on 22nd inst., and onwards, for the whole of the above personnel, in addition to 4 P.B. Men attached to R.E. Dump, and 8 men of 10th Pontoon Park.

10.   R.S.M. Cook will detail 1 N.C.O. and 3 O.R. from the above Field Company's attached Infantry to relieve a similar party at the SHALE Dump at G13.a.2.3. before 4 p.m. on 20th instant.

11.   R.S.M. Cook will take over from the outgoing R.S.M. all papers relating to the Dumps, including Nominal Roll and Pay Sheets of Civilian Employes together with any particulars and instructions regarding works in hand.

12.   8 Other Ranks from attached Infantry, 502 Field Coy., R.E., will relieve a similar Party and should report at C.R.E., 15th Corps Troops Stores Office, The Square, LA GORGUE, on 20th inst., for duty as permanent loading party.
       Rations to be carried for 20th and 21st. Accommodation will be found by C.R.E., XVth Corps Troops for this party and rations will be found on 22nd instant and onwards.

13.   Completion of Moves will be notified to this Office.

14.   C.R.E's. Office will close at MERVILLE at 10 a.m. on 21st March 1918, and will reopen at CROIX DU BAC. *at the same hour*

15.   ACKNOWLEDGE.

                                                Capt. & Adjt.,
18.3.1918.   for C.R.E., 57th Division.
Issued at   p.m.

DISTRIBUTION:-

Copy No. 1. 57 Div. "G".	Copy No. 12. C.E. XV Corps.
2. 57 Div. "A" & "Q".	13. C.R.E., XV C.T.
3. O.C. 421 Fd.Co.R.E.	14. C.R.E. 12 Div.
4. - do -	15. O.C. 57 Div. Sigs.
5. O.C. 502 Fd.Co.R.E.	16. O.C. 57 Div. Train.
6. - do -	17. A.D.M.S. 57 Div.
7. O.C. 505 Field Co.R.E.	18. A.D.V.S. 57 Div.
8. - do -	19. D.A.D.O.S. 57 Div.
9. 170th Inf. Bde.	20. War Diary.
10. 171st - do -	21. - do -
11. 172nd - do -	22. File.
	23. Spare.
	24. do.
	25. do.

SECRET.   APX 2   Copy No. 7

57th DIVISION.

C.R.E's. OPERATION ORDER No. 19.

Map Reference:- Sheet 36 N.W. 1/20,000 and HAZEBROUCK 5A, 1/100,000.

1. (a) 57th Division (less Artillery) will be relieved by 40th Division (less Artillery) between 31st March and 2nd April.
   (b) On relief 57th Division (less Artillery) will leave XV Corps Area by train. Entrainment to begin on April 2nd.

2. (a) The Field Companies R.E. will be relieved on 31st March as follows :-

    502 Field Company, H.Q., M.13.c.6.9, Transport Lines G.5.b.central, By 231st Field Company, 40th Division, H.Q., at SAILLY.
    505 Field Company, H.Q., M.13.b.3.6, Transport Lines G.10.b.9.5, By 224th Field Company, H.Q., at RUE MONTIGNY.

   (b) 421 Field Company, H.Q., G.18.b.8.8, Transport Lines G.18.b.8.8, will move in accordance with attached March Table on April 1st, and will be prepared to hand over details of work to O.C. 229 Field Company, 40th Division, when latter arrives.

3. Details of Reliefs will be arranged direct between opposite numbers and 57th Divisional Field Companies will hand over all work in hand, all maps, air photos, plans, documents etc., of work in hand or proposed. All Demolition Schemes, Bridging Schemes, Defence Schemes, Trench and Area Stores, R.E. Material in R.E. Dump, etc. Receipts for all Trench and Area Stores handed over and also Receipts for all Secret Maps and other Secret Papers to be sent to this Office in duplicate by 4th April.

4. The Attached Infantry will rejoin their respective Brigades on 31st instant under arrangements made by C.R.E., with Brigades concerned.

5. (a) Attached Infantry and R.E. Personnel at the R.E. Dump will rejoin their Units on 31st instant, viz :-

   To 505 Field Company by 8.30 a.m.
      502   - do -   by 8.45 a.m.
      421   - do -   by 5.0 p.m.

   (b) L/Cpl. Cottrell and the 8 O.R. Attached Infantry of 502 Field Company at LA GORGUE will rejoin their respective Units on the 1st April in the ESTAIRES AREA. These men to take unexpended portion of that day and the following day's rations.

6. The 2 G.S. Wagons on loan from A.D.M.S., 57th Division will be collected from the Field Companies on the morning of 31st instant.

7. On Relief, the 502 and 505 Field Companies will be grouped with the 172 Infantry Brigade, and the 421 Field Company with the 171 Infantry Brigade.

8. (a) Moves in connection with and after Reliefs will be carried out in accordance with the attached March Table.
   (b) Orders concerning entrainment will be issued separately.

9. On the March the following intervals will be observed :-

   Between Companies — 500 yards.
   ,,   Sections — 100 yards.

10. Completion of Moves, giving Map locations will be notified to this Office daily by wire.

11. C.R.E's. Office will close at CROIX DU BAC at 10.0 am. on 2nd April and reopen at a time and place to be notified later.

12. ACKNOWLEDGE.

Issued at 11 a.m.   Capt. & Adjt.,
31.3.1918.   for C.R.E., 57th Division.

DISTRIBUTION.

Copy No. 1 - 57th Division "G".
      2 - 57th Division "A" & "Q".
      3 - O.C. 421 Field Coy., R.E.
      4 -   - do -
      5 - O.C., 502 Field Company R.E.
      6 -   - do -
      7 - O.C., 505 Field Company R.E.
      8 -   - do -
      9 - 171 Infantry Brigade.
     10 - 172   - do -
     11 - 231st Field Company R.E.
     12 - 224th Field Company R.E.
     13 - 229th Field Company R.E.
     14 - C.R.E., 40th Division.
     15 - C.R.E., XV Corps Troops.
     16 - C.E., XV Corps.
     17 - 57th Divisional Train.
     18 - 57th Div. Signals.
     19 - A.D.M.S., 57th Division.
     20 - D.A.D.V.S., 57th Division.
     21 - D.A.D.O.S., 57th Division.
     22 - R.S.M. Cook, R.E.
     23 - Area Commandant, ESTAIRES.
     24 - War Diary.
     25 -   - do -
     26 - File.
     27 - Spare.
     28 - Spare.

MARCH TABLE TO ACCOMPANY C.R.E's. OPERATION ORDER No. 19.

Serial No.	Date.	Unit.	From.	To.	Route.	Remarks.
1.	March 31st.	502 Field Co.R.E.	Coy. H.Qrs.	ESTAIRES AREA.	No Restrictions.	Not to enter ESTAIRES before 4 p.m. and to be clear of Cross Roads BAC ST MAUR by 2.30 p.m. An Advance Party to be sent forward to arrange for billets with Area Comdt. ESTAIRES.
2.	March 31st.	505 Field Co.R.E.	FORT ROMPU.	ESTAIRES AREA.	- do -	Not to enter ESTAIRES before 4 p.m. and to be clear of FORT ROMPU by 2.30 p.m. An Advance Party to be sent forward to arrange billets with Area Comdt. ESTAIRES.
3.	March 31st.	251 Field Co.R.E.	SAILLY.	E.13.c.6.9.	- do -	Advance Parties to be sent forward to H.Q. 502 Field Coy. R.E.
4.	March 31st.	224 Field Co.R.E.	RUE MONTIGNY.	FORT ROMPU.	- do -	Advance Party to be sent forward to H.Q. 505 Field Company R.E.
5.	April 1st.	502 & 505 Fld. Coys. R.E.	ESTAIRES AREA.	HAVERSKERQUE AREA. STEENBECQUE	- do -	(a) To be clear of ESTAIRES by 12 noon. (b) To march under orders of 172 Inf. Bde.
6.	April 1st.	421 Field Co.R.E.	CROIX DU BAC.	ESTAIRES AREA.	CROIX DU BAC and thence North of River LYS.	Billets to be arranged by 171 Infantry Brigade.

57th Divisional Engineers

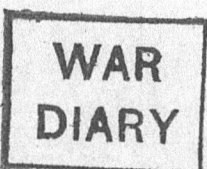

505th (Wessex) FIELD COMPANY R. E.

APRIL 1 9 1 8

CONFIDENTIAL

WAR DIARY
OF THE
505th (WESSEX) FIELD CO. R.E.
from
APRIL 1st to APRIL 30th 1918

VOLUME FIFTEEN

Brendan Wallis
OC 505th Coy RE

April 30/1918.

Army Form C. 2118.

WAR DIARY
or
INTELLIGENCE SUMMARY.
(Erase heading not required.)

APRIL 1918

Place	Date	Hour	Summary of Events and Information	Remarks and references to Appendices
NEUF BERQUIN 51 36.89	APRIL 1		PARADED at 10 a.m. passing Starting Point at I.5 48.72 at 11 a.m. on to Brigade orders & arrived at STEENBECQUE at 4-5 p.m. where an advance party met us & conducted us to the Billets around A.G.05-28. No officers being billeted in Steenbecque	Sheet 5a Hazebrouck
			Billets AF 83-11	
STEENBECQUE AF 63-11	2		Capt S.W. Floyd received orders to report to CRE 57 Div and he has been appointed to the command of the 105th Field Co R.E. & departed accordingly.	
			Received orders from 173rd Brigade to entrain, commencing midnight 2/3rd April. Train leaving at 3 a.m. - 57" Divl. & 172nd Brigade Orders attached	APX 1 + 2
	3		Entrained at Steenbecque station Steffstrah at 3 a.m. arriving at DOULLENS Sheet 11 8.m., 5.E Square, about 8.30 a.m. - Marched from there arriving at OPPY 3.E 80.05 about 6-30 p.m.	Sheet Kens 11 Capt R. SAYCE Reported to duty from the 421st (Field R.E.) by n/o A/CRE
OPPY 3.E 80.05	4		Resting all day - Received orders to move tomorrow	
SUS-ST LEGER AF 25-85	5		Leaving at 10 a.m. arrived at SUS-ST LEGER at 10-45 a.m. - Rest in afternoon	
	6		Section drill in morning + Gas lectures by O.C.	
	7		Section drill in morning & lectures by O.C. Paper chase in afternoon.	
	8		Recd orders 3 a.m. to move this morning - left Sus St Leger at 9.30 a.m. passing	

WAR DIARY
or
INTELLIGENCE SUMMARY.
(Erase heading not required.)

Army Form C. 2118.

Place	Date	Hour	Summary of Events and Information	Remarks and references to Appendices
FAMECHON 5F 52.76 & sheet 11 bis C20 c 1-1 sheet 57 D	9th		No starting point nearly 3 miles off at A.F 77.57 to time 10.25 arriving at FAMECHON 5F & arrived at billets arranged by advance party under Cpt EDSON at HURTEBISE FARM 5F.52.76 about 3 pm	Sheet 11 Keres
			The unit is under orders when to move from 8 am to 12 noon & they have orders after that. In the morning from 8 to 12 the Rechers are engaged in section drill, Physical exercise, bayonet fighting, & lectures are taken in signalling, surveying, levelling etc. In the afternoon football. Weather rainy & heavy mist.	
	10		As yesterday - Section Drill in morning.	
	11th		Fine but cold & muddy. - Training as above.	
	12th		Orders received during afternoon to move at 6 pm & advance party left at 3 pm under Staff Captain 172nd Inf. Brigade. We only had advance of 6½ miles to go i.e. to WARLUZEL 4.F 65.70 but being at the rear of the Column the journey seemed a continual halting or the slightest halt at the head of a column was a painful effect by the time it had spread to the rear of a column. We arrived at our billets at 10-15 pm	

Army Form C. 2118.

WAR DIARY
or
INTELLIGENCE SUMMARY.
(Erase heading not required.)

Place	Date	Hour	Summary of Events and Information	Remarks and references to Appendices
WARLOLEL AF 65-7.0	13th		Having taken 4¾ hours to do 8½ miles - Brigade orders Received orders to move today after 2 p.m. but actually moved at 4 p.m. - Proceeded via COUTURELLE + GAUDIEMPRÉ to HENU but on arrival found that the billets were occupied by Canadian Division who had to bivouac in a field on hill top 59.1-8 & got settled down by 11 pm - bitterly cold + liquid drizzle. Met Lt Col Neville RE by appointment at 9 a.m. at point on road SOUASTRE 59.8-8	APX 3. sheet 11 Kena "
	14		& went over new lines being dug astride village under the Sups interchange. Commenced work on new lines - The front line on our sector is completed	
	15		but support line only has which need to be continued. Then joined up boundary for my Coy on right SOUASTRE - FONQUEVILLERS ROAD to William patch A, E 13.d.3.1 - Wiring in front of support line also commenced	Sheet 57.D
	16		tuelvem from work found Coy moved to St Pierre Wood 5.f 99-50 (sheet 11 Kem) Work on new trenches - Commenced Communication Trencher on return from work found Coy half moved to HENU D 19.a.20.b5 with men billed thereline D 19.6.1-4 Work as above. Remainder being dug out as ordered	APX 4.
	17		Took over half of 502 Fld Coy's area as they are moving away - Bondon	
	18		in front of SOUASTRE - BAYEN COURT RD about D 28.6.9.9 where working	Pa —

(3)

WAR DIARY or INTELLIGENCE SUMMARY

Army Form C. 2118

Place	Date	Hour	Summary of Events and Information	Remarks and references to Appendices
HENU D.19.a.20.65 Sheet 57D	19th		Parks rendezvous - Relieved French took over area North of SOUASTRE - FONQUEVILLERS RD. Extended area to valley along South side of Square D27 d c 28 c. -	
"	20th		Completion of front line + support line + wiring support line now in hand. Communication Trenches, Platoon Dug. outs now put in hand for 172nd Brigade.	
"	21st		Reserve line East of wood D27 d.7.4 to D22 d.5.3 now put in hand. Complete Survey of all our areas lines + also those of the French commenced.	
"	22nd		Survey completed - wiring to Reserve line commenced.	
"	23rd		Work as usual - We have 1 Battalion mtd daily at D 28 day a 58 - 65 for work + half battalion every other day, rendez vous D.28.C.00.30.	
"	24th		Work as present area approaching completion. - Marked + traced out new Reserve line on the left of present area, at rear of line now held by the French - Regt Dugouts commenced by Brigade Hd at D 17.a. 5-3.	
"	25th		Commenced work on new Reserve line which runs from D 22 d 8-4 to about D 23 a.q-6 in front of SOUASTRE. - Regt Dugouts punched hand for Battn Hd qtrs at D 27 b-6-2 + D 23 b-q-q.	
	26		Work as usual but 1 Battalion only now available. -	

WAR DIARY or INTELLIGENCE SUMMARY

Army Form C. 2118

Place	Date	Hour	Summary of Events and Information	Remarks and references to Appendices
HENU D19a,b,6.5 Sheet 57D.	27		Work as usual – Reconnaissance made for emergency track for Infantry & Gathers to avoid SOUASTRE – Decided on line running from D.20.b.3.6 to D.15.c.7.3, D15.d. posts, D18.d.1-1, D17.c.4.1, D17.a.6.5-10. Thence along existing track to "WILLOW PATCH "A" at E.13.a.3-1. This is to be known as "No WILLOW PATCH TRACK"	
	28		Lieut EDSON makes a SURVEY for provision of Trenches running from BOIS ST PIERRE C.23. central to I.10.b & I.11.b. – Weather usual	
	29		Work on SOUASTRE (RED LINE) Trenches complete as far as required at present. 1 or 2 Corp Fly parties will be employed & 1 Section of Sappers obtain stores etc. Net CRE he arrived at I.11.a.6.5 & marked out line of new Plank Road running from J.5.d.2.7 to D.30.c.8.8. All observable improved. Staff Branch to be pegged out at D.17.a.6-3. Are now about 9 feet down	
	30		Only bedding of about 12 feet. Bore driving to 14' 8" below R.of. at D.27.b.6.2 are 11 ft drain spring. End of 15 feet.	

R. M...... Major
oc. co's Full CoRE

Strength on April 1st '18 – Offs. 6. O.R. 08

505th (WESSEX) FIELD COY. ROYAL ENGINEERS
No........
Date........

Evacuations.

508266.	Corpl. E. Collins,	evacuated through 53 C.C.C.		14/3/18
434344	2/Corpl. G. Rowbottom	" " " "		12/3/18
508483.	Sapper B. Morgan	" " " "		28/3/18
88666	2/Corpl. J. McKay	" "	43 "	4/4/18
180391	Sapper T. Roscoe	" "	43 "	4/4/18
52099.	Driver B. Sloane	" "	54 "	6/4/18
508400.	2/Corpl. B. Read	" "	29 "	10/4/18
508559	Sapper R. J. Clarke	" "	29 "	12/4/18
508218	Driver G. Hawkins	" "	29 "	12/4/18
426639	Sapper A. Virgo	" "	29 "	16/4/18
508517	L/Cpl. E. W. Brooks	" "	33 "	6/4/18
508067	Sapper T. Merrick	" "	29 "	15/4/18
508155	Sapper E. W. Polacker	" "	29 "	17/4/18

Transfers.

508170. Sergt. T. Duddridge ⎫
508230 Sapper T. Marchman   ⎬ Transferred to Foreways R.E. Base Depot. 16/3/18.
505160 Pioneer E. Pipe.   ⎪
508244 L/Cpl. B. H. Griffith ⎭

Captain J. W. Lloyd, transferred to 105 Field Co. R.E. 2/4/18.
508017 Driver J. Parsons   "   "   "   "   " 2/4/18.
508180 Sapper. A. E. Tucker transferred to Base on Medical Grounds 19/4/18.

POSTINGS.

526041. D.R. Y. Benson   ⎫
146233. Sapper D. Burton ⎬ Transferred to this Unit from Base Depot 3/4/18
34294.   "   G. Rickardo ⎪
166161.   "   J.A. Rose   ⎭

Capt. R. Joyce, transferred to this Unit from No 1 of Sect'n Co. P.E. on 4/4/18.
480138. Driver W.A. Davis   "   "   "   "   "   4/4/18.
241126. Sapper N.J. Deal   "   "   "   "   "   4/4/18.

#56679.   "   J. Wright   ⎫
#10307.   "   D. Stewart   ⎪
107140.   "   L. Law   ⎪
398266.   "   L. Hughes   ⎪
#38654.   "   L. Jones   ⎬ Transferred to this Unit from Base Depot.
8962S.   "   J. Walker   ⎪   26/4/18.
404454.   "   A. Lorton   ⎪
167995.   "   L. Pearson   ⎪
263056.   "   P. Duke   ⎪
267764. D." G. Hornaby   ⎪
353230.   "   W. Hopper   ⎪
52426.   "   W. Evans   ⎭

Strength on 30th Offrs 4. OR. 197

Ch. Sop 5th Wessex Co R.E.
J. Major

SECRET   172nd Infantry Brigade Operation Order   Copy No.
                            No. 45

1. Troops will entrain at STEENBECQUE Station on April 2nd/April 3rd in accordance with attached time table.

2. ARRANGEMENTS AT ENTRAINING STATION
       Vehicles and horses of each unit will be at the station of entrainment three hours and the personnel one and a half hours before departure of the train. All entrainments to be completed half an hour before train departure.

3.   ENTRAINING STRENGTHS showing:-
          (a) Officers and Other ranks
          (b) Horses and Mules
          (c) Vehicles and Number of wheels
will be handed to the R.T.O. three hours before departure of trains; loading parties will be shown separately.

4.   Units will not enter the station precincts previous to the times shown in attached table for entrainment.

5.   The D.A.Q.M.G. 57th Division will superintend the entrainment at STEENBECQUE Station. The following officers will report to the Staff Captain 172nd Inf. Bde. at Bde Hd Qrs at 10-0.a.m. April 2nd:-   Lieut J."Sillavan 2/10th Bn Lpool Regt
      1 Officer to be detailed by 9th Bn Lpool Regt
These officers will act as assistant R.T.O's and will be rationed up to and inclusive of April 4th. The name of the officer detailed by the 9th Bn Lpool Regt will reach Bde Hd Qrs by 10-0.a.m. April 2nd. Both these officers will travel to destination by the train no:19 and will keep their kits with them.
      The Staff Captain will explain to these officers the facilities for loading and the method to be employed.

6.   LOADING PARTIES consisting of 1 Company, 1 cooker and team, will be detailed as follows:-

To load train number	Report at station at	Unit	To travel by	To unload
1	April 2nd 11-30.a.m.	9th Bn Lpool R.	No: 1 Train	Nos: 1, 4, 7, and 10.
4	2-30.p.m.	2/10th Lpool R.	No:13 Train	No:13.
7	5-30.p.m.	ditto	do.	--
10	8-30.p.m.	ditto	do.	--
13	11-30.p.m.	2/4th Bn S.Lan R	No:16 Train	No.16
16	April 3rd 2-30.p.m.	ditto	No:16 Train	--
19	5-30.a.m.	2/3rd Wessex F.A.	No:19 Train	No:19

(%) Party to be at least 40 strong.
      Units detailing loading parties will make all arrangements for feeding their personnel. The cooker and team of each company acting as loaders will travel on the train with their respective Companies.

7. BILLETING PARTIES.
      Advance parties for all units in the Brigade Group will travel by train no: 1. They will be rationed up to and including of April 4th. Each Battalion will detail two cyclist orderlies to proceed with advance parties, and other units one each.

8.   Breast ropes for horse trucks will be provided by units. Ropes for vehicles will be provided by the railway company.

9. All doors of trucks and carriages on the right hand side of the train when on main lines must be kept closed.

10. Units will enforce strict discipline during the journey, and during entraining and detraining.

11. ARRANGEMENTS AT DETRAINING STATION.
All advance parties will report to the Staff Captain at station of detrainment immediately on arrival.
The Officer in command of the Company of the 9th Bn Lpool R. proceeding by train no: 1 will report to R.T.O., station of destination and will act as detraining officer for all trains.
Unloading parties will be found as shown in column 5 para 6 above.

12. GENERAL INSTRUCTIONS
One blanket per man will be taken for which special transport will be provided at station of detrainment. No other transport will be provided.

All baggage wagons and supply wagons will report to units in their present locations at 8-0.a.m. April 2nd. They will entrain with units and will remain with them until further orders.

RATIONS
Rations to accompany troops will be:-
(a) Iron ration
(b) Current day's rations.
In addition, one day's supply will travel in the vehicles of the Divisional Train and one by Div.M.T.Column.
All water bottles will be filled before entraining.

All billets in the present area will be left scrupulously clean. Billet certificates must be completed and handed in to the Mairies of the prospective Communes before leaving.

13. ACKNOWLEDGE.

Captain
for Brigade Major
172nd Infantry Brigade

Issued by Signals
1/4/1918.
Distribution:-
Copy No:1 9th Bn Lpool R.
2. 2/10th Bn Lpool R.
3 2/4th Bn S.Lan R.
4 172nd L.T.M.Batty
5 Bde Signalling Offr
6 57th Division "G"
7 57th Division "A"
8 H.Q.Dival Train ASC
9 4 H.T.Coy A.S.C.
10 S.S.O.
11 Bde Supply Officer
12 502nd Field Co.RE.
13 505th Field Co.RE.
14 C Coy 57th M.G.Bn
15 2/3rd Wessex F.A.
16 57th Mobile Vet.Sec.

17. Area Commdt HAVERSQUERQUE
18. Area Commdt STEENBECQUE
19. R.T.O., STEENBECQUE
20. 9th Lpool R. Entraining Officer
21. Lieut J"Sillavan
22. 9th Lpool R. Detraining Officer
23. G.O.C.
24. Brigade Major
25. Staff Captain
26/27. War Diary
28. File
29/30. Spare

TRAIN ARRANGEMENTS FOR ENTRAINING OF 172ND INFANTRY BDE. AT STEENBECQUE STATION APRIL 2ND & 3RD 1918.

No. of train	Units	Time of entrainment Transport	Time of entrainment Personnel	Time & date of departure.	Remarks.
1	172nd Bde H.Q. 172nd Bde Signal Sect. 9th Bn. K.L.R. (1 Coy, 1 cooker & team) "C" Coy. 57th Bn. Machine Gun Corps 172nd L.T.M.Bty.	Apl 2nd 12 noon	Apl 2nd 1-30 p.m.	Apl 2nd 3-0 p.m.	
4	9th Bn. K.L.R. (less 1 Coy, 1 cooker & team)	Apl 2nd 3-0 p.m.	Apl 2nd 4-30 p.m.	Apl 2nd 6-0 p.m.	All loading parties
7	2/10th Bn. K.L.R. (less 1 Coy, 1 cooker & team)	Apl 2nd 6-0 p.m.	Apl 2nd 7-30 p.m.	Apl 2nd 9-0 p.m.	will report with
10	2/4th Bn. S.Lan.R. (less 1 Coy, 1 cooker & team)	Apl 2nd 9-0 p.m.	Apl 2nd 10-30 p.m.	Apl 2nd/3rd 12-0 midnight	cooker and team three
13	H.Q. Divisional Train 2/10th K.L.R. (1 Coy, 1 cooker & team) 505th Field Co. R.E.	Apl 2/3rd 12 midnght	Apl 3rd 1-30 a.m.	Apl 3rd 3-0 a.m.	and a half hours before
16	No. 4 Coy. Divl Train 502nd Field Co. R.E. 2/4th Bn. S.Lan.R. (1 Coy, 1 cooker & team)	Apl 3rd 3-0 a.m.	Apl 3rd 4-30 a.m.	Apl 3rd 6-0 a.m.	train is due to depart.
19	2/3rd Wessex Fld Amb. 57th Mobile Vet. Sect.	Apl 3rd 6-0 a.m.	Apl 3rd 7-30 a.m.	Apl 3rd 9-0 a.m.	

C O P Y.   S.638.   APX 2

SECRET.

ADMINISTRATIVE ARRANGEMENTS REFERENCE 57th DIVISIONAL ORDER
                    NUMBER 77.

1. Troops will entrain from STEENBECQUE, CALONNE and MERVILLE in accordance with the Table attached.

The average interval between trains at each Station will be 3 hours.

2. ARRANGEMENTS AT ENTRAINING STATION.

The vehicles and horses of each train load will be at the Station named 3 hours, and the personnel one and half hours before departure of the train.

3. Entraining strengths shewing (a) Officers and Other Ranks
                                (b) Horses and Mules
                                (c) Vehicles and number of wheels.
will be handed to the R.T.O. or Officer detailed to assist at least 2 hours before departure of trains.

4. Units will not enter the Station precincts previous to the 3 hours mentioned in para 2.   Roads leading to the Station will not be blocked by Units, and to ensure this strict punctuality must be kept.

5. The D.A.Q.M.G. 57th Division will superintend the entrainment generally and will be at STEENBECQUE Station.   Officers as under will assist him as assistant R.T.Os.

(a) AT MERVILLE - 171st Brigade Group - 2 Officers.
(b) AT STEENBECQUE - 172nd Brigade Group - 2 Officers.
(c) AT CALONNE - 170th Brigade Group - 2 Officers.

These Officers will report to the R.T.O. at their respective Station at least three hours before the departure of the first train, and will entrain with the last train.   They are to reconnoitre at once their respective Stations, in order to get acquainted beforehand with the loading, etc., facilities, and the approaches to the Station.

6. The O.C., 57th Divisional Signal Company will detail a Motor Cyclist Orderly at each Station.

7. Each Brigade Group will detail one Company and one Cooker and Team to be at their entraining Station 5½ hours before departure of the first train, and report to the R.T.O.   These will act as loading party for all Units.   They will entrain on the last train and will be under the orders of the Officer detailed above.

8. BILLETING.

Advance Parties for billeting will be sent on in the first train from each entraining Station, under Staff Captains of Brigade Groups. Two days' rations will be taken.

9. Entrainment will be completed half-an-hour before the departure of the train.

10. Brest ropes for horse trucks must be provided by Units.   Ropes for vehicles will be provided by the Railway.

11. All doors of covered trucks and carriages on the Right hand side of the train when on the Main Line must be kept closed.

12. Arrangements at detraining Station.

The D.A.A.G. 57th Division will be in general charge at the most central Station.

Staff Captains, with billeting parties, will go by first train and will get into communication with the D.A.A.G., as early as possible.

13. ARRANGEMENTS AT DETRAINING STATION (Contd.)

Each Infantry Brigade will detail one Company, and one Cooker and Team to go in the first train and to report to R.T.O. at detraining Station. The Officer in command of this Company will act as Detraining Officer.

14. GENERAL INSTRUCTIONS.

One blanket per man will be taken. All troops will move with the normal Field Service Scale of Transport. No extra transport will be provided but arrangements will be made for the conveyance of extra blankets.

15. RATIONS.

Rations to accompany troops will be :-

(a) Iron Rations.
(b) Current Day's Rations.

In addition, two days' Rations will be taken, one in Supply Vehicles of the Divisional Train and one by Divisional Mechanical Transport Company.

All supply vehicles of the Divisional Train will move full.

16. RAILHEAD.

Railhead up to 1st April, inclusive, will be SAC ST MUER and on 2nd April LESTREM NORTH.

D.H.Q.
31st March, 1918.

(Sd.) F.W.M.Stewart, Lieut.-Colonel,
A.A. & Q.M.G., 57th Division.

Officer Commanding,

565 Field Company R.E.

Forwarded for your information and necessary action.

31.3.1918.

Thadwbe Campbell
Lieut.-Colonel,
C.R.E., 57th Division.

TRAIN ARRANGEMENTS FOR MOVE OF 57th DIVISION LESS ARTILLERY.

No. of train.	Time.	STEENBECQUE. 172nd Infantry Bde. Group.	No. of Train.	Time.	MERVILLE. 171st Infantry Brigade Group.
1.		172 Bde. H.Q. Bde. Sig. Sec. 1 Coy, 1 Cooker and Team "A" Batt. "D"Coy, M.G. Batt. 172 L.T.M.B.	3.		171 Bde. H.Q. Bde. Sig. Sec. 1 Coy, 1 Cooker and Team "A" Batt. 1 Coy, M.G. Batt. 171st L.T.M.B.
4.		"A" Batt. less 1 Coy. and Cooker.	6		"A" Batt. less 1 Coy. and Cooker.
7.		"B" Batt. less 1 Coy. and Cooker.	9		"B" Batt. less 1 Coy. and Cooker.
10.		"C" Batt. less 1 Coy. and Cooker.	12		"C" Batt. less 1 Coy. and Cooker.
13.		H.Q. Divl. Train. 1 Coy. and Cooker "B" Batt. 505 Field Coy. R.E.	15		No. 3 Coy. Divl. Train. 421 Field Coy., R.E. 1 Company and Cooker "B" Batt.
16.		No. 4 Coy. Divl. Train. 502 Field Coy. R.E. 1 Coy. & Cooker "C" Batt.	18		H.Q. Div. Emp. Coy. LATE 843 No. 1 Sec. Div. Sig. Coy. H.Q., R.E.

SECRET.   APX 3   Copy No. 5

172nd INFANTRY BRIGADE ORDER No. 47.

Ref. Map LENS 1/100,000   April 12th, 1918.

1. The 172nd Infantry Brigade will move to SOMBRIN, WARLUZEL, COULLEMONT, HUMBERCOURT, today April 12th, in accordance with attached table.
   Strict march discipline will be maintained.

2. The 172nd Infantry Brigade will be composed as follows :-
    9th Bn Lpool Reg.
    2/10th Bn Lpool Reg.
    2/4th Bn S. Lan Reg.
    172nd Light T.M. Bty.
    505th Field Co R.E.
    2/3rd Wessex Field Amb.
    No. 4 Co Divl Train.
    57th Divisional Pioneer Battn.

3. Transport will accompany Units.
   One motor lorry will report to each of the following units at their Headquarters as soon as possible :-
   9th Bn Lpool Reg, 2/10th Bn Lpool Reg, 2/4th Bn S. Lan Reg, 172nd Light T.M. Bty,-172nd Brigade Hdqrs.

   In addition to this, Battalions will have their baggage wagons available for transport purposes.

4. <u>Stragglers.</u> Seconds in Command of units will ride behind their units and will be responsible that stragglers are collect--ed in parties, and that they march into their new billeting area in their own time.

5. <u>Dress.</u> Full marching order.

6. Units will send a cycle orderly to Brigade Headquarters at 3.0 p.m. to obtain correct signal time.
   The Bde Signalling Offr will attend to this matter.

7. All billets in present area will be left scrupulously clean.
   All billeting certificates will be completed.

8. Billeting parties for units in HUMBERCOURT and COULLEMONT will meet the Staff Captain at the Town Major's Office HUMBERCOURT at 4.0 p.m.
   2/10th Bn Lpool Reg will take over their old billets in SOMBRIN.

2/9th Bn Lpool Reg billeting parties will meet Interpreter LE-BLANC at the Town Major's office at SOMBRIN at 4.30 p.m. to take over billets formerly occupied by 2/4th Bn S.Lan R. 2/4th Bn S. Lan Reg will do their own billeting in WARLUZEL: billeting parties will report to the Town Major at WARLUZEL at 4.0 p.m.

9. <u>Guides.</u> Staff Captain will send guides to meet units going into HUMBERCOURT and COULLEMONT at road junction immediately West of the H in HUMBERCOURT.
Remaining Battalions will arrange their own guides.

10. All units will report to Brigade Hdqrs by cycle orderly the completion of the move, and will give map reference of new Headqrs. These orderlies will report to Bde Signalling Offr.

11. Bde Hdqrs will close at THIEVRES at 3.30 p.m. and reopen at HUMBERCOURT upon arrival.
During the march of the Brigade group, reports will be send to the head of the column.

12. ACKNOWLEDGE.

C. Forbes - Bx

Captain.
Brigade Major.
172nd Infantry Brigade.

12/4/18.

DISTRIBUTION :-

No 1	to 9th Bn Lpool Reg.		No 17.	S.S.O.
2	2/10th Bn Lpool Reg.		18	Bd Signalling Offr.
3	2/4th Bn S. Lan Reg.		19	170th Bde.
4	172nd L.T.M.B.		20	171st Bde.
5	505th Field Co R.E.		21	G.O.C.
6	No 4 Co Divl Train.		22	Bde Major.
7	2/3rd Wessex Fld Amb.		23	Staff Captain.
8	57th Divl Pioneer Bn.		24/25	War Diary.
9	57th Div (G)		26	Captain Clements.
10	do (A)		27	File.
11	Town Major THIEVRES.		28	Interpreter LE BLANC.
12	do HUMBERCOURT.		29/35	Spare.
13	do SOMBRIN.			
14	do WARLUZEL.			
15	do COULLEMONT.			
16	Bde Supply Offr.			

172ND INFANTRY BRIGADE MARCH TABLE FOR APRIL 12TH 1918.
(To accompany Brigade Order No. 47).

Serial	Date	Unit	Starting Point	Time to pass starting point.	Route	Destination	Remarks.
1	Apl 12th	No. 4 Co A.S.C.	Road Junc. S.F.74.78 on FAMECHON-PAS Road.		PAS-MONDICOURT	COULLEMONT	To march in own time. To be clear of start-ing point by 3.30 p.m.
2	-do-	2/10th K.L.R.	-do-	4-0 p.m.	PAS-MONDICOURT HUMBERCOURT COULLEMONT	SOMBRIN	
3	-do-	9th K.L.R.	-do-	4-20 p.m.	-do-	SOMBRIN	500 yds between Battns.
4	-do-	Bde Hdqrs	-do-	4-40 p.m.	PAS-MONDICOURT HUMBERCOURT	HUMBERCOURT	100 yds between Companies.
5	-do-	2/4th S.L.R.	-do-	4-45 p.m.	THIEVRES-FAMECHON-PAS-MONDICOURT HUMBERCOURT COULLEMONT	WARLUZEL	100 yds between Battns and transport.
6	-do-	172nd L.T.M.B	-do-	5-15 p.m.	PAS-MONDICOURT HUMBERCOURT	COULLEMONT	
7	-do-	57th Pioneer Battn	-do-	5-20 p.m.	THIEVRES-FAMECHON-PAS-MONDICOURT	HUMBERCOURT	

P.T.O.

172ND INFANTRY BRIGADE MARCH TABLE FOR APRIL 12TH (continued)

Serial	Date	Unit	Starting Point	Time to pass starting point	Route	Destination	Remarks
8	Apl 12th	2/3rd Wessex Fld Amb.	Road junc. 5.F.74.78. on FAMECHON-PAS Road	5;40 p.m.	PAS-MONDICOURT HUMBERCOURT	COULLEMONT	500 yds between Battns. 100 yds between Companies. 100 yds between Battns and transport.
9	-do-	505th Field Co. R.E.	-do-	6-0 p.m.	PAS-MONDICOURT HUMBERCOURT	COULLEMONT	

NOTE: The usual ten minutes halt at 10 minutes to each clock hour will be observed.

APX 4

Section of Trenches

|← 7'0" →|← 2'6" →|← 5' at level →| +1'6"
|← 5'6" →|← 3' →|

Parapet
← 2'1' → ← 2'1' → 2'1'

← 6' →
← 4' →← 4' →

Communication Trench.

CONFIDENTIAL

War Diary

of

505th (Wessex) Field Coy R.E.

from May 1st 1916 to May 31st 1918

(Volume 16)

WAR DIARY
or
INTELLIGENCE SUMMARY.
(Erase heading not required.)

Army Form C. 2118

Place	Date	Hour	Summary of Events and Information	Remarks and references to Appendices
HENU D.19a.20.65 Sht 57D	MAY 1st		Recd orders relieving one plat 427 Field Co RE at E 28 c 9.7. Proceeded to that point & interviewed the OC who is subsequently inspecting work in hand - which is mostly in taking reserve lines of the old German trenches around & in GOMMECOURT WOOD, where the Coy is housed in one spacious dugout consisting of many galleries 30-40 feet underground. The front line held by the Brigade runs from E 10 d 4-0 to E 12 a 3.5	
	2nd			
	3rd		Capt SNOE & Lieut SAUNDERS proceed to 427 Fd Co RE to make themselves acquainted with the work carried out by them 2nd in command & other attached to Brigade - Weather change to warm & sunny.	
	3rd		Water Red line stopped - Platoon Posts at BAYENCOURT nearly complete. All work now confined to deep dugouts which are all down to required level. ORE's conference.	
	4th			
	5th		Arrangements made to relieve remaining one -	
	6th		Left billet at 5.30 pm & proceeded via SOUASTRE to GOMMECOURT WOOD E 28 c 9 6.70 relieved the 427 Field Co RE. Settled down by 12.30 midnight - Corpl G. Foreacre shot thro' thigh with 2 M.G. bullets. R.	

Army Form C. 2118

WAR DIARY
or
INTELLIGENCE SUMMARY.
(Erase heading not required.)

Place	Date	Hour	Summary of Events and Information	Remarks and references to Appendices
GOMMECOURT WOOD E 26 c & 70 Sheet 57 D N W	7th Cont'd		At 1-15 am we 'stood to' in our Battle positions for the first time, rations being untill then not delivered, & SAA 17,000 rounds having to be fetched from dump. At 3-45 am as 'daily stand-to' we again manned our battle positions. The CRE called during afternoon & arranged with Brigade that this standing to need not be continued. During morning reconnoitred site between C.T. & the new Rum Trench, also deepening locality of GOMMECOURT WOOD. Lt SAUNDERS & detail to work with Brigade until section 3+4. 1Coy working newly from Reserve Brigade + 1 Co from Res. Batt of this Brigade worked on clearing old Boch Trench for CT from K+6.1 to K+6.45.05. Interviewed with 172nd Brigade (R.O.E.) C.O. Res Battn. & Bns in line. Gas meeting all Coy Comdrs with Wood Park an urgent matter.	
	8th		Met C.O.C. 172nd Inf Brigade by appt at 9am & with him round trenches until 3 pm. Party from Reserve Brigade of 1 Coy (64 per Coy) worked on RUM TRENCH at night.	
	9th		Park 1 Co. mostly on Rum Trench, Party of 1 Co. daily in	

WAR DIARY
or
INTELLIGENCE SUMMARY.
(Erase heading not required.)

Army Form C. 2118.

Place	Date	Hour	Summary of Events and Information	Remarks and references to Appendices
GOMMECOURT N? Sect E.26.c.98.70			Gommecourt Went through, I Coy in line at night as Somme court trench	
			running on small front for the so clearing - Sappers engaged on Dist Dug out work - Run Trench badly badly damaged but no casualties.	
	10ᵗʰ		Weather usual - Interview with GOC at Bde Hq - New strong point started at K.4.c.6.6. Run trench party did little up to dark night.	
			Quiet by May shell M.G. fire. Third Army Wk. A/A/11794. AS. AQ/SS/22113.(0) received - instructions for me to proceed to England having been selected for a tour of duty at home.	
	11ᵗʰ		GOC 1/7 Brigade having ordered the wiring in f. of the Gommecourt wood corner of the q.W.Kh. B. were put into the work in four parties from E.28.d.6-1 round K.S.C.2080 to K.4.d.60.70 told 70% of the work during night. Reas brothers + the 50 odd dugouts in line with each having from 2 to 3 entrances each entrance requiring 2 screens of curtains, is a man hellion hand - Enemy shrapnel gas bombardment at 4 am on FONQUEVILLERS + the gas penetrated our trench but let the W Wind - Working parties presumably were clear of gas zone.	P.T.

WAR DIARY
or
INTELLIGENCE SUMMARY.

(Erase heading not required.)

Army Form C. 2118.

Place	Date	Hour	Summary of Events and Information	Remarks and references to Appendices
SOMME CAMPT NORD E.12.c.96.70	11th	cont'd	Bombardment finished about 10 pm but Verdun shells didn't fall until 11 pm. Sapper GRIFFITH cyclist orderley, was the only man in the Coy gassed.	
	12th		Wiring from E.28.d.5.5. front K.5.c.20.50 to R.46.c.70 completed during night. Sapper Mogg & Clarke dumps stores to #3 High Res Two forward sections are engaged mostly on deep dug-out work & in carrying through by night the GOVERNMENT TRENCH from K.10.b.85.95 to about K.10. central.	
	13th		MAJOR P.O.L. JORDAN reported ok back to Coy as Coy Command. Work arranged.	
	14th		Round Run Trench - Somme Court Wood - Beaulih - to Pruttetu Hdqrs with Major Jordan - 2 Other Cos See Ross fell at one of the entrances to the HQ Co dug-out this evening about 10-15. The firing indicated to officers who were sleeping just before. He was med'y company could be avoided. Dugout was subsequently cleared by dragoons & charged in five - M. Connally handled coy Command to Major Jordan at midnight 14/15th. P Jordan

WAR DIARY
or
INTELLIGENCE SUMMARY.
(Erase heading not required.)

Army Form C. 2118.

Place	Date	Hour	Summary of Events and Information	Remarks and references to Appendices
Gomme court Wood	15th		Major J.E. Tindall left for the A. Corps at 3 p.m. after handing over. Work as usual. Discussion with Brigadier	
E28c 96.70	16th		Work as usual. Practically no night work accomplished although parties	
do			3 Coys for wiring & digging went out as the hour for a concentrated machine gun shoot was advanced at the last moment & parties ordered back to billets	
do	17th		Work as usual. ※ Coy for work from Reserve Bde arrived an hour later than expected & did not find guide, but went to work with works of the Division. ※ Reclaiming German dugouts & improving & strengthening Wires & Front digging & wiring hindenburg C.T.s & fire trenches at midnight.	
do	18th		Work as usual	
do	19th		Work as usual. The Boy Coy onto shelled. Direct hit on cook house of Officers mess in trench at entrance. No casualties. 5 Sapper reinforcements	
do	20th		Work as usual. R.O.P. & Wittnespoele & Commstonset scantily commenced. Visit from C.O.R.	
do	21st		Saw both G.O.C. (outgoing) 172 & G.O.C. (incoming) 171 Inf Bdes. Transport shelled at Pr dump 10.15 p.m	

(2)

WAR DIARY or INTELLIGENCE SUMMARY

Army Form C. 2118.

Place	Date	Hour	Summary of Events and Information	Remarks and references to Appendices
GOMMECOURT WOOD East G.9.b.70	22nd		172 Bde relieved on night 21-22 by 11th Inf Bde. No working parties available. Sappers work by Squadron. Site temperature 10½°. Concreted through dugouts. Continued through night. Field Ambulance from adjacent	
	23rd		Work on trying change trenches, carrying party dry tape, construction of elephant shelters. Sent to Bécourt Lt Osborne returned from Leave & Lieut Sayer back to have leave.	
			Sergt Cockle joined unit from leave (just been down)	Lieut Arthur
			Sich temp ±10 10.3.5 & Recorded during night	
	24th		Rain. Lieut Street SD.2 Q.1 Co. joined Cy HQ attached temporarily to replace Lieut Butler. Sgt Hebden left for Rear HQ to report at MARIEUX for temporary duty. 1 Sapper reinforcement joined Cy HQ (Sapper Buckingham)	
	25th		Day work as usual. Work by night suspended owing to open time. USA sergeant joined for 3 days attachment	
	26th		Work Carrying dugouts, RAPs, trench impacts. Blew a crater at 2 a.m. in the PUSIEUX-GOMMICOUR Rd thrust with instructions from division. Object to prevent wheeled traffic. Work carried out in forward line under difficult conditions. Shell fire, S.A.C & unexpected ammonal 8.1.20 G.C. From Charge Three 25 lb charges in bore at 7' centre & one in lower B' behind, depth 3.6' Tamped with sandbags humidly fused electrically. Results: crater average depth 8' Tamped out to 1st Street Cpl. Hogg & 8 sappers. (N.B. Jake a filling axe) Gas Bombdr. by German batteries 2am no on our artillery & other positions. Continuous down from 2am. 3am —	

505 M.R.E.

WAR DIARY
or
INTELLIGENCE SUMMARY.

Army Form C. 2118.

Place	Date	Hour	Summary of Events and Information	Remarks and references to Appendices
GOMMECOURT WOOD E.28.c.9870	27th May 1918		Work as usual. U.S.A. Engineer Sergt returned to ranks & o/c 3 days inshrtional attachment.	
	28th		Work as usual. Six Sapper reinforcements joined Coy. One U.S.A. Sergt attached from 302 Coy U.S.E.R.	
	29th		No Sapper Casualties. Shrapnel wound left thigh (slight) when taking messages down STOUT TRENCH. Less Artillery activity than usual. 12 N.C.O's & men attached from 502 Field Co. R.E. Sgt for connecting up gallery communication in Dug out # 15117 in the GOMMECOURT LINE. Sparking tools 1 N.C.O & 14 men of 2/5th Leinster Fusiliers attached to Reserve Bn of Brigade for permanent work.	
	30th		Officers & 3 N.C.Os reported from 427 2d Co R.E. to make acquaintance with sector. Rear HdQrs & horse lines shelled, no Casualties.	

R. L. Jordan
Major R.E.
O.C. 505th M Co R.E.

506th (Wessex) Field Co R.E.

INS

505279	Corpl Spry. J	Posted to unit from Base	30/4/18
85290	Sapper Godfrey H		
352838	" Beyer A.C.		9/5/18
446077	" Boyd JV		
106171	Pioneer Burgess J.C.		
57826	" Knifton H.C.		9/5/18
51322	Driver Jones. E		
48126	Sapper Smith J.H.		
49663	" Kirk H.		
155579	" Betts J.		
180692	" Gamble F.		
552124	" Surrey A.G.		
520015	" Sinlett DJ		
470632	2/6/L Henderson JR	Posted to unit from Base	18/5/18
471,150	Driver Lennon J		
60723	" Scott. R		
209312	" Tinker H		
422,767	" Bathgate J.		
83409	" Moore H.		
31336	" Jenkins F.		
51383	" Kerr W.		
219889	" Keep E		
450,140	2/6/L Jenkins T.	" " " "	21/5/18
440427	Driver Chadwick A		
219864	" Cliff WN	" " " "	21/5/18
404021	" Donaldson W		
51554	Sapper Buckingham RG		
650644	" Good SS		
416,834	" Bacon. A		
426672	" Pendlebury W	" " " "	25/5/18
495164	" Warburton F		
519695	" Harrington R.		
440432	" Halkyard F		
Major Gadow POL		Joined Coy from Base on	13/5/18
Lieut Dodds WH		" " " "	23/5/18

OUTS

508210	Driver	Talbot C	Evacuated through CCS	25/4/18
508189	"	Rutty F	" " "	"
508250	Sgt	Williams JB	} Transferred to Base on	
508174	Cpl	Chivers W	} medical grounds	3/5/18
450140	2/Cpl	Jenkins J	Evacuated (sick) through CCS	4/4/18
176576	Sapper	Wheatley J.M.	" " "	30/4/18
524426	Driver	Evans W.G.	" " "	30/4/18
508219	Sapper	Shedden R	" " "	1/5/18
505643	A/Sgt	Chitty L.W.	" " "	2/5/18
16040	S.M.	Street W	" (injured) "	4/5/18
506430	Cpl	Fowacre G	" (wounded) "	4/5/18
508463	Driver	Board H.	" (sick) "	5/5/18
202906	"	Ward W.D	" (sick) "	8/5/18
508471	Sapper	Griffiths C.H.J	" (gassed) "	19/5/18
508611	"	Radford A	" " "	20/5/18
138652	"	Jones L.	" " "	20/5/18
508231	"	Mogg H.R	" (acc.injury) "	19/5/18
508172	Sgt	Maggs C	" (sick) "	22/5/18
508622	L/Cpl	Selwood C	" " "	22/5/18
188851	Sapper	Barker G.A	" " "	23/5/18
508468	"	Hartland G	" " "	22/5/18
49663	"	Kirk E	" " "	26/5/18
504460	"	Hunt L.J	" " "	31/5/18
	Lieut	Saunders S.J.R	" " "	23/5/18
	"	Butler L.G	" " "	26/5/18

Major Tindall J.E. MC Transferred to England for tour of duty on 18/5/18

Strength on 31/5/18   Offr 6 } 213
                       OR 207 }

Haige Capt

31/5/18   for OC 505 Field Co RE

Confidential.

WAR DIARY.

of

505 (Wessex) Field Company R.E.

From 1st June 1918 to 30th June 1918

Volume 17

Volume 18

WAR DIARY
or
INTELLIGENCE SUMMARY.

Army Form C. 2118.

505. F.A. 10.

Place	Date	Hour	Summary of Events and Information	Remarks and references to Appendices
GOMMECOURT WOOD E2B & G.9870.	31st May 1918		Three killed & three wounded both heads gone (W Cpl J Mc Shane & Sp Bunton). The Galleries in DUGOUT B117 GOMMECOURT TRENCH reported to meet & leading to chambers commenced. Considerable shelling of R.E. Dumps & vicinity in evening & much shelling from about 3 a.m. to 5 a.m. on morning of the 1st. The enemy making a raid on our left front Polish sector, which was successfully repulsed with a few casualties on both sides & a few prisoners left in our hands. Working parties at night much interrupted —	weather warm & fine
	1st June		Took no round. From about 2 a.m. to 3 a.m. on the night of the 1st-2nd the Boche put over 30 gas shells (Mustard & Phosgene) & M.E. over the whole of the GOMMECOURT area. Gas curtains in dug outs effectively kept it out & prevented casualties. Lt Skinner sent down to have him with trench fever.	— —
	2nd June		GOMMECOURT wearily heavily shelled. Major Fox (O.C. 502) went round area prior to taking over.	
	3rd June		Lt Eden & Pearse (502 F.A.Co) reads blown up in STO 2 TR. Both suffered slightly from shell shock.	
	4th June		505 F.A. 10 R.E. relieved in the line by 502 Field Co. R.E. on the 4th of the 4th Company sent out of the line in small detachments of 6 to 8 men at 400 yds distance from 6 p.m. to 7 p.m.	
COIGNEUX, 57D NE, J3B34.	5th June		The men were given 24 hours rest badly needed after 1 month in the line during which daily working parties during that period —	

WAR DIARY
or
INTELLIGENCE SUMMARY.
(Erase heading not required.)

Army Form C. 2118.

Place	Date	Hour	Summary of Events and Information	Remarks and references to Appendices
CONTENT 57 D N.6 J.5 B.34.	6 June 1918		The coy employed as follows:- Construction of large elephant shelters in the Third line system, clearing CTs in forward area (via sappers employed on excavating, no Inf working parties being available.) (night work) Rifle range target erection, cradles etc. The coy & Q.M.T Sections together in camps situation about 2500 yds behind our front line.	booklet. first form
	7 June		Work as above. H.E.D reservoirs filled up by acting from lorries	
	8 June		worked in sections	
	9 June		" "	
	10 June		" " Captain Soppe transferred to 421 Coy R.E. Sgt Pelletier taken on Strength	
	11 June		" "	
	12 June		" " 17 men on sick list with Spanish flue	
			Sgt Twigg rejoined unit – two Sappers reinforcements (Strength of unit 7 officers 252 O.R.) Officers arrived 1st Lt R.E.V.A. 2 Kings	
	13 June		St Eloi. Sick trench fever outbk. Orders to relieve 421 Coy in line received	Ditto
	14 June		Left brigade in line sector by C.R.E. reference work to be carried out	
	15 June		Relief of 421 Bn Coy carried out, in small parties of 8 to 10 at 400' intervals between hours of 5pm & 7pm. Lt Gibson left in charge of horse lines. Strength of Coy into advn. Coy H.Q. 3 officers (Major Jordan, Lt Dodds & Lt Skinner) + 98 O.R.	Lt D

WAR DIARY
INTELLIGENCE SUMMARY

Army Form C. 2118.

(3)

(Erase heading not required.) 505 Th Co. R.E.

Place	Date	Hour	Summary of Events and Information	Remarks and references to Appendices
GOMMECOURT WOOD E.28 d.75.80	16 June 1918		Work in left forward Brigade sector on following lines:- Trench digging, cleaning & wiring carried on as usual by parties who only submit indents & obtain advice from R.E. Officer each morning, (except in case of working parties from Moore Bde who work directly under R.E.) Sapper employed in construction of "Minced trolls elephant" shelters, opening up & gas proofing deep dug outs etc.	Fine
	17 June		Work as usual. Hostile artillery active 6th day searching for forward batteries near our dug out	—
	18 June		ditto ditto Night working parties employed on repairing damage to trenches	—
	19 June		Work commenced on chamber in dug out "MATTHEWS POST". Lt. Butler & Saunders rejoined from L.Q.	Hot
	20 June		Lt. Butler joined coy H.Q. Bde quiet	Wet
	21 June		Work as usual	Fine
	22 June		Sgt Watton awarded "Meritorious Service Medal." Lt. Saunders joined coy Coy H.Q.	—
	23 June		Work as usual. Lt. Scott returned to coy coy H.Q.	—
	24 June		Enemy intercepted ordering Saxon troops to stand to at 6 am. Precautionary measures in consequence	—
	25 June		No events of importance except considerable hostile artillery activity — Two reinforcements from base	—
	26 June		Chamber for shelter cases 8'x12'x6 completed at MATTHEWS POST. Tunnelling in SALMON TR. handed over to tunnellers — Sgt Watton to have time with	—

P.V.D.

R. Ranger R.E.

Army Form C. 2118.

WAR DIARY
or
INTELLIGENCE SUMMARY.

(Erase heading not required.) 505th Fld. C. R.E.

Instructions regarding War Diaries and Intelligence Summaries are contained in F. S. Regs., Part II. and the Staff Manual respectively. Title pages will be prepared in manuscript.

(4)

Place	Date	Hour	Summary of Events and Information	Remarks and references to Appendices
GOMMECOURT WOOD.	27 June		ROSSIGNOL WOOD shelled all day by all sorts of our artillery from 12" to TMs -	June
E 28 d 75.80	28 June		Little retaliation & Rossignol wood still stands.	
	29 June		Battle position practice.	June
			Major Jordan returned to Rear H.Q. - Boche quiet.	June
	30 June		Lt. Saunders sent to take over new billets at I 24 a centrel Ry map 1/20000 - Boche quiet	
			57 D, preceded by 3rd Fld Cy R.E. N.Z. Div. - Boche quiet.	This

STRENGTH RETURN

accompanying War Diary of June 1918.

STRENGTH on 1st June, 1918;-   Offrs. 8   O.R. 207

ARRIVALS.

504860.	Sapper	Hunt, F.J.	to Unit from	C.R.S.		1/6/18.
508191.	Sergt.	Maggs, C.	" " "	Base		11/6/18.
402274.	Sapper	Miller, W.	" " "	"		"
550183.	"	Stutely, S.H.	" " "	"		"
508215.	"	Clark, W.	" " "	C.R.S.		9/6/18.
98512.	"	Dobinson, J.W.	" " "	Base		
154993.	"	Cooper, R.)				
155561.	"	Owen, J.R.)	" "	Base		17/6/18.
142099.	"	Southwell, W.)				
164703.	"	Hutchinson, J.)				
16010.	Sergt.	Street, W.	" "	Base		20/6/18.
304744.	Sapper	Tait, A.)	" "	Base		25/6/18.
471153.	Barrier	Maughan)				
428399.	Sapper	Coakley, F.	" "	Base		25/6/18.

DEPARTURES.

412784.	L/Cpl.	Little, W.	Evacuated through C.C.S.	31/5/18.
508511.	Sapper	Howe, E.	" " "	31/5/18.
146233.	"	Burton, D.	" " "	31/5/18
169483.	"	Webber, A.	" " "	2/6/18
508252.	"	Salway, H.	" " "	3/6/18
508165.	"	Gready, R.	" " "	3/6/18
508229.	"	Chappell, P.	" " "	3/6/18.
508216.	"	Walker, A.	" " "	3/6/18.
508209.		Ahern, J.	" " "	29/5/18.
508455.	L/Cpl.	Chappell, A.W.E.	" " "	15/6/18.
506632	"	Smith, H.	" " "	15/6/18.
508215.	Sapper	Clark W.	" " "	6/6/18.
402374.	"	Miller, R.W.	" " "	20/6/18.
420454.	"	Porter, A	" " "	17/6/18.
508191.	Sergt.	Maggs - to Base on Medical grounds-		19/6/18.
508175.	Sapper	Gibbs, L.	Evacuated through C.C.S.	24/6/18.
398266.	"	Hughes, H.	" " "	26/6/18

Capt. R. Sayce - posted to 421st (W.Lancs) Fd. Co.R.E. with effect from 9/6/18. (C.R.E. Routine Order No.47, 10/6/18.

Strength on 31st June 1918.   7 Offrs.   204 O.R.

Confidential

War Diary

of the

505 (Wessex) Field Co. R.E.

July 1st – July 31st 1918

Vol 18

M.T. Jordan
Major R.E.

Army Form C. 2118.

WAR DIARY
or
INTELLIGENCE SUMMARY.
(Erase heading not required.) 505th Fld Coy R.E.

Place	Date	Hour	Summary of Events and Information	Remarks and references to Appendices
WARNIMONT WOOD I.24.a.6.7 1/2	1/July		Company moved into Billets at I.24 Central in WARNIMONT WOOD	Fine
	2		Horse Lines at I.24.a.6.2. Relief completed by 10 P.m.	Fine
	3		Billets located in 505" Fld Coy in GORRE-COURT WOOD were taken over on the 1st Inst by the 1st Auckland Inf. Batt.	Fine
	4			Fine
	4	9 W	Company employed preparing Camp for habitation & transporting Company Stores with Remounts up to Antry. Major Gordon approved of RE Gardens	Fine
	5	3		Fine
	5	4		Fine
	6	5	Right Half Company employed on training. Until completing yesterdays work. Half Company employed in transporting Camp Ulysses & E.23 entrusted for Riffe & Rigte. Rus. Movement H.Q. & transporting Cp. Hopkins	Fine
	6	6	Do.	Fine
	7		Do.	Fine
	8		Do.	Fine
	9		Company employed as yesterday. August's Remounting arrangements made for Half Coy by & this on 30 oph. truck at I.8.d.	Showery
	10		Right Half Company & Mess, & Coys, Routine 1.7.d.11. (Made by Regt.) Remainder of company as usual.	Wet

Army Form C. 2118.

WAR DIARY
or
INTELLIGENCE SUMMARY. 505th Fld. Coy. R.E.
(Erase heading not required.)

Instructions regarding War Diaries and Intelligence Summaries are contained in F. S. Regs., Part II. and the Staff Manual respectively. Title pages will be prepared in manuscript.

Place	Date	Hour	Summary of Events and Information	Remarks and references to Appendices
WARNIMONT WOOD	July 1st		Strenuous forenoon spent clearing up & packing of transport	Fine
			for inspection by the Corps Commander.	
24 area	July 2nd		The 1st Eschelon Inspection at 6.30pm by C.R.E. Woke on Chepouts Suspended	Wet Storm
	July 3rd		Corps Commander made to pass Inspection at 10.30 am	
			by the Chief Engineer. To troops held at 118 C.C. tent	Storm
			were carried out by Sappers in march. Army & Corps tot	
			Trenches C.E. Corps Expressed his entire satisfaction	
	July 4th		172 inf. Bat. Spots to which the 505th	Wet
	July 5th		Work recommenced nightwork by Right Half Coy	Wet
			Coy engaged on Infantry training. Left Half	Wet
	July 6th		Work in support of Left Ref. New H.R. Right Lay log a Infrpt Tramway	
			Lt. Woods + 2 O.R. motored down to 15th & C. under Instns	Very hot
	July 7th		R.E. Spots at 118 C.cent. 505th Inf. By had hard pass them over 1st proper	SE
	July 8th		Inspection held for the 1st 43rd Middlesex Regt.	

Kept. D. Dust + Marcher Bats.

Army Form C. 2118.

WAR DIARY
or
INTELLIGENCE SUMMARY.
(Erase heading not required.)

Place	Date	Hour	Summary of Events and Information	Remarks and references to Appendices
BOIS du WARNIMONT I 24 c on July 20 central.	1918. July 20		Divisional System changed to movements of Arty Front m/c R.E.	
	21st		57th Divisional Horse show & sports	fine
	22nd		—	fine
	23rd		Half coy on at stables (reorg to FS) starting fires	cloudy
	24th		Fires pm musketry onwards Jam for orders rec'd.	" "
	25th		Prisoners taken by Allies on Champagne counter offensive stated to be 25,000 & 400 guns	Showers
	26th		Visitors night - toy to be held note work begun. Monday EK 407 Pl to O.R. note now to Zabunyart	Showery
	27th		51st Div'l System reported. View to see note on Maston Lepousse & continued	boy workd
	28th		Return to duty one piece of s Division cancelled Leave now been front on morn —	dull
	29th		Practised part of tattoo at 9 a.m. & proceeded by route march with 172 Bgd, 13th Hows div wright [ADTHIE - PAS Y ZOUTOR 2015] HARBAR Eq. ETRUN boy keft	
SOMBRIN Front Returns (LENS II 4 F)	30th		Practised home-road tattoo in village built the 12th grade by AVESNES LE COMTE	
ETRUN (LENS II 3 I)	31st		The coy starts night of 30 & 31st in Y rest camp HodEt 12 to Canadian Engineers & C coy begtd of 12th & 13th R.E. with a view to taking over part of the System in the line maintained held by the 4th Canadian Division just N. of ARRAS. Considerable bombing activity in vicinity of ETRUN by night. 57th Division from IV to VII Corps	

J. M. Jackson
Major R.E.
O.C. 505 Field Coy R.E.

War Diary of

505. Field Co. R.E.

Vol. 19

August 1918.

505th Field Coy RE
July 1918

INS

410,044	Sapper	Bolton A.	
512,582	"	Baele W.H.	Joined unit from
515,155	"	Crossley W.F.	RE Base Depot on 5/7/18
470,899	"	Hendhough J.	
330,092	"	Glassman H.	-do- -do- on 20/7/18

OUTS

236638	Sapper	Lucas F.	Evacuated thro' CCS	1/7/18
471,153	Farrier	Maughan H.	" " "	1/7/18
488,588	L/Cpl	Walker H.P.	" " "	7/7/18
99,818	Sapper	Carnes G.	" " "	8/7/18
504650	"	Westcott W.	" " "	10/7/18
488,078	"	Wright J.	" " "	11/7/18
65533	"	Newton A.	" " "	12/7/18
157,826	Pioneer	Knipton A.	" " "	16/7/18
518,350	Sapper	Sinclair J.	" " "	16/7/18
138,695	Driver	Baguley G.		
526,041	"	Benson S.	Transferred to 502nd	
267,764	"	Hornsby J.H.	Field Co RE 17/7/18	
471,150	"	Lennon J.		
534009	"	Moore H.		
31338	"	Jenkins J.	Sferred to 21st Fld Co RE 17/7/18	
504632	2/Cpl	Webb B.G.	Evacuated thro' CCS	17/7/18
508215	Sgt	Webber W.F.	Sferred to Base	19/7/18
554416	L/Cpl	Smith J.G.H.	" 511 Fld Co RE	26/7/18

Strength Offs 7 OR 191

WAR DIARY
or
INTELLIGENCE SUMMARY

Army Form C. 2118.

Vol 19.

Place	Date	Hour	Summary of Events and Information	Remarks and references to Appendices
ST NICHOLAS (ARRAS) G15 & 77 [51 D NW] 1/10,000	Aug. Thursday 1st		Dismounted Coy H.Q. & Sections marched from Y Camp ETRUN to billets in the evening at 8.45. Arr'd relieving C Coy 12 13th Canadian Engineers of R.C. Div. Billets about 4 miles behind front line entailing long marches to work. Taking over the trench system took considerable time. Coy H.Q. (French shelter, shower bath etc.) 1 section present comfort & above ground. 1½ (French shelter, shower bath etc.) 1 Section forward for work in forward area accommodated in cellars NE of ARRAS on the railway at the SCARPE.	
	Friday 2nd		Visit area in morning with O.C. C Coy 12/13th C.E. R.E.) Reconnaissances & arrangements for work, reorganizing sector from the Canadian form system to the Field Co R.E system. The different organization making relief difficult.	very hot
	Saturday 3rd		G.H. Capt Marshall 2C/h R.E. posted to visit from 502 H/C Co R.E. as second in command	very hot
	Sunday 4th		Visit orn to new H.Q. in modern Div. dug out. T Group & demolition relieved in forward sector by Lt Skinner Capt Marshall to forward H.Q. visited area from 5.30 a.m - 1.30 p.m only seeing a small portion. to 13 HQ for interior work, inspections and work	wet
	Tuesday 6th		Walked northern part of area with C.R.E. visiting CHANTICLER SWITCH TEXAS POST, MISSOURI etc, work on CHANTICLER SWITCH by Lt. & 9 13th Scot. regiment	showers
	Wed 7th		Visited BDe in evening reference working parts from N.L.R. etc	Fine
	Thurs 8th		Visited northern boundary – CHANTICLER SWITCH – BROWNTR etc. McD dug out decided on on GAVRELLE road. AMIENS offensive commenced	Fine

Vol 19

Army Form C. 2118.

WAR DIARY
or
INTELLIGENCE SUMMARY.

(Erase heading not required.)

Place	Date	Hour	Summary of Events and Information	Remarks and references to Appendices
ST NICHOLAS (ARRAS) G.16.b.77	Friday 9th	Aug	Mondo dropped all round section billets — one within 8 yards of sentry — Reconnoitred for forward sec^{tn} billets & support shelter for machine gunners TOP AVE POST	Fine
	Sat 10th		Commenced work on GAVRELLE ROAD M.G. Dug out. Visited forward sectⁿ & 13th H.Q. 9/K.L'pools. 17,000 prisoners & 100 guns reported from AMIENS.	Fine
	Sun 11th		Hostile raid repulsed 3.45 a.m. Visited dug out etc in company with Pte. 172. Saunders Cpy. for purpose of heading over work — Visited 13th H.Q. etc. Forward station moved to H.1.C.60.35	Very Hot
	Mon 12th		C.R.E. called in at Coy H.Q.	Weather very good
	Tues 13th		Visited with 13th H.Q. Box & Saunders area (Saunders having gone to section)	"
	Wed 14th		Visited new the SNOUT in connection with demolition of Traverses	"
	Thurs 15th		Charges of 25 lbs of G.C. fired at 2 a.m. in Two traverses in the SNOUT in front of Block in C.T. across no mans land. Traverses kept 21' through by 10' x 10' approx. & This charge proved about correct to level Traverse & block Trench. Lt Skinner & Sgt Foy fc of demolition nearly blown up by a 4.2" shell which burst in the fire bay between Traces killing a man of the 2/4 K.R.Rs —	
	Frid 16		Orders received to go into G.H.Q. Reserve	"
	Sat 17		Major Depenb (Pte 400 nightwd) Jdn'd Co Pte 51st Divⁿ went round the line prior to taking over.	"
	Sun 18		Bangoat marched out of LOUEZ 7 a.m. Coy relieved by 400 Fd Co & proceeded by light railway at 8.30 am from St NICHOLAS TO LA NEUVILLE (near S^t POL) arriving about 10 pm —	—

Vol 19

Army Form C. 2118.

WAR DIARY
or
INTELLIGENCE SUMMARY.
(Erase heading not required.)

Instructions regarding War Diaries and Intelligence Summaries are contained in F. S. Regs., Part II. and the Staff Manual respectively. Title pages will be prepared in manuscript.

(10)

Place	Date 1918	Hour	Summary of Events and Information	Remarks and references to Appendices
LA NEDVILLE (N. ST POL)	Aug Mon 19		All officers & orderly Together in CHQ reserve - Inspections, Training etc	Some rain
LENS 11 & 45.25	20th		ditto - Lt. Eben evacuated to hospital with high temperature -	
	21st		Snipers marched about 8 miles there to & from rifle range in heat of the day - Ret Officers & Stinson dined at Officers Mess A.C.	
			Club Aubigny, returned about 10.30 p.m. to find orders to march forthwith. Cadre & left came within the hour	Heavy morning mist
			Marched about 12 miles, arriving WWK (FOUSSEUX) about 5 a.m. Snipers frightfully done up - saw many old blown	
			in men who should not be Cat Egy A. Reports of fall of BAPAUME & capture by us of 10,000 prisoners	
			(NB untrue)	
FOUSSEUX (c AVESNE LE COMTE & BARLY)	22nd	8 p.m	received orders to be ready to march at short notice, but only received marching orders at 12.30 a.m (22-23)	Fine
			starting point 5 miles away. Left Squad at 12.45 a.m. also 4 miles out of direct route. Assumed mistake	
			on part of Staff & marched direct route, finding roads congested because anxious about disregard of orders, however	
			got clear of block & later discovered I was justified & mistake had been made - marched 15 miles via BARLY	
			SOMBRIN & LUCHEUX to BOUQUE MAISON arriving about 6 a.m	
BOUQUEMAISON	23rd -		Informed we should probably spend night in Billets but marched off at short notice about midnight back through	
			IVERGNY, SOMBRIN, BARLY to BAVINCOURT arriving about dawn 5 a.m	
BAVINCOURT	24th		Spent day & night 24-25th in rest -	
"	25th		Marched 12 noon about 5 miles to BELLACOURT (172 J 18 15 c concentrated in close billets)	
BELLACOURT	26th		Marched 9 p.m about 6 miles & bivouacked just NW of MERCATEL about 1000× W of the British front	
			line of July 19.18 -	

WAR DIARY
or
INTELLIGENCE SUMMARY.
(Erase heading not required.)

Army Form C. 2118.

Vol 19.

Instructions regarding War Diaries and Intelligence Summaries are contained in F. S. Regs. Part II. and the Staff Manual respectively. Title pages will be prepared in manuscript.

Place	Date	Hour	Summary of Events and Information	Remarks and references to Appendices
MERCATEL	Aug 27. 1918		Cycled round HENIN, BOIRY, NEUVILLE VITASSE etc. that O.C. 410 Fd Co R.E. (52nd Div) & galloped details on to work in hand. Leaving M.Q. Transport behind moved with 13th to assembly point N.E. of NEUVILLE VITASSE just after dark. 132td moved up & relieved successfully relieved 13th of 52 Div'n during night. Coy bivouacked in German trenches near NEUVILLE VITASSE. Capt COTELLOE R.A.M.C. joined unit.	Quiet at night.
ST MARTIN-SUR-COJEUL (HINDENBURG LINE)	Aug 28th		Parties at work on water supply at HENIN & on roads. Coy HQ transport reported. 172 Inf Bde attacked at 12.30 p.m. w/E/E 4 hours barrage. 2nd objective HENDECOURT, RIENCOURT, BULLECOURT (approx.) First objective including FONTAINE-LES-CROISILLES taken. About 600 casualties in Bde. 1 Sect Z/Coy up in contact with rear Bde H.Q. Started on repair of Bridge over HINDENBURG LINES just before dark.	Fine + cool.
	Aug 29th		Work on Road to FONTAINE LES CROISILLES. Commenced a deviation bridge over HINDENBURG trench (span 5' spans & struts 8'). Heavy traffic of 9"x3" (unknown) 5'x3" R.S.J.'s for R.B.'s. to carry 4 tanks.{sic}	Some rain later.
	Aug 30th		170 Bde arrived by 11 a.m. attacked & gained R I—MCOURT. Canadians attacked & made good progress. Enemy counter attacked retaking HENDECOURT, RIENCOURT &c.	—
			BULLECOURT — Z/H Coy employed on bridge & deviation.	—
	Aug 31st		Comparatively inactive day. By nature completed bridge & employed on water supply at FONTAINE LES CROISILLES.	—

[signature]
Major R.E.

RETURN OF STRENGTH FOR WAR DIARY.

AUGUST 1918.

505th (Wessex) Field Company R.E.

Strength on 1st August 1918 ;- Offrs. 7, O.R. 192.

INS.

Capt. G. Marshall, D.C.M.   Posted to this Unit for duty as 2nd in Command, 4/8/18.

471770.	Sapper H. Ludlow.)	
470258.	" R. Liddell.)	Reported to this Unit from
471440.	" R. Smeaton.)	R. E. Base Depot 4/8/18.
474485.	" F. Longbone.)	
524673.	" F. Taylor.)	
396657.	" H. Roberts.)	
450016.	L/Cpl. R. Parking.)	
91665.	Pioneer R.G. Keeble.)	
65111.	" R. Graham.)	

C.R.S.

488679.	Sapper J. Wright.)	Posted to this Unit from R.E. Base
457826.	Pioneer H. Knifton.)	Depot 4/8/18.
425715.	Sapper J. Gibson.)	Posted to this Unit from R.E. Base Depot
522792.	" G. Osborne.)	Rouen 7/8/18.
508209.	" J. Ahern.)	
508605.	" C.H. Edney.)	
540744.	" A. Martin.)	
546616.	" E. Small.)	

562297.	" J. Ellis.)	
552786.	" F. Wardill.)	Posted to this Unit from R.E. Base
524542.	" L. Lake.)	Depot 15/8/18.
478586.	" J. Earnshaw.)	
508308.	" S.J. Beaby.)	
49848.	" P. McGarth.)	

508455. L/Cpl. A.W.E. Chappell - Posted to this Unit from R.E. Base Depot, 26/8/18.

OUTS.

W.O.
430138. Driver R.S. Davies - Transferred to 421st W.Lancs Fd.Co.R.E. 9/6/18. (C.R.E. 57 Div.R.O. 10/6/18)

540961.	Sapper C. Cheesman	- Evacuated (sick)	25/8/18.
440432.	" F. Halkyard	-do-	27/8/18.
508261.	Driver R. Davis	" (Acc.Inj)	28/8/18.
508548.	" A. Copping	" (G.S.Wds.)	29/8/18.
504632.	2/Cpl. B.G. Webb	" (sick)	27/8/18.

Strength of Coy. on 31/8/18 ;- Offrs. 8   O.R. 210.

Major.

Commanding 505th (Wessex) Field Co.R.E.

31/8/18.

Vol 20

CONFIDENTIAL

WAR DIARY
of the
505th (Wessex) Field Coy. R.E.
September 1st – 30th 1918

Volume 20

555 Wessex Field Co. R.E.   Army Form C. 2118.

WAR DIARY
or
INTELLIGENCE SUMMARY.
(Erase heading not required.)

Vol 20. Sept 1918

Instructions regarding War Diaries and Intelligence
Summaries are contained in F. S. Regs., Part II.
and the Staff Manual respectively. Title pages
will be prepared in manuscript.

Place	Date	Hour	Summary of Events and Information	Remarks and references to Appendices
ST MARTIN SUR COJEUL	Sun 1st/Sept 1918		(Embodied on Aug 31st) Casualties 2nd/Cpl. GREGORY, Dr. COPPINGS wounded both legs & arm respectively. 3 casualties amongst horses from same shell.) Work on bridge over HINDENBURG TRENCH completed — Repairs to plank road between ST MARTIN & HENNEL — both sinking at FONTAINE LES CROSSELLES commenced. Attempted to excavate to B alts. in stages, work afterwards delayed by fallo	Fine
	2nd Sept 1918		teller to case from start — Prepared mobile charges against HINDENBURG TUNNEL (not used) Work as above. Big advance BULLECOURT RIENCOURT HENDICOURT CAGNICOURT Taken	
HENDICOURT	3rd Sept		at dawn of 3rd Moved up to HENDICOURT in the evening. 57 R. Div" taken out	
HENDICOURT	4th Sept 5th Sept		Our line advanced up to CANAL DU NORD. Coy employed on filling in shell holes on roads etc. Work on roads & tracks & well at FONTAINE in bed of SENSEE river — Coy fello intercepted the work & it would have been better, to have closed Zealand from the station as the had to be done in the end — track extended at about 20' & work points made (L&F pumps supply)	
	6th Sept		Training orders to reliefs — Saw OC 249 Coy re work in hand — Transport of many works finished for far forward & shelled where situation settled —	Heavy Hostile shelling
	7th Sept		Relieved Division in line — Dry weather tracks being had on account of rain —	
between RIENCOURT & QUEANT	8th Sept		1 Sect. found fruitfully employed on snofsmoking dugout & repairs to tracks Coy HQ & 3 Section employed on filling up rear road J.Q. at ECOUST (much Bosche material slightly available) Work on tank tracks, repairs to troops & humps etc Coy HQ & rampart about 800 yds behind the line, shelled once or twice but not so much demand as impartial filling in rear	repl.
	9th Sept		Work as above. Work on watrpoints urgently required much infested so all tanks. Slightly slight, troops etc. region before approached before dawn although avurlable start at hand (BULLECOURT)	
	10th Sept		Railways from wd to QUEANT (broad gauge) Work as above —	

255 Field Co RE

Vol 20 Sept 1918

Army Form C. 2118.

WAR DIARY
or
INTELLIGENCE SUMMARY.
(Erase heading not required.)

Instructions regarding War Diaries and Intelligence Summaries are contained in F. S. Regs., Part II. and the Staff Manual respectively. Title pages will be prepared in manuscript.

Place	Date	Hour	Summary of Events and Information	Remarks and references to Appendices
Between PRONVILLE & QUEANT	11th Sept		Coy working on Rear Div H.Q. (completed & then informed not required!) repair of pumps & erection of troughs in HIRONDELLE VALLEY, New Decauville track between QUEANT & PRONVILLE, & the improvement of Infantry dugouts — Attack at 6.15 p.m. by 57 Div. R.E. to establish 1 Sect. forward on Infantry dugouts — 170 Bde took & held objective, 171 took & found to give up objective line on CANAL DU NORD — owing to losses.	Wet
	12th Sept		Erection of Stores, Tank Filling point at LONGATTE commenced., 3 Trucks reconstructed & Decauville repaired at PRONVILLE 1 Sect. Geophysy — Attack at American attack on St MIHIEL SALIENT drawn by 11 Corps Show Battle rejoined from leave	Very wet
	13th Sept		Work as above continued 5000 gallon & canvas tank fixed on Tractor staging (25 uprights 5×5) Sapper Howard 1 2 "reading", & "conversation" & delivery to Hase Trough, 2" ditto for mot. carts Sapper Howard arrived 12 hours a day for all arteries the period since operations commenced on Aug 27th.	Stormy
			Lt Skinner proceeded on leave SF	
	14th Sept		Work of 13th continued — Sapper MASTERS casualty scalp wound (slight) from shell fragment when working on the DECAUVILLE RAIL at PRONVILLE.	Some showers
	15th Sept		Work of 13th & 14th continued & completed. Opposite numbers of 413 Field Co. R.E. 52 Division invited by It Q with a view to taking over —	
BOIRY	16th Sept		Company relieved by 413 F.d Co. 52nd Div. Moved off at 11.15 am, Marched to BOIRY, arrived at Fine.	
	17th Sept		6.5 p.m, Went into Billets	
	18th Sept		Resting — Repaired pumps at Bdn. Baths Boulevard & Saulty, reconnaissance range at Bailleulmont & Bailleulval. Few men employed, remainder resting & cleaning up.	
	19th Sept		One Section constructing Range, one Section repairing billets. Afternoon, recreation afternoon Recreation. Football Match. Remainder Physical Training.	

WAR DIARY or INTELLIGENCE SUMMARY

Army Form C. 2118.

505 Field Coy R.E.

Place	Date	Hour	Summary of Events and Information	Remarks and references to Appendices
Boisleux	20th Sept.		Whole Coy on Physical Training in morning. Recreation in afternoon.	Fine
"	21		Physical Training in morning. Recreation afternoon.	Wet
"	22		Church service	Wet
"	23		Physical Training etc. Sent Lt. Downer to BULLECOURT	Some Showers
"	24		Packing up. Billeting to Pack Ponies, Equipment	
"	25		Transport moved off to LAGNICOURT, VAUX X RAICOURT and moved to LAGNICOURT	Showers
HAGNICOURT	26		Remained at LAGNICOURT. Coy moved by train 12 noon. arrived LAGNICOURT and arrived at Camping Ground ar 5.0 pm	Fine
BOURSIÉS	27		Section road to NORD CANAL & 1 Corp Pioneer Coy H.Q. CAMBRAI Road. Coy H.Q to move to BOURSIÉS	Fine
CAMBRAI ROAD	28	H.Q 10:0	Left BOURSIÉS and marched to Factory on CAMBRAI ROAD, near ANNEUX. Section moved to GRAINCOURT employed on water supply in GRAINCOURT and repairing road from GRAINCOURT and CANTAING. Reconnoitred Village of CANTAING for water supply found several wells	
CAMBRAI Road			one ready for testing	
Nr FONTAINE NOTRE DAME	29		Coy & 2 Section employed on Water supply in GRAINCOURT, two on road and developing water supply in Cantaing. Order from CRE to return Section to Coy H.Q. at once. Two sections of party Pioneers L.N.L.R under Lt Butler were sent out to village to Purge L'ESCAUT CANAL at Section. (Question successfully carried out, and section) Cont. P.2	

F.2 A(10656) W W5300/1713 750,000 2/17 Sch. 53 Forms/C2118/10 D.D. & L., London, E.C.

WAR DIARY
or
INTELLIGENCE SUMMARY.

Army Form C. 2118.

Place	Date	Hour	Summary of Events and Information	Remarks and references to Appendices
Cambrai Road N' FONTAINE NOTRE DAME	29.9.18		Section returned to H'Q.C. without casualties at 4.30 am 30/18.	
"	30.9.18		Re work Coy sections standing Fp	

STRENGTH RETURN FOR WAR DIARY.

SEPTEMBER 1918.

Strength on 1/9/18.

Offrs. 7   O.R. 209

INS.

496486. 2/Cpl. Barnes, W.	Transferred from 57th Divl. Signal Co. 26/8/18
430009. Driver J. Smith	Transferred from H.Q. 57th Divl. R.E. 19/9/18

159047.	Sapper	E. Soper.)	
440127.	"	N. Knott.)	Joined Unit from R.E. Base Depot
92722.	"	W. Benson.)	
520009.	"	E.N. Hanson.)	23-9-18.
167056.	"	T.H. Smith.)	
40199.	"	W. Burridge.)	

OUTS.

508188. 2Cpl. O.E. Beard	Evacuated through C.C.S.	1-9-18.
512512. Sapper Bache, W.H.	" " "	1/9/18.
508236. " Dade, G.	" " "	29/8/18.
546616. " Small, E.T.	" " "	30/8/18.
508169 " Hawkins, H.J.	" " "	30/8/18.
508506. L/Cpl. Gregory, F.	" " "	4/9/18.
Lieut. F. A. Sheen M.C.	Transferred to H.Q., 57th Divl. R.E.	23/9/18.
219889. Driver Keep, E.A.	Evacuated thro' C.C.S.	3/9/18.
508496. L/Cpl. Jones, E.T.	" " "	15/9/18.
508550. Driver Blackmore, F.	Transferred to H.Q., 57th Divl. R.E.	19/9/18
508428. Sapper Sweetland W.	Evacuated through C.C.S.	19/9/18.
Souter, C.H.	" " "	19/9/18.
480680. Sapper Smith		

Strength on 30/9/18:-   Offrs. 6   O.R. 206.

Capt.

Act/O.C. 505th (Wessex) Field Co. R.E.

30/9/18.

C O N F I D E N T I A L.

WAR DIARY OF THE

505th (Wessex) Field Company R.E.

October 1st 1918 to October 31st 1918.

VOLUME 21.

Captain.

31st Oct.1918.   Act/O.C. 505th (Wessex) Field Co. R. E.

WAR DIARY
or
INTELLIGENCE SUMMARY

Army Form C. 2118.

(Erase heading not required.)

Instructions regarding War Diaries and Intelligence Summaries are contained in F. S. Regs., Part II. and the Staff Manual respectively. Title pages will be prepared in manuscript.

Place	Date	Hour	Summary of Events and Information	Remarks and references to Appendices
FONTAINE NOTRE DAME	1-10-18		The company moved from the Sugar Factory Cambrai Road to FONTAINE NOTRE DAME A Section preceded to L'ESCAUT CANAL at FOLIEWOOD to make a watering point for horses, had to leave work owing to hostile artly fire.	
"	2-10-18		Resumed work at 5.30am on watering point. Laid light Railway to bring up ballast and armd trough. C.S.M. proceeded on leave. Complete Paint and Ballast for horse standings.	
"	3-10-18		Two sections laying ballast for standings. One section laying bridge 152 Div attacked on our right. Recommoitred for water in PROVILLE. Found six wells and thought samples of water down for testing. Water trevs'd (mag gun in 4 men party) trenches on each side. Bosch shelling unfortunately had to come out.	
"	4-10-18		12 Men attached to Batt for looking out Enemy Snipers were noticed to unit. Sections standing by. Brig Gen Paynter + Brig Major wounded.	
"	5-10-18		C.R.E. rounds dump with Brig Gen Longbourne. Improving Water Area Supply in Proville. Some shelling.	
"	6-10-18		Took over work from 52nd Div: of improving wash house area in CANTAING. Enemy Shelling area ahead + Bombing in Vicinity. Rain in evening. Very cold. Rain.	

Army Form C. 2118.

WAR DIARY
or
INTELLIGENCE SUMMARY
(Erase heading not required.)

Instructions regarding War Diaries and Intelligence Summaries are contained in F. S. Regs., Part II. and the Staff Manual respectively. Title pages will be prepared in manuscript.

Place	Date	Hour	Summary of Events and Information	Remarks and references to Appendices
FONTAINE NOTRE DAME	7-10-17		Improvement of Water Supply in CAMBRAI. Lt Dodds and section were in the 63rd Div R.E. Lt Butler Making a water supply up to the Pontoon Bridge put across by the N of the Canal (not). This was a very good bit of work and enabled us to get across unseen before it was only fit for foot traffic. Lt Skinner made good the Inspain on the N. side of Canal & also a great amount of repairing.	
"	8-10-17		Coy standing to. 57th & 63rd Div attacking to the S. of CAMBRAI.	
"	9-10-17		Lt Butler put in a Dam but lock gates. Very successful during the morning. I received orders to Reconnoitre CAMBRAI for water supply by C.R.E. I took Lt Butler with me & we entered CAMBRAI at 10.0 am. Our troops had entered that morning. We completed our reconnaissance and sent in report to C.R.E. Lt Dodds was sent off to EAST of CAMBRAI to place Bridging troops from 172 Brigade Area. He completed his survey but found no bridges. We received orders to move	

Army Form C. 2118

WAR DIARY
or
INTELLIGENCE SUMMARY
(Erase heading not required.)

Instructions regarding War Diaries and Intelligence Summaries are contained in F.S. Regs., Part II. and the Staff Manual respectively. Title Pages will be prepared in manuscript.

Place	Date	Hour	Summary of Events and Information	Remarks and references to Appendices
FONTAINE NOTRE DAME	10.10.18		Company moved to BOURSIES. (Sunken Road)	
Bourses	11.10.18		Transport wag and ff same Lt Dodds at 10.0 am to ARRAS en route VERQUIN. Company remained, awaiting orders.	
"	12.10.18		Company marched to HERMIES station to entrain for BETHUNE. Kept waiting till 9.0 o'clock before entraining	RAINING
VAUDRICOURT	13.10.18	12.30 p.m	arrived at BETHUNE detrained and marched to VAUDRICOURT. Billeted in Nissen huts.	
FROMELLES	14.10.18		Received orders to move at 8.0 am, marched to VERQUIN + entrained. Lorries took us to PONT DE HEM. detrained & marched to FAUQUISSART. to relieve the 518 F.C. R.E. 47 Div; orders were altered + we moved on to FROMELLES to relieve the 517 F.C. R.E. 47 DIV. Duty arriving at 5.0 p.m. Relief completed. Boxes wiring	
	15.10.16		Company arranging lists & repairing billets, overhauling tools & company equipment. Met C.R.E. 47th Div. sec; orders to reconnoitre area which I did in the evening, along with a dir 47th Div & O.C. 515 F.C. R.E. 421 F.C. R.E. best moved into our camp	

1875. Wt. W593/826 1,000,000 4/15 J.B.C. & A. A.D.S.S./Forms/C. 2118.

Army Form C. 2118

WAR DIARY
or
INTELLIGENCE SUMMARY
(Erase heading not required.)

Instructions regarding War Diaries and Intelligence Summaries are contained in F.S. Regs., Part II. and the Staff Manual respectively. Title Pages will be prepared in manuscript.

Place	Date	Hour	Summary of Events and Information	Remarks and references to Appendices
FROMELLES.	16/10/18		Two sections employed filling craters near RADINGHEM & one reconnoitring for Bosche troops & machine gun posts on sq. road left by retiring enemy. (Bosche still retiring. No contact with our Section was obtained.) Lt Doods with No 1 Brigade.	
FROMELLE LAMBERSART.	17/10/18		3 Section repairing the road (filling in craters & looking for Booby traps. Bosche evacuated LILLE. I reconnoitred the area as far as the PONT DE CANTELIEU LILLE, found a lot of big craters blown up, also bridges over the CANAL DE LA HTE DEULE destroyed. All work down the road was being repaired by 59th Div. R.E. J.Rohner to FROMELLES and moved the coy up to LAMBERSART. Pontoons + 2 Sections went forward to bivouac at St ANDRE about (K20 d Sheet 36.) I went forward with from the 3 other Field Coys had already started, so I stated to reconnoitre another site. Section had not arrived by 12.0 M.N.	
FROMELLES.	18/10/18		Lt Doods Pont. 2 Pontoons across canal to get inf. across or on PONT DE CANTELIEU. I reinforced the bridge, which Bridge L. Burke had not arrived but received note to say he had not been able to bridge yet as had orders to clear a road along the railway or to allow any to pass. He had completed it	

WAR DIARY
INTELLIGENCE SUMMARY

Army Form C. 2118.

Place	Date	Hour	Summary of Events and Information	Remarks and references to Appendices
LANDERSART.	16/10/16		has completed it. Meanwhile M/CRE who ordered him to bridge on R.11.6.v.30. Meanwhile I had sent for Lt Stevens to repair a foot bridge over the Citerne. Mr. M/CRE and reconnoitred some as far as LEMARIAS, he decided to stop Lt Bulls bridge, as the first place was occupied. In R.10.v.30.20 (Sheet 36). Lt Bulls on the bridge over Lt Stevens section. Pontoon trestle bridge completed to carry Fd Guns on 7.0 pm. Lt Docks started Heavy bridge over culvert vp 2.0 pm.	
	17/10/16		Orders from M/CRE to take over Pontoon bridge at R.10.6.50.20. Trestles completed at midnight. Coy moved to Loos in afternoon. Too late to go on to HELLEMES. Lt Docks completed Heavy Bridge to take H.T. at 5.0 pm started sufficient to take Lorries.	
	22/10/16		Moved to HELLEMES. Got forage collected CRE 17 BT 18.	
WILLEMS			Lt Docks completes way to Lake Louisa at 2.0 pm repairing road in afternoon.	

WAR DIARY
or
INTELLIGENCE SUMMARY.
(Erase heading not required.)

Army Form C. 2118.

Place	Date	Hour	Summary of Events and Information	Remarks and references to Appendices
HELLEMMES	21/10/18		Col Groom called. Sent for 10 men and had them taken to 421 F.C. R.E. at WILLEMS. C.R.E. moved to WILLEMS	Rain
Ronbaix	22/10/18		Moved to Roubaix. No work	Cold
"	23/10/18		Paid Coy at 8.0 am CSM Redmond for hour. Received warning order to be prepared to move at 172 hours. Coy moved to BLANDAIN to relieve 421 Fd Coy relief complete. Received order to attack meet O.C. 9th Kings. Lt Butler & myself went to FROYENNES & met O.C. 9th K Rs. Same night at 11.30 I attempted to make a reconnaissance to the CANAL on O.3.U.10.50. (Sheet 37) nearly collared by the Boche. Had to get back. Lt Butler made a reconnaissance at D.10.b.10.50. Could not bridge as Bosch held canal bank. Lt Doods & section formed escort.	

WAR DIARY or INTELLIGENCE SUMMARY

Army Form C. 2118.

Place	Date	Hour	Summary of Events and Information	Remarks and references to Appendices
BLANDAIN	25/10/18		Divine service from Reconnaissance at 5.0 a.m. sent in report to CRE. All hands on constructing Light foot bridges. Lt Dodd reports to 2 Bridge with 9 men and took down all light bridging material to enemy's bank in area of vicinity of Mairieux dumps at FROYENNES O.14.a.9.7. (Sheet 37)	
"	26/10/18		Lt Dodd returned at 5.30 a.m, he had made a reconnaissance and found it impossible to bridge at O.3.d.4.0.35. A bridge and all sappers were left in charge of the bridging equipment, to be ready in case of emergency. Instructions given to 2nd Lt R.W.R with reference to footbridge. Bridging material shifted from O.14.a.9.1 to O.6. cent. making for temporary bridge on embankment O.14.a.9.7. Boche shelling in neighbourhood of Rue de Tournai at 10 pm casualties? Sapper Turner, 2nd Lt Segg, Sipley finishing 2nd R. Road. Coy employed on making light trussed footway 15'11" long, for use as light infantry Bridge when required. Lieut. Ukenatt sent with the remainder of his section to R.W.R. Lieut Rhodes returned to Garoby Leois at WILLEMS. Three footbridge completed and sent down to Lieut Ukenatt.	One 9.2 gun 2.10 pdr gun with 9th KRL R.W.R. in readiness for bridging operation.
"	27/10/18		Shelling in vicinity of Willems. N.E. & Ero – 4.0pm 6.5.0pm no casualties.	

Army Form C. 2118.

WAR DIARY
or
INTELLIGENCE SUMMARY.
(Erase heading not required.)

Instructions regarding War Diaries and Intelligence Summaries are contained in F. S. Regs., Part II. and the Staff Manual respectively. Title pages will be prepared in manuscript.

Place	Date	Hour	Summary of Events and Information	Remarks and references to Appendices
BLANDAIN	28/10/18		Lieut. W. Dodds proceeded on leave from Transport Lines. Sergt. R.H. Parker sent down to take over. GPS proceeded 10.30am. Material arrived from S/N Dump 5.0pm — 2 wagons under Lieut. Callinan — heavily shelled at the Dump. Callinan - Vicinity heavily shelled at the Dump, but transport got away without mishap, with the exception of a wheel coming off one of the wagons. Material reported all delivered to forward Dump by 9 pm. Callinan returned at about 8.0pm. Message from Lieut. Benner to say Rd. front N. to South at O.5.c.95.35 was impassible, as the position was covered by enemy machine gun. Telegraph poles at O.8.b.80.35 have been cleared from road. BLANDAIN subjected to heavy bursts of shell fire at frequent intervals during the day.	FINE
BLANDAIN	29/10/18		To 1.1.b. 517 Divn. with OR 4 + 7 Divn. called at 11.0 am. Lieut Butler reconnoitred road from N.17.b.1.7. to O.1.c.1.3. to O.14.a.70.90. and found same passable for transport. Movement order and details regarding relief of Divn. on 30/10/18 received from CRE. In evening BLANDAIN shelled at intervals during the day. Lieut. Skinner (Advanced section) reported two gas casualties, (Spr Parkin & L/Cpl Lamb). Casualties at 11.0 am, one man (Sapper Lister) slight. L/C/W Hunt, who was admitted Ambulance for A.S.F. injection, & returned to Unit.	
BLANDAIN	30/10/18		Lieut. Butler proceeded re advance party to ST MAURICE to take over rest billets. Officer i/c advance party 517 Field Coy. R.E. arrived at Coy. Hqrs. 6.0 P.M. to take over. Lieut. Skinner and Advance section were relieved by section 517 Fd Coy. R.E. in evening, & returned to Coy Hqrs. Some shelling of BLANDAIN during day.	FINE
BLANDAIN	31/10/18		Relieved by 517 Field Coy. R.E. All stores maps &c. correctly handed over. Coy. clear of billets by 16.00 hours. Handed to ST MAURICE arriving at billets. N.35.c.3.5. at 20 p.m.	Dull, slight rain.
ST MAURICE				

[signature] Act O/c 506th (Wessex) Field Coy., R.E.

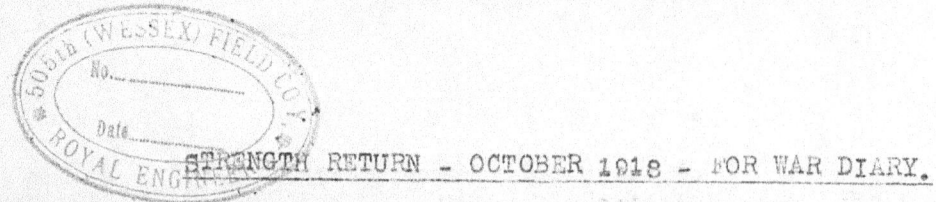

STRENGTH RETURN - OCTOBER 1918 - FOR WAR DIARY.

Strength on October 1st;- Offrs. 7   O.R. 206.

ARRIVALS.

No. 526035. Driver Crofts, A.   ) Joined Unit from R.E. Base
 " 526088.   "   Spencer, W.S.) Depot 14/10/18.

 " 508506. L/Cpl. Gregory, F.   ) Joined Unit from R.E. Base
 " 466431. Sapper Storey, F.C.   ) Depot 21/10/18.

Capt. W.J.M. Davison - 502nd Field Co. R. E. - posted to
this Unit for duty as Officer Commanding with effect from 21/10/18
No. 43038. A/Sgt. S. Rowntree.   )
 " 539213. Sapper A.S.V. Kent.   ) Joined Unit from R.E. Base
 " 212351,   "   C.W. Hadden.   ) Depot, 29/10/18.
 " 465857.   "   J. Alty   )

DEPARTURES.

No. 508224. L/Cpl. H. Hasell - Evacuated :struck off strength, 8.10.18

 " 508573 Sapper S. Dayman -   "   "   8/10/18.
    508512.   "   H. Marsh   "   "   6/10/18.
    508457 Cprl.   H. Montacute   "   "   12/10/18
    508268. Sapper A.J. Westlake   "   "   14/10/18.
    508072. Driver F. Passmore T'ferred to H.Q.R.E.   23/10/18.
    508507.   "   J.H. Dove.   "   "   23/10/18.
Lieut.Col.P.O.L.Jordan taken on strength of H.Q.R.E.   10/10/18.

Strength on October 31st;- Offrs. 7, O.R. 207.

------------o------------

CONFIDENTIAL.

War Diary

of the

505th (Wessex) Field Coy. R.E.

November 1st to November 30th 1918.

Volume 22.

W. Muller — Lieut.
Act. O.C. 505th (Wessex) Field Coy. R.E.

WAR DIARY
or
INTELLIGENCE SUMMARY.

(Erase heading not required.)

Army Form C. 2118.

Instructions regarding War Diaries and Intelligence Summaries are contained in F. S. Regs., Part II. and the Staff Manual respectively. Title pages will be prepared in manuscript.

Place	Date	Hour	Summary of Events and Information	Remarks and references to Appendices
ST. MAURICE	1/11/18		Troops employed in cleaning up and improving billets generally.	
ST. MAURICE	2/11/18		Two sections employed in constructing rifle ranges and firing targets at FORT MONS EN BAROEUIL. Working parties from 172nd Infantry Brigade (1 Platoon from R. Munst. Fus.; 1 Platoon from Leino; 1 Platoon; 5 Platoon from G. K. Trigr.)	
		9.0 a.m.	Two sections overhauling and packing tool carts.	
		12.0		
		1.0 p.m.	" " General inspection - equipment, rifles, ammunition, S.B.R., iron rations	
		3.0 p.m.	Lieut. Skinner reconnoitred district BAVOREUIL with Staff Capt. 286 Bde. for purpose of selecting site for baths. Site previously selected by 286 Bde. was found unsuitable owing to poor water supply.	
ST. MAURICE	3/11/18		Work on rifle ranges continued. Working parties from 172nd Inf. Bde. = 2 Platoons Leins Regt. 2 Platoons R. Munst. Fus.	
		9.0 to noon	Two sections, O.C's inspection. General fatigues. Lieut. Skinner reconnoitred site for spray baths at BARVEUQ. Site selected at Dye Works BIZOCQ.	

Army Form C. 2118.

WAR DIARY
or
INTELLIGENCE SUMMARY.
(Erase heading not required.)

Instructions regarding War Diaries and Intelligence Summaries are contained in F.S. Regs., Part II. and the Staff Manual respectively. Title pages will be prepared in manuscript.

Place	Date	Hour	Summary of Events and Information	Remarks and references to Appendices
ST MAURICE	4/11/16		Went on rifle range at FORT MONS EN BAROEUL. - no working parties from 173 Bde this day.	
		9.0/6	Two sections at Coy. Billets on physical training, squad drill, & musketry.	
		13.00		
		13.00	Lectures and demonstrations on use of spurs and construction of light bridges.	
		8.00	Work on Spray baths at Dye Works BROUCQ - fixing heating apparatus, arranging dressing rooms &c.	
			Casualties: Hopt Pollard was admitted hospital suffering from delayed effects of gas poisoning. Sapper Bacon admitted hospital suffering from injury to left ankle (accidental).	
ST MAURICE	5/11/16		Went on rifle range at FORT MONS EN BAROEUL. 8 baths at BROUCQ & spray baths taken down from HELLEMMES baths, and re-erected at DYE WORKS BROUCQ.	WET.
			Sections at billets employed in morning on squad drill and bayonet fighting, musketry, map reading and road reconnaissance, with lectures by section officers on road making & repairs and road drainage.	

WAR DIARY or INTELLIGENCE SUMMARY

Army Form C. 2118.

(Erase heading not required.)

Place	Date	Hour	Summary of Events and Information	Remarks and references to Appendices
ST. MAURICE	6/12		Fitting of army boots at 0940 hrs. BPESCO. Complete with dressing toms & completed by 1.0 pm. Section at Billets employed on Squad Drill with arms and Company Drill with arms in morning. Monastery in afternoon. MAJOR DAWSON reports for duty.	WKT.
ST. MAURICE	7/12	0900 to 10.00	Coy. on recreational training at Coy. Billets.	
		10.15 to 1300	Lectures and demonstration on use of Companies bridging equipments and various types of light bridges.	
		1300 to 1500	Swimming.	
ST. MAURICE	8/12	0900 to 1200	Coy. on physical training, bayonet fighting, and demolition, including removal of road mines, booby traps etc.	
		1300 to 1500	Knots and lashings. Open order drill.	

Army Form C. 2118.

WAR DIARY
or
INTELLIGENCE SUMMARY.
(Erase heading not required.)

Place	Date	Hour	Summary of Events and Information	Remarks and references to Appendices
ST MAURICE	9/11/18	10.00 to 12.00	Company employed on Entraining and demolition.	
		13.00 to 15.00	Inventory and instructional training.	
			Orders received from O.R.E. of Divn to be in readiness to move at short notice.	
			Casualties:- Sapper W Lord knocked down by motor car whilst standing outside billet at 5.30 hrs and severely injured. Admitted Field Ambulance.	
			Orders to move $\cong$ at 8.0 am 10/11/18, received at 11.40 am	
FROYENNES 10/11 Sheet 37 1/40,000	10/11/18		Company moved at 8.0 am and to FROYENNES - O.2.d.9.1, Sheet 37, arriving 13.30 hrs Fdns Recce party to move in good tickets and to push ahead will the way as for sees able. Saw OC 5-20 Field Coy R.E. & C.R.E. 47 Divn on way to find places for dt taking over new billets etc along JC and Buttos. Reconnaissance of mines at O.16.d.0.22.5.95 as 1st Div had sent [illegible] as reconnaissance of mine farm O.16 d R O.10.a	
			bridge Lt Tamblin found reconnaissance of mines [illegible] as noted. However at crater in Approach to [illegible] above a broken of mine recorded. Houvealin at crater in approach to winery by the broken of mines recorded. bridge at O.10.a.9.8. blown. 5-20 Fd. Cy R.E. Reconn bridge from O.15 to bridge ridge at O.23 b. O 05.60. Three under-carefully take. went then ept my bridging C.P.E O.90 to O. 4/ Divn to assist in more absolute emptime of in the bridge to be more further in O.23a. Saw C.R.E. 47 Divn. R.E. reconn in charge O.R. both of 1st Div transport stateth bridge	
	12/11/18			

Army Form C. 2118.

WAR DIARY
or
INTELLIGENCE SUMMARY.

(Erase heading not required.)

Instructions regarding War Diaries and Intelligence Summaries are contained in F. S. Regs., Part II. and the Staff Manual respectively. Title pages will be prepared in manuscript.

Place	Date	Hour	Summary of Events and Information	Remarks and references to Appendices
Sheet 37 1:40,000 FROYENNES	13/11/18	0700	L/Cpl BUTLER with 10 small party of men to O.23.a.6.0. No take the counterships of river and prepare for bridge. Sets found immediately owing to stiffness in length of planks, men set to work.	
		0800	Men 1,2,3 & 4 continue station work as carpenters of bridge.	
	14/11/18		By 16 hours no bridge. 3 arches of the 50.4 ft of 16 reported forward as bridge.	true 2/9/xy 81
			Bridge 131 ft across, the total length being 2614". Roadway 9', cantilevers about 18'. Standard was in anchorages at D.O.O 93 the side-anchorages connected to O.P.E.	V. [illeg] 2/9/xy 89
	15/11/18		Gp at work on bridge 70% Junction at [illeg] on branches Lt DODDS wounded.	true 2/9/xy 81
	16/11/18		Bridge at O.23.a 25.35. 80% complete.	
			Roads from bridge at O.23.a.25.35. 80% complete.	
			Roads from bridge at O.3.a.3.4. demolition and also cleared at O.10.c to 0'0 a landmines on feet of trestle to place, and to the stairway bridge at O.23.a landmines Hemming her team is about 2 every approach bridge.	
	17/11/18		Bridge at O.23.a Completed.	
	18/11/18	10.00	Major Unwin proceeded in [illeg] to U.K. Notice board showing direction of Luelle Bridge fixed at O.22.6.70.20 L/cpl Pallender L.P awarded the M.M.	

Army Form C. 2118.

WAR DIARY
or
INTELLIGENCE SUMMARY.
(Erase heading not required.)

Instructions regarding War Diaries and Intelligence Summaries are contained in F. S. Regs., Part II. and the Staff Manual respectively. Title pages will be prepared in manuscript.

Place	Date	Hour	Summary of Events and Information	Remarks and references to Appendices
SHEET 36 FIVES. Q.50.d.20.70	19/11/18	8.30	Company moved to billets at FIVES Q.50.d.20-70. Move completed by 15.15.	
	20/11/18	9.00 to 16.00	Whole Company on repairs to billets.	
	21/11/18	9.00 to 16.00	Repairs to Billets.	
	22/11/18	9.0-0 15.00	Repairs to Billets.	
	23/11/18	9.00	Lt Butler & a party of 16 O.R. proceeded to ARMENTIERES by Motor Lorry to look over trenches & work which had been done by 303rd Field Coy when in that area. Lt. Saunders was evacuated to Hospital.	
	24/11/18	8.45 10.00	Advanced party proceeded to LOUEZ. 2 N.C.O & 14 O.R. Church Parade.	
	25/11/18	9.00	Company Route March.	
	26/11/18		Capt. Marshall inspected billets at Bivouac Baths HELLEMMES & condemned same.	
	27/11/18	9.00 13.00	Company Training	
		9.00 15.00	Company Training.	

Army Form C. 2118.

WAR DIARY
or
INTELLIGENCE SUMMARY.
(Erase heading not required.)

Instructions regarding War Diaries and Intelligence Summaries are contained in F. S. Regs., Part II. and the Staff Manual respectively. Title pages will be prepared in manuscript.

Place	Date	Hour	Summary of Events and Information	Remarks and references to Appendices
SHEET 26 I FINES O5d 20.70.	28/11/18	9.00 13.00	Company Training	
	29/11/18	9.00 13.00	Company Training	
		13.00	Capt. Marshall proceeded on leave to U.K.	
	30/11/18	9.00 13.00	Company Training	

30/11/18

[signature]
Lieut.
A.P.O. 605 c/o (Abased) Field Coo. R.E.

HONOURS AND AWARDS.   NOVEMBER 1918.

Extract from X1. Corps Routine Orders dated 19/11/18.

"Under authority delegated by the Field Marshal-Commanding-
"in-Chief, the Corps Commander has awarded the decoration
"as stated to the undermentioned N.C.O. for gallantry and
"devotion to duty in the Field.

Date of Award:- 18/11/18.

THE MILITARY MEDAL.

No.508447. Driver (Lce.Corpl.) L. CALLENDER, Royal Engineers
(T.F.)

STRENGTH RETURN FOR WAR DIARY - NOVEMBER 1918.

Strength on 1st Nov.1918.:-   Offrs. 7   O.R. 197

ARRIVALS.

552838. Sapper A.C.Beyer)	Discharged from Hospl.& taken on strength
425705. " J. Gibson)	11 - 11 - 18.

454607.   "   L. Hawkins.) Joined from R. E. Base Depot
466100.   "   T. Hordon.)   12 - 11 - 18.
187012.   "   A. Aspland.)
174218. Driver H. Reay   )

422486. L/Cpl. J.H.Elder.   )
285099. Sapper J.M.Trotter.) Joined from R. E. Base Depot.
40199.   "   W. Burridge.)   20 - 11 - 18.
508579.   "   H. Dash.   )
534147.   "   J. Ely.   )
526035. Driver A. Crofts.   )

DEPARTURES.

209315. Driver S. Sanderson	Evacuated		2/11/18.
508508. Sapper F. Thyer.	"		3/11/18.
508509. Driver A. Dare	"		4/11/18
508258. " J. Cridland	"		7/11/18.
255230. " W. Hopper.	"		4/11/18.
38461. " J. Simpson.	"		5/11/18.
508276. " H. Jennings.	"		5/11/18.
508271. " C. Sargent.	"		7/11/18.
508269. " A. King	"		2/11/18.
167872. Sapper H.J.Turner.	"		6/11/18.
450016. L/Cpl. R. Parkin.	"		6/11/18.
508203. Sapper F. Gamble	"		30/10/18.
508181. Sapper T. Baiss	"		2/11/18.
488442. " J. Mann.	"		3/11/18.
476824. " A. Bacon.	"		4/11/18.
508626. L/Cpl. E. Pollard	"		4/11/18.
508535. Driver E. Woodland	"		5/11/18.
353838. Sapper A. Beyer.	"		2/11/18.
435765. " J. Gibson.	"		3/11/18.
508248. " W. Gould	"		9/11/18.
16010. Sergt. W. Street.	"		22/11/18.
508168. Sapper J. Maggs.	"		22/11/18.
488679. " J. Wright.	"		23/11/18.
508506. L/Cpl. F. Gregory.	"		23/11/18.
155164. Sapper W. Hardman.	"		25/11/18.
508457. Driver L. Callender	"		26/11/18.
550644. Sapper S.T.Good.	Transferred 520th Field Co. R.E.		13/11/18.

Strength on 30/11/18;-   Offrs. 7.   O.R.182.

Lieut.

Act/O.C. 505th (Wessex) Field Co. R. E.

30/11/18.

VOLUME 23.

VIII 23

CONFIDENTIAL.

WAR DIARY

OF THE

505th (WESSEX) FIELD COY. R.E.

DEC. 1st to DEC. 31st 1918

P/m D. Dundas Major.
O/C 505th (Wessex) Field Coy R.E.

WAR DIARY or INTELLIGENCE SUMMARY

Army Form C. 2118.

Place	Date	Hour	Summary of Events and Information	Remarks and references to Appendices
SHEET 36. FIVES. Q5d 20.70	1/12/18	10.00	Church Parade.	
LENS 11. 1L 30.85	2/12/18		Cleaning and packing Transport for move.	
LENS 11. 3 I 60.75	3/12/18	7.45	Company moved to CARVIN. & Work on billets from 421st Fld. Coy. R.E.	
	4/12/18	7.45	Company moved to LOUEZ. G.O.C. 57 Div. inspected Transport & expressed his appreciation.	
	5/12/18		Lt. Dodds & 18 O.R. proceeded to CAMBLAIN L'ABBE to work on billets for 57 Div. Artly. This party to be billetted & rationed by the Artillery. Sergt. Morgan & 17 O.R. proceeded to ACQ. to work on billets for 57 Div. Artly. This party to be billetted & rationed by the Artillery. Lt. Skinner & 30 O.R. working in billets for the 9th K.L.R. 172nd Bde. at ETRUN. Remainder of Company employed on work on 505th Fld. Coy. Billets.	
	6/12/18		Lt. Dodds & 18 O.R. on work at CAMBLAIN L'ABBE for Artillery. Sergt Morgan & 17 O.R. on work at ACQ. for Artillery. Lt. Skinner & 30 O.R. on work at ETRUN for 172 Bde. Remainder of Company employed on 505th Coy. Billets.	
	7/12/18		Major Warren returned from leave from U.K.	

WAR DIARY or INTELLIGENCE SUMMARY

Army Form C. 2118.

(Erase heading not required.)

Place	Date	Hour	Summary of Events and Information	Remarks and references to Appendices
LENS 11. 1:100,000 51 60.75	9/12/18		Nothing of interest to report.	
	8/12/18		OC & 2Lt Butler to CAMBLAIN L'ABBÉ 9 ACQ to see men in hut by detachment. All ready for photo candles. Voluntary Church parade will be attended.	See appx 84
	9/12/18	11.30		
	9/12/18		OC worked mostly indoor work on plans chiefly of making the Infantry camp comfortable & fit, more dry and of keeping in temper & cheery for the men's Christmas dinner.	See appx 84
	10/12/18		Went as usual to the OC's office with various schedules relating to advancing subscriptions etc. went to see how the OGs during the coming months. Received news that GOC's emphatic orders were Troops could get to Christmas.	See appx 84
	11/12/18		Arrangements made for a party of German prisoners (about 25 in number) to report here daily for work in camp, in all now we are employed on work for the Infantry. Boots ready for last demands.	See appx 84
NOTE.			As the 15/12/18 Demobilisation started for men, La Gl HILLS, & establishing from 4410 SOMER-MORTON, and Home.	

WAR DIARY
or
INTELLIGENCE SUMMARY.

Army Form C. 2118.

Place	Date	Hour	Summary of Events and Information	Remarks and references to Appendices
LENS 11 - I/100,000 37 60 15	12/12/18		Went to march. Received instructions from Col. H.Q. to send a party to search latrine camp of 1st R.M.F. Dicks's R.M.F. most resigned in my birth, inevitably only 3 sent papers.	Appx.
	13/12/18		Visit from O.P.E. (2nd Col. P.L. JORDAN) who is having as to when to to England. The departure being felt by all ranks of the Bty.	Appx.
			Went to march.	
	14/12/18		1 N.C.O. 3 men at march in 1st R.M.F. Camp. No 3 section finished up work for birthday Bugles, and returned to H.Q. from CAMBLAIN L'ABBÉ & 9CD Remainder of Bty at work to not march.	J. Jan 81
	15/12/18		Sunday. No work. No parades. Bells not arrange church parade.	J. Jan 81
	16/12/18		Bty at work as usual. Nothing of interest to report. CAPT. MARSHALL returned from U.K. Leave.	J. Jan 81
	17/12/18		Started 2 sections on Sunday a camps, (4 NISSEN hut's, cookhouse & latrine) for the want of suitably R.E. timber at LOUEZ. These hut's are erected in 30 2 Coy Camp.	J. Jan 81
	18/12/18		Work as usual. Lt. C. H. was to CAMBLAIN L'ABBÉ to fit up a deep well pump. Do not think same is very urgent, but am told site when gone available.	J. Jan 81

Army Form C. 2118.

WAR DIARY
or
INTELLIGENCE SUMMARY.
(Erase heading not required.)

Instructions regarding War Diaries and Intelligence Summaries are contained in F. S. Regs., Part II. and the Staff Manual respectively. Title pages will be prepared in manuscript.

Place	Date	Hour	Summary of Events and Information	Remarks and references to Appendices
LENS II	19/5/16		10.5 A.M. 2nd Lt. S.J.P. SAUNDERS returned from R.E. BASE DEPOT after an absence of about 3 weeks. (On course with Tunnellers.)	
57.60.95	20/5/16		Had a visit from Sir AMYA's 3rd DIVISION's from 6th armies to enquire into the urgently wanted supply of earth of nature & to report	
	22/5/16		Visit from General Barton. (No news at present to weaken or weaken armies)	
	23/5/16		Started the march parade B.on the (try source at course attention to our same 2 our 5th Company	
	24/5/16		Informed by Division weakly all men on detachment at a same attachment to reconnoitre courses handing up and help to keep to pursue the offices moving to these notes. Set up camp content to be moved further when ...vacation was to set notes ...of us. as far ...he might but overhead 3 occur	
	24/5/16		Harness act. Carpenter for Grinders. the army but mounted	
	25/5/16		Another day. The cavalry had ambulance among trees ...of what, all the more Advanced to that you ... wounds through hilly of BOESINGHE. Avenues	

WAR DIARY
or
INTELLIGENCE SUMMARY.

(Erase heading not required.)

Army Form C. 2118.

Instructions regarding War Diaries and Intelligence Summaries are contained in F. S. Regs., Part II. and the Staff Manual respectively. Title pages will be prepared in manuscript.

Place	Date	Hour	Summary of Events and Information	Remarks and references to Appendices
LENS 11	25/2/18		concert held in the evening was a great success. 120th officers attended	
27 60.45	26/2/18		Started as usual. received football competition, were my business. Regiment supplied in the ground. Lt BUTLER & SKINNER left for 7 days leave.	
	27/2/18		Received more transport today, e.g. battn at 26N42, jumping plant at 24N13 & 19N17.	
	28/2/18		today left for the afternoon.	
	29/2/18		Arranged to take officers journey, 2 NCO's & 9 men got a 2 day trip to LILLE. Arranged Officers to Quennes. Inter-coy football in the afternoon.	
	30/2/18		Went as usual. today. Inter coy football GOC's inspection on the 6th January. speaks in afternoon.	
	31/2/18		Had the S.of A. gave any member or 1 or two expect pros, was that ordinary	

R. W. Darnell Major

STRENGTH RETURN FOR WAR DIARY.   DEC.1918.
505th (Wessex) Field Company R. E.

Strength on 1st Dec. 1918.;-   7 Offr.   182 O.R.

ARRIVALS.

508457. Corpl. H. Montacute - Joined Unit from R.E.Base, 9/12/18.
176872. Sapper A.J. Turner.   )
488442.   "   J. Mann.   )
241445.   "   J. Fryer.   )
563781.   "   W. Ukin.   )
89937.   "   W. Dickinson.   )
495164.   "   F. Warbutton.   )
438678.   "   R. Jones.   )
349731. Pnr.   C. Harper.   )
145848. Sapper H. Dickinson,H.C.) Joined Unit from
508181.   "   T. Baiss.   ) R.E.Base Depot
353307. Pnr.   G. Thompson.   ) 11/12/18.
141050. S.S.   G. Lewington.   )
17793. Driver F. Kedge   )
522036.   "   A. Spencer   )
534368.   "   W. Butchers.   )
173471.   "   T. Gledhill.   )
522768.   "   A. Stone.   )
404310.   "   C. Crawford.   )
550407.   "   W. Hook.   )

14121. 2/Cpl. W. Marsh   )
508626. L/Cpl. E. Pollard.   )
450016.   "   R. Parkin.   )
508506.   "   F. Gregory.   ) Joined Unit from R.E.Base
426765. Sergt. T. Millington   ) Depot 18/12/18.
370457. Driver J. Bailey.   )
370436.   "   R.J. Smart   )
169242. Sapper H. Evans   )
23870.   "   A.W. Roberts.   )

508446. L/Cpl. L.G. Callender   Joined Unit from Base 25/12/18

80401. Driver W. Thompson   )
508535.   "   E. Woodland   )
450055.   "   W. Edmunds.   )
550226.   "   H. Roberts   ) Posted to Unit from R.E.
412443.   "   D. Johnson.   ) Base Depot, 30/12/18.
64096.   "   W. Hamilton   )
480297.   "   A. Rooke.   )
504479.   "   A. Bailey.   )
476824. Sapper A. Bacon   )

DEPARTURES.
532213. Sapper A.V.S. Kent   Evacuated (sick) 1/12/18.
508593.   "   A.D. Dean   "   "   4/12/18.
508308.   "   S.G. Beaby   "   "   6/12/18
508252. L/Cpl. L. Mills (Minnr) - To Dispersal Area - 10/12/18.
466431. Sapper F. Storey   Evacuated (sick) 12/12/18.

Strength on 31st Dec.1918;-   Offrs. 7   O.R. 216

                                                     Major.
                           Commanding 505th (Wessex) Field Co.R.Em

31/12/18.

CONFIDENTIAL.

WAR DIARY

OF THE

505th (WESSEX) FIELD COY. R.E.

JAN 1st to JAN 31st 1919.

Volume 24.

Army Form C. 2118.

WAR DIARY
or
INTELLIGENCE SUMMARY.
(Erase heading not required.)

Instructions regarding War Diaries and Intelligence Summaries are contained in F. S. Regs., Part II. and the Staff Manual respectively. Title pages will be prepared in manuscript.

Place	Date	Hour	Summary of Events and Information	Remarks and references to Appendices
JENA'S H - 1:100,000 LOOZ 3.I.60.y3	1/1/19		In accordance with D.R.O. the necessary gear to facility to enable to attend the General Officer's tour. We had 3 entries on Lorries, 2 three & 1 mule, but none were successful. Lt BURRELL & 2 Co. rushy 1st. O.C. Coys. felt as the jumps were badly arranged.	Seen 4/1/19 Seen 4/4/81
	2/1/19		2nd day of the races. Lure entries today, also unsuccessful. Men turned up in great numbers and cheered the competitors the race itself. 5 men demolished. Jdrn HINDHAUGH, BURGESS, GRAHAM & DRIVERS SCOTT & SPENCER. Preparation for C.R.E.'s inspection on the 4th & 6.0 Co. inspection on the 6th. All the messing arrangements	Seen 4/4/81
	3/1/19		are to the lines. Stepmanly the bars above arranged difficulties as it has been wet into the masses, from the G. meals. Staff offices the open area & the mains LTS BUTLER & SKINNER returned from leave & unacle PARIS (7 days) 5 officers & n.c.o.s at turkey, viz :- Lieut ROUNTREE. I Col PEARSON. Sapper BENSON " OSBORNE " SEAL.	Seen 4/Jan/81
	4/1/19	10.00	Parade as general of 4 Coys. for C.R.E's inspection. The 3 Field companies drawn up in line. C.R.E. inspected. As the inspector, the C.R.E. approved and disapproved as to state of turn-out as men appeared, to march to inspect. The C.R.E. approved. Men marched equipped order, were left impressed themselves.	Seen 4/Jan/81
	5/1/19		Inspection for 6.0 Co. inspection. Different conference at C.R.E's my lunch. Turning in to the 5 to as a feeling of Infantry officer umpire has towards the SO's arbitrary in forbearing in 90 and we had the same of transport the as generally longer erects.	Seen 4/Jan/81

Army Form C. 2118.

WAR DIARY
or
INTELLIGENCE SUMMARY.
(Erase heading not required.)

Instructions regarding War Diaries and Intelligence Summaries are contained in F. S. Regs., Part II. and the Staff Manual respectively. Title pages will be prepared in manuscript.

Place	Date	Hour	Summary of Events and Information	Remarks and references to Appendices
LENS 11 LOUEZ 3J.60.45	1/1/19	1.00 9.00 10.00 A.M.	Parade to inspection by G.O.C. 51st Div. The G.O.C. expressed himself and the Bgy marched past in excellent style. Men undoubtedly had great pride in their turnout. Two men selected Sapper FOURACRE & PALFREY.	[initials]
	6/1/19		Started having a few lectures & addresses, based on Pont examn, which lasted 2½ hours per day having a 1½ hours interval.	[initials]
	8/1/19		" " " " " "	[initials]
	9/1/19		" " " " " "	
	10/1/19		Lecturing as per programme.	
	11/1/19		Today is the programme. Visit of CRE to camp, after seeing the men at games. The men have been very keen indeed on the Authorities and Borderley constructions in help of Ambulances Bus & They also continued to shot down two German aeroplanes and the several guns on by the A.S.C. Men give as the enemy 10 men decorated Sgs. ug. Col. MONTACUTE Sapper HATERS L.Col. CHAPPELL " PAIN L.Col. PARKIN " BOLTON L.Cpl. GODFREY Driver MILLS L.Cpl. HENDERSON " DONALDSON	[initials]
	12/1/19	11.15	Church parade Lebro en rum saw Revelation hit Rev. W. CRESSWELL went & Rev. were at march of mass SERVICE. 2 N.C.s Rendell 9 WS Sapper READ 9 PENDLEBURY	

Army Form C. 2118.

WAR DIARY
or
INTELLIGENCE SUMMARY.
(Erase heading not required.)

Instructions regarding War Diaries and Intelligence Summaries are contained in F. S. Regs., Part II. and the Staff Manual respectively. Title pages will be prepared in manuscript.

Place	Date	Hour	Summary of Events and Information	Remarks and references to Appendices
LENS H. LOUEZ 3I 60.45	1/00/00 13/1/19		Training & Reorganisation. OPE came down lines to inspect mens kit at 10am OPE & COO went out. BLANGY plan, that 31.8 & 40,070 GIRL 90 30.16 one the work required to reinstate lines of the scoppered billets, also class at 6.15 & 90 30 mins two teams by the melting watch as manly of ploughing the scoppered by many instruction equipments. 9 men demobilised viz Spoken DICKMAN Spoken HARDMAN Sapper TAIT EVANS ELLIS Driver PRICE BETTS FRYER LOCKE	three sgn B/
	14/1/19		Training & Reorganisation. 21 men demobilised viz Sergt POTHEN Sapper TEMPLEMAN WINDSOR MUTTON BROWN Lee Cpl POLLARD BRINSON BLACKMORE WESCOTT BAILEY Driver TINNER SUPER MIEO DASH STATELY ASPLAND ROGERS WILLIAMS SMEATON MYNARD THORNTON	4 men B/
	15/1/19		Training as per programme. Nothing of interest to report.	
	16/1/19		Nos 10 & 2 sections training as per programme. Nos 3 & 4 sections absent on demolition of 616.123. Estimated time to do the job is about another three days & also on the business of 3/2 — H days	
	17/1/19		Nos 1 & 2 sections at work on MAROEUIL nothing as long for DA DOS for use dumolished signs- most no 3 of section on plan at BLANGY. Men demobilised viz Sapper HUMMELL, SHAW, LONGBONE, DOBINSON, WARDMAN COOPER, TAYLOR, BARNESS, ELHARTE W. BROWN S	three sgn B/

ad JONES

A8834 Wt.W.4973/M687 750,000 8/16 D. D. & L. Ltd. Forms/C.2113/13.

WAR DIARY
or
INTELLIGENCE SUMMARY.
(Erase heading not required.)

Army Form C. 2118.

Instructions regarding War Diaries and Intelligence Summaries are contained in F.S. Regs., Part II. and the Staff Manual respectively. Title pages will be prepared in manuscript.

Hour, Date, Place		Summary of Events and Information	Remarks and references to Appendices
LENS 11. 1:100,000 LOUEZ 51.60.95	18/1/19	Went to work. 1760 completing Lethbridge Camp at ECOIVRES & for drainage. 6 men demobilized viz. Sappers BURRIDGE, GILLARD, DIVALL, EARNSHAW, TROTTER, COAHLEY. Present in camp by the JETS arrival, party will always remain separated.	See Pm 81
	19/1/19	Church parade in recreation hut. Lieut BUTLER arrived to U.K.	Arrived to man Pm 81
	20/1/19	Rations rather difficult to obtain, not as much Remoleyance & assistance as camps L.b. c.c. etc.	Met Pm 81
	21/1/19	Went to work. Strength of an D.A.D.O.S. above completed. Released the S.O.S. Lee & R.E. of these employed 170/172. Ettes. 9 who meet at Div H.Q. SAPs on leave to U.K. Major FOX Y/CRE 10 men the sapper eng — I Col NASH, Lee Col TUDBALL Sapper WARBUTTON, Sewers BAKER, OUTB HANSLIN, HARLEY, ROWLEY, COLEMAN & WHEELER.	Leave 10 Pm 81
	22/1/19	Went to work. "FRAGMENTS" Concert party came down to give us a concert. Well attended & appreciated.	Knee Pm 81 Up Pm 81 Comp front
	23/1/19	Went to work.	Camp front Up Pm 81
	24/1/19	" " Four more Sappers relieved (ations) at ST MARTS CAMP. On men demobilized Cpl JENNINGS.	Up Pm 81 From & Ecole
	26/1/19	Went to work. L/Cpl DODDS demobilized. Emergency orders issued. To do work. L/Cpl and 66 Standby write. I Col HERB, Bueler JONES. G.RUSSELL	Sup 4, 81

WAR DIARY
or
INTELLIGENCE SUMMARY.

(Erase heading not required.)

Army Form C. 2118.

LENS 11 1/100,000
LOUEZ
3 I. 60.45.

Hour, Date, Place	Summary of Events and Information	Remarks and references to Appendices

26/11/18 No church parade as no trains reported. 11 am Intelligence class for Lce Cpl HUDSON & 2/Cpl HUTCHINSON & ALLAM from SPENCER. For the first time the motor lorries over the platter.

NOTE Lt SAUNDERS on PARIS leave from 24/11/18.

27/11/18 OC to CRE's and march to WALNES & BERNEVILLE. Work progressing well, where no alterations expected to the way of the work.

28/11/18 Went as usual OC to ANZIN jumping ale him to see horses & transport etc. Board of officers composed of MAJOR DAWSON, LIEUT DIXON & SKINNER met to enquire into loss of kit of Sapper WRIGHT SHOTER & 2: SMITH demolished. Work arranged. OC on Court of Enquiry re fire in MRPPS. Too busy instruct to inspect.

30/11/18 CPL inspection work done by Coy on dam at G16 d 9.3. Sunset and earthworks inspect that the work done was not sufficient to tend the newly made away over the ride cannot wait to inspect.

3/11/18 Went as usual. No test done as the enemy round the 502. Coy. Very successful. One was demolished as Lce Cpl BAGG.

N.J.A. Avery MAJOR RE

Forms/C. 2118/10.

STRENGTH RETURN FOR WAR DIARY.
JANUARY 1919.

Strength on 1st January, 1919;- Officers;- 7   O.R.217

DEPARTURES.

106671. Pioneer J. Burgess	)	
470899. Sapper H. Hindhough.	)	
65111. Pioneer R. Graham.	) Proceeded to Dispersal Stations	
60723. Driver R. Scott.	) 2/1/19.	
522036. " A.B. Spencer.	)	

43038. Sergt. S.B. Rowntree.	)
167995. 2/Cpl. C.J. Pearson.	) Proceeded to Dispersal Stations
24126. Sapper H.T. Seal.	) 3/1/19.
92722. " W. Benson.	)
522279. " G. Osborne.	)

508489. " F. Palfrey.	) Proceeded to Dispersal Stations.
508203. " A. Fouracre	) 6/1/19.

550407. Driver W. Hook   Transferred to 520th Field Co.R.E. with effect from 27/12/18.

450016. L/Cpl. R. Parkin.	)
85290. " H. Godfrey.	)
508455. " A.W. Chappell.	)
89625. Sapper J. Waters.	) Proceeded to Dispersal Station.
428679. " W.G. Pain.	) 11/1/19.
422486. L/Cpl. J.H. Elder.	)
410444. Sapper A. Bolton.	)
508472. Driver W. Mills.	)
404021. " W. Donaldson.	)
508457. Corpl. H. Montacute.	)

522805. Sapper A. Read.	) Proceeded to Dispersal Station.
426672. " W. Pendlebury.	) 12/1/19.

169242. " H. Evans.	)
155164. " W. Hardman.	)
502297. " J. Ellis.	) Proceeded to Dispersal Station.
242445. " H. Fryer.	) 13/1/19
89937. " W. Dickman.	)
304744. " A. Tait.	)
508259. Driver R. Locke.	)
508440. " F. Rice.	)
155579. Sapper J. Betts.	)

508626. L/Cpl. E.H. Pollard.	)
508462. Sapper J. Mico.	)
508623. " P.J. Wescott.	)
508253. " G. Mutton.	)
164273. " G. Thornton.	) Proceeded to Dispersal Station
187012. " A. Aspland.	) 14/1/19.
508442. " W.G. Brown.	)
508579. " H.C. Dash.	)
187566. " G. Blackmore.	)
458034. " H.C. Templeman.	)
508220. " E. Brinklow.	)
508018. " F.G. Windsor.	)
471440. " R. Smeaton.	)
217682. " A. Mynard.	)
428678. " W. Rogers.	)
159047. " W. Soper.	)
550183. " S.H. Stutely.	)
209372. Driver H. Tinker.	)
504479. " A. Bailey.	)
164981. " H.E. Williams	)
508015. Sergt. N.H. Parker.	)

2.

DEPARTURES" Contd.

508171. Corpl. A.W.Jones.	)	
524673. Sapper F. Taylor.	)	
508215. " W. Clarke.	)	Proceeded to Dispersal Station
508184. " H. Barnes.	)	
508463. " S. Brown.	)	17/1/19.
552786. " F. Wardill.	)	
154993. " R. Cooper.	)	
426643. " C. Shaw.	)	
474486. " F. Longbone.	)	
98512. " J.W.Dobinson.	)	
428682. " A. Murrell.	)	

425705. Sapper J. Gibson — Evacuated through C.C.S. and struck off strength 17/1/19.

285099. Sapper J.M.Trotter.	)	
40199. " W. Burridge.	)	Proceeded to Dispersal Stations
428678. " G. Runham.	)	
428399. " F. Coakley.	)	18/1/19.
540760. " E. Divall.	)	
508204. " C. Gillard.	)	
478586. " J. Earnshaw.	)	

508506. L/Cpl. W. Tudball.	)	
508408. 2/Cpl. S.G. Marsh.	)	
508060. Driver C. Wheeler.	)	Proceeded to Dispersal Stations
508198. " L. Hamblin.	)	
210864. " W.H.Cuff.	)	20/1/19.
508159. " G. Harvey.	)	
508563. " C. Baker.	)	
508487. " F. Rawles.	)	
504781. " S. Coleman.	)	

495164. Sapper F. Warbutton.) Proceeded to Dispersal Station
450140. Corpl. T. Jenkins) 24/1/19.

504632. 2/Cpl. B.G.Webb.	)	Proceeded to Dispersal Stations
51322. Driver E. Jones.	)	23/1/19.
213586. " C. Russell	)	
Lieut. W. H. Dodds		

526088. Driver W. Spencer.	)	Proceeded to Dispersal Station
522829. Sapper J. Allen.	)	26/1/19.
508195. L/Cpl. G. Hudson.	)	
164702. Sapper R. Hutchinson	)	

263856. Sapper P. Shuter	)	Proceeded to Dispersal Station.
440127. " N. Knott.	)	28/1/19.
430009. " J. Smith.	)	

508552. L/Cpl. W. Bagg — Proceeded to Dispersal Station 31/1/19.

ARRIVALS.
508405. Driver E. Burt - Transferred from 502 Field Co.R.E.12/11/18.
508693. Sapper A.D.Dean - Joined from R.E. Base Depot, 31/1/19.

Strength on 1/2/19 ;- Officers 6   O.R. 123.

Vol 25

CONFIDENTIAL

WAR DIARY
of the
505 (Wessex) Field Company R.E.

From Feby 1st 1919   To Feby 25th 1919

Volume 25

Army Form C. 2118.

WAR DIARY
or
INTELLIGENCE SUMMARY.
(Erase heading not required.)

Instructions regarding War Diaries and Intelligence Summaries are contained in F.S. Regs., Part II. and the Staff Manual respectively. Title pages will be prepared in manuscript.

Hour, Date, Place		Summary of Events and Information	Remarks and references to Appendices
LENS 11. 1/100,000	1/2/19	Work as usual. Major Davies proceeds on PARIS leave	Very cold snow
LOUEZ S.I. 60.75		Nine Seaners returned from PARIS leave	
	2/2/19	Nine OR discharged. Capt Marshall T. No church service.	Very cold.
		Chaplain are now away until 12 Noon.	
	3/2/19	Work as usual. 2 OR discharged. Sgt Hughes H. to hos. (M) Very cold	
	4/2/19	Work as usual. OC visited dam	Very cold
	5/2/19	Work as usual	
	6/2/19	Work as usual. One OR discharged. Sgt Smith T.H.	Heavy fall of snow
	7/2/19	Work as usual. 2/Cpl Thorpe demobilized	cold
	8/2/19	Work as usual. Dr Bailey demobilized. C.R.E. visited camp + dam on River SCARPE. Capt Marshall Msjbah	

Army Form C. 2118.

WAR DIARY
or
INTELLIGENCE SUMMARY.
(Erase heading not required.)

Hour, Date, Place	Summary of Events and Information	Remarks and references to Appendices
LENS 11. 1/100,000. LOUEZ 3.I. 6o. 75.		
9/2/19	Church Service held in Advan Hut.	Very cold.
10/2/19	Men's account. LT SAUNDERS & party of 7 men laid cement at GUINCHY-LE-NOBLE and transportation plant.	" frosty "
11/2/19	Men's account. Returned of 1 non-orderlies to H.Q. from BERNEVILLE. 1 man died 2/Lt a Hopkins died at Gas.	Work going out of.
12/2/19	Major Quance returned from PARIS. Men's account.	Clerk & 2 drivers to [?]
13/2/19	Men's account. 2 sappers & 1 driver demobilised.	Travelling on [?]
14/2/19	Men's account. 60 to CAZÉS for a Service YMCA Lect at ARRAS.	
15/2/19	Men's account. Travelling to cinema & lecture trouble, concert at ANZIN & GREENHOUSE. Engineers at CREWE schedules of emeraldite & new furnished.	Not [?]
16/2/19	Test drew DUTCHES for pay stubs (GREENHOUSE) demobiled. Worthy Sgt. O went sick to spot. Church Service in ADVAN HUT 9hrs & lecture Hew forms Hr Laser Sgt W?	get [?]
17/2/19	Mens. on Duties. attend Hygiene lecture. One man demobed Lt. STONEMAN and 3 men attended ARRAS YMCA Lt. Lectures.	Some [?]
18/2/19	Work in men's C.	

WAR DIARY
or
INTELLIGENCE SUMMARY.
(Erase heading not required.)

Army Form C. 2118.

Instructions regarding War Diaries and Intelligence Summaries are contained in F. S. Regs., Part II. and the Staff Manual respectively. Title pages will be prepared in manuscript.

Hour, Date, Place	Summary of Events and Information	Remarks and references to Appendices
LENS 11. 1/100-000	19/2/19 Forged document Release many going to list of Trouble. C.S.M. evened [Kith plant of the Bde Hg was 9,082 men who boarded west of the whole	time of
LOUEZ 3.I. 60. 75.	20/2/19 23 at YESSEN plumbing gas with 100	this. Pasteboards were to this of
	1/3/19 proof award 3.R. Chocolate Soup	
	21/2/19 " Supply of such Whisky & D.H.Q. on the Divisions	time of
	22/3/19 " cont'd to send Pearlsstocks were much as the 2 times, also gave	ment of
	are to front	ment of
	23/3/19 SUNDAY. No fresh can get to drunk. 100 stampdoor	ord of
	24/3/19 Mon Tues Wed SCORPE complete. Civil prisoners being sign of 2 9	keep out of
	Railway started C	"
	25/3/19 Rifle ranges arranged at. Party of Officers + 3.R.P. to SUFFIELD, ok	Out of
	NOBLE, Transportation. BC Res to VALENCIENNES + guarantee	
	report. Chamelles of EQUIPMENT	
	26/3/19 Court assisted 209 Hawkeston	61
	" " "	4,
	27/3/19 " " "	
	28/3/19 Inspection of armoured 16 occasion. Horse Transport by C.R.E. mat Ford. Out of	
	and of activity	
	Conference of ads Repr. of C.R.E.s	

a/L.T.R. Hunter S/Col. M.C.
O.C. 103 Pioneer Bde C.E. M.C.

505th (Wessex) Field Coy. R.E.

ARRIVALS AND DEPARTURES FOR MONTH OF FEBRUARY. 1919.

Departures.

185504.	Sapper.	Masterson.	T.E.	Despatched to Div'l Reception Camp for demob. 2/2/19.
508605.	"	Edney.	C.H.	" " " " 3/2/19.
471770.	"	Ludlow.	H.	" " " " "
167056.	"	Smith.	T.H.	" " " " 6/2/19.
508156.	2/Corpl.	Thomas.	W.O.	" " " " 7/2/19.
370057.	Driver.	Bailey.	J.	" " " " 8/2/19.
470632.	L/Corpl.	Henderson.	J.R.	" " " " 12/2/19.
242099.	Sapper.	Southwell.	W.	" " " " "
470259.	"	Liddell.	W.F.	" " " " 13/2/19.
534147.	"	Ely.	J.	" " " " 13/2/19.
513901.	"	Boulger.	A.C.	" " " " "
370436.	Driver.	Smart.	R.J.	" " " " 14/2/19.
550236.	"	Roberts.	H.	" " " " 16/2/19.
508199.	"	Witcombe.	H.	" " " " "
536320.	L/Corpl.	Read.	A.M.	" " " " "
508181.	Sapper.	Baiss.	T.	" " " " 17/2/19.
48126.	"	Smith.	J.H.	" " " " "
203359.	"	Hart.	T.	" " " " "
426765.	Sergt.	Millington.	T.E.	" " " " 20/2/19.
508243.	C.S.M.	Evered.	F.L.	" " " " 21/2/19.
508239.	Sapper.	Harding.	W.G.	" " " " "
508245.	L/Corpl.	Taylor.	S.H.	" " " " "
141167.	Sapper.	Guttridge.	H.A	" " " " 16/2/19.
344025.	Driver.	Reay.	H.	" " " " 24/2/19.
23870.	Sapper.	Roberts.	A.W.	" " " " 27/2/19.
155561.	"	Owen.	J.R.	" " " " "
508197.	"	Wise.	C.	Demobilised whilst on leave in U.K.
396657.	"	Roberts.	H.	10/1/19.
496586.	2/Corpl.	Barnes.	R.W.	Sent to A.A.G.'s Office at the Base and struck off strength 22/2/19.
508576.	Sapper.	Smitham.	N.G.	Evacuated through C.C.S. 9/2/19.
508209.	"	Ahern.	J.	" " " "
508429.	"	Vickery.	J.	" " " 14/2/19.
508279.	Serg.	Fry.	T.	Despatched to Div'l. Reception Camp. 21/2/19.

Arrivals.

549700.	Sapper.	Wooster.	J.H.	Transferred from 421st Fld Co.R.E. on 24/2/19.

	Offrs.	O.R.
Strength 1/2/19.	6	123.
Departures.		33
	6	90
Arrivals.		1
Strength 28/2/19.	6	91.

Nov 26

Confidential

War Diary

of

505" (Wessex) Field Coy R E

from 1/3/19 to 31/3/19

Volume 26

Army Form C. 2118.

WAR DIARY
or
INTELLIGENCE SUMMARY.
(Erase heading not required.)

Instructions regarding War Diaries and Intelligence Summaries are contained in F.S. Regs., Part II. and the Staff Manual respectively. Title pages will be prepared in manuscript.

Hour, Date, Place	Summary of Events and Information	Remarks and references to Appendices
LENS 11. 1:100 000 3.I. 67.89.		
1/3/19	Work as carried on per progress report	
2/3/19	Church parade 11.30 service in Divisional Tent.	
3/3/19	Draft in march 750 3 feet legs and two officers men and two care	
4/3/19	Arrived at OOS. Men on in clothes.	
4/3/19	Lt. SPINNER left draft to U.K. Received instruction O.R.E. Reinforcements at 17/3/19 ST. HUBERT 9. 20. U.E.Z. not reaching 20.U.E.Z. Factory here till billet at ST. HUBERT 9. 20. U.E.Z.	
5/3/19	to be completed by the 6.	
6/3/19	Report to march large numbers to OOS Bn for newly obtaining refitting	
7/3/19	for 8 " " as OOS Bn. O.RE. men arrive to be	
8/3/19	fitted " " O. P. O. O.R.E.	
9/3/19	" "	
10/3/19	Draft is march	
11/3/19	"	
12/3/19	"	
13/3/19	"	
14/3/19	"	
15/3/19	" All ready to come due to leave for England at any moment. Reserves in short O.R.E. to be sent off from O.RE. Reinforcements	

WAR DIARY
or
INTELLIGENCE SUMMARY.
(Erase heading not required.)

Army Form C. 2118.

Hour, Date, Place	Summary of Events and Information	Remarks and references to Appendices
LENS II 1:100,000 3.I. 6 & 8.9.		
16/3/19	Church parade. 11.30 Lieut Col Atkins Ltd.	[illegible]
17/3/19	Pct. to march. Lent over to type the night's programme of work. 3 O.R. of unit attached leave to U.K.	[illegible]
18/3/19	24 O.R. NUMBERS leave to U.K.	[illegible]
19/3/19	16 O.R. privileged (pro rata) leave to Belgium & Spain + 3 O.R. men from 145 Co. 1st Army.	[illegible]
	Orders to all Divisions from the RE point for forms indicating the views on Athletic events.	
20/3/19	Party of the annual sports. Leave to cancel to the maximum num. Ensured that HQ encourages respect.	[illegible]
21/3/19	Went to a review. Some munitions required for the Country from Hampshire. Was an order to II Corps conventions and forward all players.	[illegible]
22/3/19	3J 421 handed over to B.C. 421 Bty.	[illegible]
23/3/19	" " " " "	[illegible]
24/3/19	A.D.O.S. II Corps down to enquire and General equipment etc.	[illegible]
25/3/19	Everything fixed up. Nogheenaur manoeuvre gone to.	[illegible]
26/3/19	About parade. 11.30 Leave Lt. SKINNER acknowledges leave	[illegible]
27/3/19	Went to mess.	
28/3/19	" " " Capt. MARSHALL Lt R Gai. p. J.O. 218 Fd. C. RE	[illegible]

WAR DIARY
or
INTELLIGENCE SUMMARY.

(Erase heading not required.)

Army Form C. 2118.

Instructions regarding War Diaries and Intelligence Summaries are contained in F.S. Regs., Part II. and the Staff Manual respectively. Title pages will be prepared in manuscript.

Hour, Date, Place		Summary of Events and Information	Remarks and references to Appendices
LENS 11. 1:100,000 3 I 67 80	26/3/19	Work dormant.	
	27/3/19	" "	
	28/3/19	" " - C.R.E. (2/Lt Col Goodwin) left for 6 A Div.	
	29/3/19	" " - Lt. Stemen transferred to cadre of the 572 Fd. Co. R.E.	
		Received no dispatches of transference of Lt. (A/Capt.) Parker to H.Q. R.E. from 14/3/19	
	30/3/19	Wind of the church parade.	
	31/3/19	Reconnaissance Lt. Short's and unserviceable for demolition of 2 of 3/24	
		Left Morley.	

J.J.P. Davey Major R.E.
OC 500 Area Fd. Co. R.E.

WAR DIARY.   March 1919.

505th (Wessex) Field Coy. R.E.

INNS.

------------NIL------------

OUTS.

404310.	Driver.	Crawford.	C.	Demobilised 23/1/19.
504660.	Sapper.	Hunt.	F.J.	Evacuated.(sick) 6/3/19.
508475.	Corpl.	Knight.	C.	Transferred to H.Q.R.E.57thDiv.4/3/19
508582.	L/Cpl.	Buzza.	H.	Demobilised. 23/1/19.
438678.	Sapper.	Jones.	R.)	
524542.	"	Lake.	L.)	
303896.	"	Lingwood.	G.H.)	Transferred to 455th Field Coy.R.E.
186161.	"	Rose.	S.A.)	11/3/19.
520015.	"	Sinnett.	D.J.)	
504613.	Corpl.	Trythall.	F.	" " 497th Fd. Co. 11/3/19.
508624.	2/Corpl.	Bray.	J.W.)	
14121.	"	Marsh.	J.)	
508606.	L/Corpl.	Gregory.	F.)	
508175.	"	Tripp.	C.W.)	
508456.	Sapper.	Biddiscombe.	H.)	
107140.	"	Law.	E.)	
508492.	"	Parkman.	A.)	
141050.	S/Smith	Lewington.	G.)	Demobilised 18/3/19.
450055.	Driver.	Edmunds.	W.)	
64096.	"	Hamilton.	W.)	
412443.	"	Hohnston.	D.)	
17793.	"	Kedge.	F.A.)	
51383.	"	Kerr.	W.)	
508260.	"	Lawrence.	A.)	
508016.	"	Pattemore.	V.)	
209005.	"	Whittaker.	J.)	
180387.	"	Turkington.	F.	Evacuated 13/3/19.
349731.	Pioneer.	Harper.	C.G.)	
353307.	"	Thomson.	G.)	Transferred to XI Corps Concen-
179926.	Sapper.	Woods.	W.)	tration Camp. 22/3/19.
199476.	Driver.	Clark.	H.)	
508535.	"	Woodland.	E.)	

Lieut. (A/Capt)	Marshall.	G.H.	Transferred to 218th Fd Coy. 26/3/19.
Lieut.	Skinner.	F.	" " 502nd Fd.Coy. 27/3/19.
Lieut (A/Capt)	Butler.	L.G.	" " HQRE 57th Div 14/2/19

	Offrs.	O.R.
Strength. 1/3/19.	6	91.
Decrease during month.	3	32
Strength 31/3/19.	3	59

_____ Major. R.E.

O.C. 505th Field Coy. R.E.

Vol 27

CONFIDENTIAL

War Diary
of
505 (Wessex) Field Coy. R.E.

from 1st April 1919 to 30th April 1919

Volume 27

WAR DIARY
or
INTELLIGENCE SUMMARY.

(Erase heading not required.)

Army Form C. 2118.

Hour, Date, Place	Summary of Events and Information	Remarks and references to Appendices
LENS 11 1.100.000 51.67.89		
1/4/19	Parade as usual	
2/4/19	" " "	
3/4/19	" " "	
4/4/19	" " "	
5/4/19	Lectures to Officers available for Church parade	
6/4/19	Started all available men notifying persons where various	
	above are church there. Rumours & much for getting the men	
	above are church there. Rumours & much for getting the men away. Leave to U.K.	
7/4/19	Lt. SAUNDERS reported from leave to U.K.	
8/4/19	Parade as usual	
9/4/19	" " "	
10/4/19	" " "	
11/4/19	G.R.O. cancelling 6% entrainments for Canada etc.	
12/4/19	Given 3 men for draft to be sent to the Details Athies & Tambour	
13/4/19	Parade as usual.	
14/4/19	Orders to fill to Colonel Carlos this kant -	
	Lt. Col. MARTIN to be a/Col.	
	2 Lt. Col. CALLENDER to be 2 i/c Col.	
	Lt. Col. DEMSEAP " " Col.	
	Sgt. " " Sgt.	

WAR DIARY
or
INTELLIGENCE SUMMARY.

(Erase heading not required.)

Army Form C. 2118.

Hour, Date, Place	Summary of Events and Information	Remarks and references to Appendices
LENS. 1. 1.30 a.m. 31.5.19.	MAJOR W.M. DAVISON wounded en route to UK LIEUT. J.R. SAUNDERS takes over temporary command of Coy.	
	Went as usual - forward of dugouts	
4 a.m.	Went as usual.	
5 a.m.	Went as usual	
6 a.m.	Went as usual	
7 a.m.	Went as usual	
8 a.m.		
9 a.m.	Quiet 5.45 p.m. Artillery active enemy	
	No observers sent out for bomb. terrain	
	quiet	
9 p.m.	Movement of troops on the forward M.T. road	
10 p.m.	Fairly busy - Artillery. Received no. of shell dropping	
	in our own supply line	
	found sufficient troops on relay to enter	
	the post. Special party sent out to supply	
	our B.Coy. prior. Letter sent to J.O.R out	
	patrols out quietly and some of them of their share	
	activity - all return.	
21.6.19	Lent. M! Phillips photos taken.	

Army Form C. 2118.

WAR DIARY
or
INTELLIGENCE SUMMARY.
(Erase heading not required.)

Hour, Date, Place	Summary of Events and Information	Remarks and references to Appendices
LENS. 11.		
1 Nov. 1918	Work resumed as usual. Partly by vehicle.	Fine weather
3.1.67.89.	Work as usual	All
21.7.19	" " "	All
23.7.19	" " "	All
26.7.19	" " "	All
27.7.19	Sunday. No duties available to Unit. Parade.	All
28.7.19	Routine as usual. No available men posting by vehicle	All
29.7.19	" " " "	Stormy weather all day
30.7.19	" " " "	Very stormy weather all day

M. Dempsey
Lt.
Officer i/c of Fieldcoy. R.E.

505th (Wessex) Field Coy. R.E.,

April. 1919.

508209. Sapper. Ahern. J. Rejoined unit from Base 12/4/19.

179926. Sapper. Woods. W. Re-t'ferred from XI Corps Conc.Camp as and from 3/4/19.

OUTS.

458660. F/Sergt. Clapham. W.)
508021. Corpl. Honey. J.) Demobilised 5/4/19.
422767. Driver Bathgate. J.)

145848. Sapper. Dickeson. H.C. Demobilised while on leave in U.K. 8/1/19.

173471. Driver. Gledhill. T. " " " " " " 23/1/19.

508182. Corpl. Brady. T. Transferred to A.A.G.'s Office Base 4/4/19.

Lieut. G.E. EDSON, Transferred to H.Q.R.E. 57th Div. 1/4/19.

	Offrs.	O.R.
Strength 1/4/19.	3	59
Increase		2
	3	61
Decrease.	1	6
Strength 30/4/19.	2	55

St. Aubin.
30/4/19.

Lieut. R.E.,
Acting. O.C. 505th Field Coy. R.E.,

WAR DIARY
or
INTELLIGENCE SUMMARY.
(Erase heading not required.)

Army Form C. 2118.

Hour, Date, Place	Summary of Events and Information	Remarks and references to Appendices
LENS. II. 1/100,000 2 I 67 89.		
1.5.19	HQ Coy distributed to No's Coys and to School.	
2-5-19	H/Cpl DAVISON returned from UK leave. Routine as usual.	
3-5-19	" " "	
4-5-19	" " "	
6-5-19	" " "	
7-5-19	Orders to reduce cadre were received to 50 ORs.	
8-5-19	Losing heavy numbers, 3 Offs and Othr Ranks & Soldiers to Northern were demobilized.	
8-5-19	Routine as usual.	
9-5-19	Cadre established. Further reduction No 2 Offr and OR & Sgt, Cpl, 2/Cpl, L/Cpl, throughout. Lt/Col Liddell Two Cooks, Mess Orderlies &c.	
10-5-19	Routine as usual.	
11-5-19	Entraining of 51st Regiment Cadre Guard commenced 10 am. Train left HANGEST.	
12-5-19	Routine as usual.	
26-5-19		
27-5-19	Orders received to reduce Establishment to 1 Offr 15 ORs. Strength to return Part 3 of Demobilization Scheme.	

Army Form C. 2118.

WAR DIARY
or
INTELLIGENCE SUMMARY.

(Erase heading not required.)

Instructions regarding War Diaries and Intelligence
Summaries are contained in F. S. Regs., Part II.
and the Staff Manual respectively. Title pages
will be prepared in manuscript.

Hour, Date, Place	Summary of Events and Information	Remarks and references to Appendices

505th (Wessex) Field Co. R.E.

May. 1919.

INNS.

OUTS.

506178.	A/L/Cpl.	Powell. H.S.)	Demobilised.	1.5.1919.
556168.	Driver.	Northcott. R.)		
188418.	Sapper.	Mann. J.)	,,	3.5.1919.
505691.	S & O.S.	Abbott. A.J.G.)		
55843 ?	Sergt.	Moss. E.)		
505601.	L/Cpl.	Tidball. R.C.)		
WR3124.	2/Cpl.	Sarry. A.J.)	,,	10.5.1919.
138501.	Sapper.	Crosling. G.)		
540178.	Sapper.	Martin. A.)		
505220.	Sapper.	Andrews. T.K.)		
???.	Sapper.	Solly. E.L.)		
???.	Sapper.	Chaffe? W.G.)	,,	??.5.1919.
???.	Pioneer.	Knifton H.E.)		
???.	,,	Finns. K.)		

of 502nd. Field Company. RE.
Lieut.   E.J.R. Saunders.   Transferred to Adm. Establishment, vice
                            Lieut. E. Rayner M.C. as from ??.?.??.

	Offrs.	O.R.
Strength ?.?.???		55.
Demobd.	1	14
Strength 31.5.???		

"ST AUBIN."

MAJOR.

Army Form C. 2118.

WAR DIARY
or
INTELLIGENCE SUMMARY.
(Erase heading not required.)

Instructions regarding War Diaries and Intelligence Summaries are contained in F.S. Regs., Part II. and the Staff Manual respectively. Title pages will be prepared in manuscript.

Hour, Date, Place	Summary of Events and Information	Remarks and references to Appendices
LENS II 1/100,000 3 I 67 89		
1/6/19	Orders received cancelling the further demobilisation of men, due to insufficient means of conveyance being available.	O i/c D
2/6/19	Orders to move on the 3rd received.	O i/c D
3/6/19	Det. moved by rail to HARDECOURT STN. for embarking.	O i/c D
4/6/19	Arrive at HARDECOURT at 15.30 hours. Entrain for DUNKIRK at 2/34 HR. hrs where the	O i/c D
5/6/19	Arrived DUNKIRK at 02.30 hours, detrained 09.30 hours, marched all men through Refugee camp & then proceeded to No. 3 EMBARKATION CAMP.	O i/c D
6/6/19	awaiting orders	O i/c D
7/6/19	"	O i/c D
8/6/19	"	O i/c D
9/6/19	Orders received to commence embarking 08.00 hours 10/6/19. Leaving party of 20 O.R. details.	O i/c D
10/6/19	Embarked for England at 16.00 hours aboard the S.S. MULTHER.	O i/c D

C. B. Cumming Capt RE
OC SOS Works Det Co RE

10/6/19

www.ingramcontent.com/pod-product-compliance
Lightning Source LLC
Chambersburg PA
CBHW080847230426
43662CB00013B/2042